# POETRY AND THE RELIGIOUS IMAGINATION

# Poetry and the Religious Imagination

## The Power of the Word

*Edited by*

FRANCESCA BUGLIANI KNOX AND DAVID LONSDALE
*Heythrop College, University of London, UK*

ASHGATE

Published by
Ashgate Publishing Limited
Wey Court East
Union Road
Farnham
Surrey, GU9 7PT
England

Ashgate Publishing Company
110 Cherry Street
Suite 3-1
Burlington, VT 05401-3818
USA

www.ashgate.com

**British Library Cataloguing in Publication Data**
A catalogue record for this book is available from the British Library

**The Library of Congress has cataloged the printed edition as follows:**
Poetry and the religious imagination : the power of the word / edited by
 Francesca Bugliani Knox and David Lonsdale.
     pages cm
 Includes bibliographical references and index.
  ISBN 978-1-4724-2624-6 (hardcover) – ISBN 978-1-4724-2625-3 (ebook) –
  ISBN 978-1-4724-2626-0 (epub) 1. Religion and poetry. 2. Imagination – Religious
aspects. 3. Religion in literature. 4. Spirituality in literature. 5. Experience (Religion)
in literature. 6. Christianity and literature. I. Bugliani Knox, Francesca, 1953- editor. II.
Lonsdale, David, 1944- editor. III. Title: Power of the word.

 PN1077.P59 2015
 809.1'9382–dc23

2014023586

ISBN 9781472426246 (hbk)
ISBN 9781472426253 (ebk – PDF)
ISBN 9781472426260 (ebk – ePUB)

Printed in the United Kingdom by Henry Ling Limited,
at the Dorset Press, Dorchester, DT1 1HD

# Contents

*Notes on Contributors*                                                    *vii*

*Preface and Acknowledgements*                                              *xi*

    Introduction                                           1
    *Francesca Bugliani Knox*

## PART I: THEOLOGY AND LITERATURE IN CONTEXT

1    Theology and Literature in the English-Speaking World    9
      *Michael Kirwan*

2    Why Theologians Are Interested in Literature:
      Theological-Literary Hermeneutics in the Works of Guardini,
      Balthasar, Tillich and Kuschel                         31
      *Georg Langenhorst*

## PART II: THE RELIGIOUS IMAGINATION: FROM
## THOMAS AQUINAS TO WALLACE STEVENS

3    Identifying a Religious Imagination                      53
      *Michael Paul Gallagher SJ*

4    Religious Imagination and Poetic Audacity in Thomas Aquinas   67
      *Olivier-Thomas Venard OP*

5    Dante and the Indispensability of the Image              91
      *John Took*

6    Law and Divine Mercy in Shakespeare's Religious Imagination:
      *Measure for Measure* and *The Merchant of Venice*       109
      *Paul S. Fiddes*

7      Wallace Stevens on God, Imagination and Reality          129
       *John McDade*

PART III: INSPIRATION: POETRY AND POETRY READING

8      Poetry as Scripture, Poetry as Inspiration               151
       *Jay Parini*

9      The Poet as 'Worldmaker': T.S. Eliot and the Religious
       Imagination                                              161
       *Dominic Griffiths*

10     *Non tantum lecturi sed facturi*: Reading Poetry as
       Spiritual Transformation                                 177
       *Antonio Spadaro SJ*

11     Reading as Active Contemplation                          189
       *Jennifer Reek*

PART IV: POETS AND SPIRITUAL EXPERIENCE:
            MYSTICAL GESTURES

12     'There Is a Verge of the Mind': Imagination and Mystical
       Gesture in Rilke's Later Poems                           209
       *Mark S. Burrows*

13     'The Pulse in the Wound': Embodiment and Grace in
       Denise Levertov's Religious Poetry                       221
       *Sarah Law*

PART V: POETRY, RELIGIOUS IMAGINATION AND
            RELIGIOUS BELIEF

14     Images of the Virgin in the Late Sixteenth Century: The Catholic
       Devotional Poetry of Henry Constable                     239
       *Lilla Grindlay*

*Index*                                                         *257*

# Notes on Contributors

**Mark S. Burrows** is Professor of Historical Theology in the faculty of the University of Applied Sciences in Bochum, Germany. His research focuses on the monastic literature of the medieval West, with a special focus on mystical and visionary texts, and the field of poetics. Recent publications include a new translation of poems by Rainer Maria Rilke, *Prayers of a Young Poet* (2013), and another collection of translated poems by the Iranian/German poet SAID (2013). Professor Burrows was the recent recipient of the Witter Bynner Fellowship at the Santa Fe Art Institute, where he served as writer-in-residence in the summer of 2013.

**Paul S. Fiddes** is Professor of Systematic Theology at the University of Oxford, and Director of Research at Regent's Park College, Oxford. His research interests include work on the interface between modern theology, literature and continental philosophy. Among his many publications are: *The Creative Suffering of God* (1988), *Past Event and Present Salvation: The Christian Idea of Atonement* (1989), *Freedom and Limit: A Dialogue between Literature and Christian Doctrine* (1991), *The Promised End: Eschatology in Theology and Literature* (2000), *Participating in God: A Pastoral Doctrine of the Trinity* (2000), and *Seeing the World and Knowing God: Hebrew Wisdom and Christian Doctrine in a Late-Modern Context* (2013).

**Michael Paul Gallagher** is an Irish Jesuit priest, now Emeritus Professor of Fundamental Theology at the Gregorian University, Rome. Before moving to Rome in 1990 he had been a lecturer in English literature at University College, Dublin. His specialization is in frontier areas of theology, such as relations with art, unbelief and culture. He is the author of ten books of spiritual and fundamental theology, including *Dive Deeper: The Human Poetry of Faith* (2003), *Clashing Symbols: An Introduction to Faith and Culture* (2nd edition, 2003), and *Faith Maps: Ten Religious Explorers from Newman to Joseph Ratzinger* (2010).

**Dominic Griffiths** received his PhD in Philosophy from the University of Auckland in 2012. He is currently working as a research associate in the English and Philosophy departments at the University of Auckland. He has published a number of articles, most recently in the *Yeats Eliot Review* and *Philosophy and Literature*.

**Lilla Grindlay** completed a PhD at University College London, studying iconography of the Virgin Mary in post-Reformation literature. She has spoken on the topic at conferences in both the UK and the USA. Dr Grindlay works as an independent scholar, teacher and lecturer specializing in early modern literature.

**Michael Kirwan** is a British Jesuit priest who hails from Leeds, of Irish parents. His undergraduate studies in English Language and Literature led to a lifelong interest in the work of William Blake and in literary modernism, as well as a readiness to explore the relation between literature and theological meaning. His doctoral studies on theologies of martyrdom brought him into contact with the work of the French American cultural theorist, René Girard, whose 'mimetic theory' about culture, religion and violence continues to be a research priority. Another area of interest is contemporary political theology. Dr Kirwan is lecturer and head of theology at Heythrop College, University of London, and is the author of *Discovering Girard* (2004), *Political Theology: A New Introduction* (2008) and *Girard and Theology* (2009).

**Georg Langenhorst** is Chair of Didactics of Roman Catholic education/ religious pedagogy at the Catholic-Theological faculty of the University of Augsburg, Germany. His main areas of research are theology and literature, religion in children and youth literature. He is also editor of the website <www.theologie-und-literatur.de>, as well as numerous publications, including *Theologie und Literatur: Ein Handbuch* (2005) and *Ich gönne mir das Wort Gott: Annäherungen an Gott in der Gegenwartsliteratur* (2009). He has also edited *Gestatten: Gott! Religion in der Kinder- und Jugendliteratur der Gegenwart* (2011), as well as (together with Christoph Gellner) *Blickwinkel öffnen. Interreligiöses Lernen mit literarischen Texten* (2013).

**Sarah Law** is a Senior Lecturer in Creative Writing and English Literature at London Metropolitan University. Her interests include explorations of mysticism in contemporary poetry and culture. Publications include essays on Julian of Norwich: 'In the Centre', in *Julian of Norwich's Legacy* (2009); 'In a

Hazelnut: Julian of Norwich in Contemporary Women's Poetry', *Literature and Theology* (2011). She has also published five collections of poetry, the latest of which, *Ink's Wish* (2014), was inspired by medieval visionary Margery Kempe.

**John McDade** was Senior Lecturer in Theology and Principal of Heythrop College, University of London. He now lectures in Theology at St Mary's University Twickenham, London.

**Jay Parini**, a poet and novelist, is Axinn Professor of English at Middlebury College. He is the author of *Why Poetry Matters* (2008) and his most recent book of poetry is *The Art of Subtraction: New and Selected Poems* (2005). He has written many novels, including *The Last Station* (2001) and *The Passages of Herman Melville* (2011). His biographies include the lives of John Steinbeck (1996), William Faulkner (2005) and Robert Frost (2000). In 2013, he published *Jesus: The Human Face of God*.

**Jennifer Reek** received her PhD in Literature, Theology and the Arts from the Centre for Literature, Theology and the Arts, Department of Theology and Religious Studies, University of Glasgow, in 2013. Her thesis, 'From Temple to Text: Reading and Writing Sacred Spaces of Poetic Dwelling', sought to articulate a poetics that might transform how we imagine 'Church'.

**Antonio Spadaro**, an Italian Jesuit priest, is the editor of *La Civiltà Cattolica*. He teaches at the Pontifical Gregorian University and is consultant to the Pontifical Council for Culture and the Pontifical Council for Social Communication. One of his areas of expertise is the languages of contemporary culture. In 1988 he founded the creative writing association *BombaCarta*. He is the author of a number of books on contemporary culture and in particular on literary criticism. He has edited the collected writings of G.M. Hopkins (2008), Walt Whitman (2009) and Flannery O'Connor (2011), and has dedicated more than a decade to the study of digital culture from an anthropological and theological perspective. He is also the author of an extended interview with Pope Francis, published in *La Civiltà Cattolica* and other Jesuit magazines in September 2013.

**John Took** is Professor of Dante Studies at University College London. Author of a number of books on Dante's philosophy and theology, he is at present at work on a comprehensive study of his life and work for Princeton University Press.

**Olivier-Thomas Venard OP** is Associate Professor of New Testament at the Ecole Biblique et Archéologique Française de Jérusalem, where he serves as the vice-director. He is the author of a trilogy on literature, scripture and theology entitled *Thomas d'Aquin, poète-théologien* (2003, 2004, 2009). He publishes in the fields of biblical studies and systematic theology and contributes regularly in the field of inter-religious studies. His most recent book is *Terre de Dieu et des hommes, écrits de Jérusalem (200–2012)* (2012).

# Preface and Acknowledgements

An important movement in recent and contemporary scholarship in Europe, North America and elsewhere, in literary studies, philosophy and theology, is devoted to revisiting and exploring in fresh ways possible relationships between, on the one hand, literature and theology, and on the other, ethics and religious practice. This scholarly interest is reflected in the UK, for example, in the founding of the journal *Literature and Theology* (1987), the establishment of a Centre for Literature, Theology and the Arts at Glasgow University and the Institute for Theology, Imagination and the Arts at St Andrews University in Scotland, the series Ashgate Studies in Theology, Imagination and the Arts, and a string of academic publications on the relationship between religion, ethics, spirituality and literature from a range of publishers.

The Power of the Word project can be seen as a contribution to and extension of these debates – with a difference. It aims to revisit in fresh ways the vital connections between poetry, theology and philosophy following specific criteria. Firstly, theology and philosophical reflection, albeit essential to the understanding of poetry, should not appropriate the study of literature; nor should literature attempt to take the place of theology or philosophy. Hence each of the volumes published by the project participants shows scholars of different disciplines, together with creative writers, tackling common issues in conversation with each other. Second, extreme postmodern views should be treated with caution. Third, a closer co-operation should be promoted between continental Europe and English-speaking worlds in reviewing common traditions of religious, philosophical and poetic experience – hence the focus, in this volume, on European and North American cultures and religion, and on text-based discussion.

The editors would like to thank Heythrop College for hosting the first 2011 International 'Power of the Word' conference, from which the essays in this volume derive, and the Heythrop College Research Committee for funding the conference. The Institute of English Studies, University of London, kindly co-organized the conference together with Heythrop College, and so helped the interdisciplinary project get under way successfully.

Colleagues at Heythrop College, especially Anna Abram, Michael Kirwan and Michael Lacewing, and, at the Institute of English Studies, Sandra Clark, Warwick Gould and Jon Millington have advised us throughout on matters practical and intellectual. Dilwyn Knox, Sarah Lloyd and John C. Ross kindly helped prepare the present volume for publication, the first, we hope, in a series of publications arising from the project and its conferences.

The Editors

# Introduction

Francesca Bugliani Knox

Co-authored by theologians, philosophers, literary critics and creative writers from various European countries, as well as from the English-speaking world, this collection of essays aims to bring together, along the lines of the project which inspired it, the study of poetry on the one hand, and of theology, philosophy and Christian spirituality on the other. Like other volumes concerning the imagination (notably those of Kearney and Warnock), it challenges the legacy – inherited, it has been argued, from the Protestant Reformation, Cartesianism and the Enlightenment – of a disjunction between imagination and reason, and the notion that the latter alone can serve as a vehicle of objective knowledge.

The case for reclaiming the 'truth-bearing' potential of the poetic imagination has been made from different quarters – by poets (for instance, Blake, Coleridge, Wallace Stevens and Seamus Heaney), by literary scholars (notably, Northrop Frye, Frank Kermode and George Steiner) and by theologians (such as John Henry Newman, Hans Urs von Balthasar, Paul Tillich, Karl Rahner and Karl-Josef Kuschel). This volume addresses not so much the 'truth-bearing' potential of the poetic imagination as the relationship between poetry and the religious imagination. Indeed it identifies the religious imagination as the appropriate common ground for a new conversation between poetry, philosophy and theology.[1]

By focusing on the concept of the religious imagination and its role in poetry, the contributors to this volume have avoided the temptation, evident in the dialogue between theology and literature, to subordinate theology to literature or vice versa. They have explored the following questions in particular. What are the main features of a religious imagination? How close can the secular and the religious be brought together? What is the role of spiritual experience in poetry? How do poetic imagination and religious beliefs interact? They also explain,

---

[1]    Warnock ('Religious Imagination' 150–1) makes interesting remarks on the relationship between the aesthetic and the religious imagination. For a discussion of the concept of 'religious imagination', see, among others, Mackey and Green.

by way of historical examples, the primary role of the religious imagination in writing, as well as in the reading, of poetry.

The first part of the volume sets the context of the debate. It explains what has been done in the field of theology and literature in the last 30 years on the Continent – in particular in Germany and the English-speaking world – and shows that the new conversation between theology and literature, heralded in 1987, is still looking for a balanced, unprejudiced and impartial way forward. In his critical overview of the studies on the relationship between literature and theology in the Anglophone world, 'Theology and Literature in the English-Speaking World', Michael Kirwan elucidates that the claim to a new convergence between literature and theology, as signalled in 1987, developed against a historical background of mutual antagonism. Over the last 20 years or so, theologians, he writes, have increasingly come to terms with the importance of narrative, myth, language and semiotics, while literary critics have become aware of the reappearance of metaphysical issues. The work of Northrop Frye (1912–91), Frank Kermode (1919–2010) and George Steiner (b. 1929) has been particularly significant, Kirwan suggests, for the relationship between literature and theology. But where, he asks, have these overtures taken us? And what is the challenge today, when a new threat to dialogue comes from the indifference to religion in secular culture? We are left with the impression of, in his words, 'a symbiotic but uncomfortably tense proximity: a conjoined twinning, tolerated at best, but never free of suspicion and resentment'. What is needed is a positive relationship between religion and literature and theology and literature, where neither is subservient to the other.

Contrary to what has happened in the English-speaking world, where literary critics have made the most important overtures towards theology, the study of the relationship between literature and theology in the German-speaking academy, according to Georg Langenhorst, has been largely initiated by theologians. Langenhorst's essay, 'Why Theologians Are Interested in Literature', discusses three of the main protagonists in the academic field of 'theology and literature', Balthasar, Tillich and Kuschel, while also emphasizing a further difference between English- and German-speaking discourse about the relationship of theology and literature. German scholars, that is, refuse to open up to postmodern hermeneutics of the kind that has set the tone for the English-speaking debates for more than 20 years. A common way forward must, in Langenhorst's view, start from a readiness to tackle the following question: how can an authentic Christian theology recognize the autonomy and value of literature in its attempt to define the grounds for a shared discourse?

CH 3-7

As a response to Kirwan's and Langenhorst's concluding remarks, the essays in the second part of the volume consider the religious imagination inherent in the poetic experience as a way forward for a balanced conversation between literature, theology and philosophy. In his essay, 'Identifying a Religious Imagination', Michael Paul Gallagher explains the concept of religious imagination, examining converging insights from thinkers who, among many others, have highlighted a religious dimension for imagination, for example, John Henry Newman, Paul Ricoeur, Martha Nussbaum, Charles Taylor, William Lynch and William Desmond. He suggests that there are many kinds of religious imagination. We can refer to the religious imagination in a broad sense to denote an openness to 'wonder'. Or we can speak of religious imagination more narrowly, applying it to artistic expression that is consciously religious. But even if we do not limit the religious imagination just to this second variety, identifying a religious imagination still requires discernment. What remains crucial is the tension between self-transcending moments of wonder and the sense of a divine gift, a reverent acceptance of which many regard as the distinctive trait of a religious imagination. The religious imagination emerges as having a double reality: a 'gesturing towards mystery' on the part of the author and a spiritual disposition on the part of the reader or audience. More often than not poetry both mirrors such gesturing and also conveys such disposition. A poem, concludes Gallagher, is an act of religious imagination as long as it suggests a movement towards mystery and invites the reader towards a threshold of transformed sensibility, even when it is not written in a self-consciously religious vein.

As the poet Czesław Miłosz, however, pointed out, the way in which religious imagination expresses itself cannot be as it was in the Middle Ages. Indeed it must differ also from the religious imagination of a hundred years ago or even less. What is commonly known as the 'Scientific Revolution' modified its more traditional features. Copernicus removed the earth from the centre of the cosmos; Newton (according to Miłosz) introduced the idea of infinite, eternal space and eternal, infinite time; Darwin introduced the idea of natural evolution. To these we might add Freud's and Jung's ideas of the unconscious. Gone, says Miłosz, is the privileged place of man, 'created in the image of God and saved by that very resemblance, i.e. through the Incarnation' (142). But despite the erosion of its traditional setting, the religious imagination has nevertheless been and still is at work in poetry. The essays following Gallagher's exemplify how the religious imagination has been at work in poetry at different times and in different ways, explicitly, implicitly and remotely, in Thomas Aquinas, Dante Alighieri, William Shakespeare and Wallace Stevens.

Thomas's religious imagination is explicit. It is characterized by a vision of the world in terms of beauty, pre-eminently the intelligible beauty of God. The principal instrument of his religious imagination through which Thomas reaches towards the beauty of God is language. Olivier-Thomas Venard's essay, 'Religious Imagination and Poetic Audacity in Thomas Aquinas', explores precisely the language of Thomas the theologian and philosopher in the poem *Adoro devote*, showing that poetry can become a monstrance displaying God to the faithful. The beauty of a poem disposes the listener or reader to theological truth. Thomas's religious imagination does not reduce poetry to a propositional illustration of eternal truths, but leads the readers to experience his poems and more generally his theological writing as mediations between the Word and our words.

Dante's religious imagination in the *Divine Comedy* is also explicit. Its essential instrument is the image. John Took, in 'Dante and the Indispensability of the Image', argues that in Dante's works the image conducts us not merely into the vicinity of the truth, wherein lies both the power and the poverty of the proposition, but into its still centre, into the very heart of its divine substance. In the degree to which the essential gives way to the existential as a means of proposing and pursuing the theological project, the image comes into its own as that whereby the theologian and poet is able to explore most succinctly the moods of being in its 'lostness' and homecoming.

Shakespeare's poetic imagination is perhaps less explicitly religious than Thomas's and Dante's, but it is religious nonetheless. In his 'Law and Divine Mercy in Shakespeare's Religious Imagination', Paul Fiddes argues that in, for example, *Measure for Measure* and *The Merchant of Venice*, Christian theological concepts are brought into imaginative tension with everyday questions of, respectively, law and mercy and law and grace. Shakespeare opens up a space in which the audience may envisage what Fiddes calls a 'human approximation' to transcendent justice and mercy, to the grace, that is, transforming law. Finally, Wallace Stevens exemplifies a poetic imagination that may ultimately be called religious (Williams 186), even if his poetry favours self-transcending moments of wonder rather than a reverent acceptance of a divine gift. Exploring the status of God and the imagination in Stevens's writings, John McDade explains, in 'Wallace Stevens on God, Imagination and Reality', how, for Stevens, imagination is the source of both the idea of God and of poetry, a poetry which eventually replaces the idea of God.

Religious imagination also surfaces as a spiritual alertness and responsiveness on the part of the poet, as well as on the part of the reader. Accordingly, the third part of the volume begins with an exploration of the concept of inspiration. After suggesting that poetry may be regarded as inspirational in much the same way as scripture, Jay Parini, in 'Poetry as Scripture, Poetry as Inspiration', argues that inspiration encompasses many features. It can be understood as a moment of rapture accompanied by a language which is 'revelatory'. It may also be experienced as an alert and attentive appreciation of the spirit breathing through the visible forms of the universe. Finally, inspiration includes the reaching of the poetic word into areas of the spiritual and contemplative lives of the readers. The essay following Parini's offers an example of the inspiration entailed in the creative process. In 'The Poet as "Worldmaker": T.S. Eliot and the Religious Imagination', Dominic Griffiths engages with the 'poetic event' as described by T.S. Eliot and explains it in relation to Heidegger's and Ricoeur's thought. The next two essays look at the reading process as spiritual transformation. Following Henri Bremond's suggestion that the spiritual and poetic experiences share some activities of the deeper self, Antonio Spadaro, in '*Non tantum lecturi sed facturi*: Reading Poetry as Spiritual Transformation', assesses to what extent the experience of Ignatius Loyola's *Spiritual Exercises* helps us understand the full meaning of the reading process as a moment of inspiration and spiritual transformation. In 'Reading as Active Contemplation', Jennifer Reek elaborates further on poetry reading as a type of active contemplation, a pilgrimage, in both its form and content. She explores movements from immobility to motion, from death to new life, in the texts of three strange 'word-fellows': Hélène Cixous; the French poet, Yves Bonnefoy; and the founder of the Society of Jesus, Ignatius Loyola.

Religious imagination and the dynamics of inspiration generate what is often thought of as a mystical quality in poetry. The fourth part of this volume offers two very different examples of this quality in nineteenth- and twentieth-century poetry. Mark S. Burrows, in '"There Is a Verge of the Mind": Imagination and Mystical Gesture in Rilke's Later Poems', reads Rainer Maria Rilke's late 'Sonnets to Orpheus' as 'sites' of a peculiarly modernist mysticism. The choice of these poems is not arbitrary. Guided by William James's description of the mystical as a consciousness at the 'verge of the mind', Burrows shows how the poems stand as mystical 'gestures' amid the largely abandoned ruins of pre-modern metaphysics. Unlike, Levertov is known for the attention she pays to the domestic and natural world about her, and for her poetry of political protest. Yet Sarah Law, in '"The Pulse in the Wound": Embodiment and Grace in Denise Levertov's Religious Poetry', shows how Levertov also engages in the imaginative poetic depiction of other figures, from biblical characters to medieval mystics to more modern figures of faith, and shows increasing affinity with the Christian mystical and contemplative tradition.

The fifth and final part of the volume deals not so much with the common sources of the poetic and the religious word as with tensions that appear inherent in the interaction between religious imagination and religious belief as expressed in poetry. The case study here is images of the Virgin in the works of a devotional poet of the post-Reformation, the Catholic convert Henry Constable. After Constable's conversion to Catholicism in 1591, the secular beloved as muse recedes from view, and is replaced by the Virgin who, in a series of spiritual sonnets, is adored as Queen of Heaven. Constable's images of the Virgin were as triumphalist as they were polemical. His poetry, quite different in tone from John Donne's and George Herbert's, can be seen both as counteracting the Protestant representation of Mary as a humble handmaid and as a personal apology for his former secular poetic voice.

## Works Cited

Green, Garrett. *Imagining God: Theology and the Religious Imagination*. San Francisco: Harper and Row, 1989.

Kearney, Richard. *The Wake of Imagination: Ideas of Creativity in Western Culture*. London: Hutchinson, 1988.

Mackey, James P., ed. *Religious Imagination*. Edinburgh: Edinburgh University Press, 1986.

Miłosz, Czesław. 'The Fate of the Religious Imagination'. *New Perspectives Quarterly* 21 (2004): 141–7.

Warnock, Mary. *Imagination*. London: Faber, 1980.

—— 'Religious Imagination'. In *Religious Imagination*, ed. James P. Mackey. Edinburgh: Edinburgh University Press, 1986, 142–57.

Williams, Rowan. 'Religious and Poetic Imagination'. *Theology* 80 (1977): 178–87.

# PART I
## Theology and Literature in Context

# Chapter 1

# Theology and Literature in the English-Speaking World

Michael Kirwan , SJ

This chapter, a survey of the relationship between literature and theology in the Anglophone academy, is intended to some extent as a companion piece to that of Georg Langenhorst who, in the next chapter, offers a survey of the same theme in Germany. However, comparative generalizations would need to take into account the daunting complexity of Irish, North American and post-colonial literatures, which resist any narrow conception of what is English. Elisabeth Jay tacitly acknowledges the challenge when she introduces *The Oxford Handbook of English Literature and Theology* (2007) with a phrase from T.S. Eliot: 'Now and in England' (3). She and her co-editors admit that a subsequent volume would be needed to encompass the full range of geographical contexts; in the meantime, they include a chapter on James Joyce, the lone non-English representative. The present overview, unfortunately, will similarly have to confine itself to the identification of some key themes in the British and North American academies, to the exclusion of other English-language settings.

A map of the territory, however incomplete, shows quite discernible contours and even fault-lines. In a chapter entitled 'The Rise of English', in his book *Literary Theory*, Terry Eagleton asserts that 'if one were asked to provide a single explanation for the growth of English studies in the later nineteenth century, one could do worse than reply: "the failure of religion"' (*Literary Theory* 20). A steadily deepening crisis of religious belief and literacy in contemporary Britain continues to alter the shape of the dual entity which I shall henceforth refer to as 'literature-and-theology'. In the United States, arguably, there has not been a comparable collapse of religious culture. Nevertheless, the academy has historically shown similar anxieties. We need think only of the insistence of the New Critics, from the 1930s onwards, that the individual literary work, and literature in general, have an absolute autonomy vis-à-vis non-literary judgements and influences. The various developments of, and reactions against, New Criticism have shaped the academic study of literature, including its religious dimension, in the American academy and beyond, for much of the twentieth century.

These examples demonstrate some of the nervousness that accompanies the juxtaposition of literature and theology. We are left at times with the impression of a symbiotic but uncomfortably tense proximity: a conjoined twinning, tolerated at best, but never free of suspicion and resentment. In what follows, I propose to explore four tracks. In the first section of this chapter, I sketch a map of the territory, with particular attention to the conversation as it has been emerging over the last 25 years. The contributions of three critics, Northrop Frye (1912–91), Frank Kermode (1919–2010) and George Steiner (b. 1929), illustrate the contrast between the German-speaking academy, where the conversation has been largely initiated by theologians – Georg Langenhorst's essay discusses three of the main protagonists, Hans Urs von Balthasar, Paul Tillich and Karl-Josef Kuschel – and the English-speaking academies, where it is the literary critics who have made the most important overtures to theology, rather than the other way round.

The third track seeks to identify in the 'English voice' a distinctive lightness of touch which has contributed greatly to the flourishing of literature-and-theology over the past 50 years; a quality best described as the Aristotelian virtue of *eutrapelia*, the mean between the extremes of boorish rudeness on the one hand and frivolity on the other. I will focus here on an essay, 'A Reading Against Shakespeare', in which Steiner seeks to make sense of Ludwig Wittgenstein's anguished attempts and failure to appreciate Shakespeare's drama. My intention is to see whether the notion of *eutrapelia* sheds light on this perplexity.

The concluding section acknowledges the delicacy of this balance between frivolity and boorishness. The new *Kulturkampf* – between believers and the 'new atheists' – has endangered this precious conversational ideal of *eutrapelia* and requires the proponents of an interdisciplinary dialogue to reposition themselves again.

## 'What Country, Friends, Is This?'

We begin with an attempt to chart the terrain of literature-and-theology, by identifying two chronological markers: the inaugural number of the British journal *Literature and Theology* (1987) and the appearance in 2007 of the *Oxford Handbook of Literature and Theology*. In the first of these, the editors intend not merely a return to past controversies, but 'also a recognition of a distinctively contemporary convergence between the two disciplines' (Jasper et al., iii). On the one hand, theologians now acknowledge the importance of narrative and figurative discourse; on the other hand, literary theorists recognize the proximity of their own hermeneutical questions to those of traditional biblical hermeneutics. In addition, metaphysical issues concerning 'presence' in literature seem to prompt either a distinctively theological or an anti-theological resolution. While dealing primarily with Western traditions, the new journal 'will not be inhospitable' to those of the East (iv). The editors assert that *Literature and Theology*, 'far from dealing with matters that only overlap at the margin, will situate itself at the theoretical centre of both disciplines' (iv).

Given this confidence, it is surprising to read David Jasper's assessment 20 years later:

> The study of literature and theology is alive and well, though it remains unsystematic and patchy. The texts of English literature and the doctrines of theology continue to enjoy creative conversations, though perhaps not much more than that, and the fundamental terms of the two fields of study remain unchanged. (Hass et al. 24)

This description is somewhat low-key. Jasper certainly anticipates change, as the institutional and cultural influence of Christianity continues to recede. He follows Eagleton, therefore, in taking the decline of religiosity as an important variable. Briefly, Eagleton argued that the decreasing effectiveness of religion as ideological control was a concern for the Victorian ruling class, anxious about the loss of a 'social cement' (Eagleton, *Literary Theory* 20) which was, for Victorian Christianity at least, a pacifying influence, fostering meekness, self-sacrifice and the contemplative inner life. A substitute was needed, Eagleton explains, and sought in literature, with 'English' henceforth being constructed as a discipline. Matthew Arnold proposed a scheme of cultural enrichment of the middle classes, which would empower them in turn to shape and direct the working classes, thus averting social disaffection and anarchy. Behind such a project lies the recognition that literature has the potential to inherit the immense emotional and experiential power of religion, and to carry forward its ideological task of preserving the political and economic status quo.

Variants on this theme of religion as a recognized force for ethical and social stability include Eliot and F.R. Leavis. In his 1935 essay, 'Religion and Literature', Eliot sought to balance the relative autonomy of literary and religious judgements; even so, his admonition that 'literary criticism should be completed by criticism from a definite ethical and theological standpoint' threw down a gauntlet for theorists through the subsequent 50 years (*Selected Prose* 97). Eliot's championing of a European, royalist-classical Catholic tradition contrasted with Leavis's articulation of a 'Great Tradition', which espoused the elemental 'English' energies of writers such as G.M. Hopkins and D.H. Lawrence. These involve very different cultural and existential commitments. Nevertheless, both are taken to task by Eagleton for not breaking free of Arnoldian anxieties about shoring up cultural defences against society at large, and therefore for being prescriptive and exclusivist in their canonical choices (*Literary Theory* 27–37).

With regard to the post-war period, Jasper lists the important *dramatis personae* on both sides of the Atlantic. He highlights in the United States the influence of Tillich in the 1950s and of three very different scholars in the 1960s, William F. Lynch, Nathan A. Scott Jr and Thomas Altizer (Hass et al. 19–20).[1] Jasper's survey also includes some British theologians – Austin Farrer, Martin Jarret-Kerr, John Coulson, Ulrich Simon and others – whose contribution has been comparatively overshadowed (Hass et al. 21–3); a corrective, perhaps, to the generalization mentioned above that in the English context it is critics and not theologians who have been making the overtures to dialogue.

In 2005 Terry Wright offered another typology of Anglophone literature-and-theology studies, once again identifying representative figures, in this case Nathan A. Scott Jr, George Steiner and Robert Detweiler. The shift here is from modernism/modernity to postmodernism/postmodernity. Wright follows Robert Venturi in seeing the modern as self-consciously 'heroic and original', whereas the postmodern is content to be 'ugly and ordinary' (3). Wright argues that the field of literature-and-theology in the USA and the UK was founded on modernist principles in the 1950s, Scott and Steiner being representative figures, and underwent a transformation under the pressure of postmodernity in the 1980s, a shift which is exemplified in the work of Detweiler.

It seems fair to say that the innovation of the study of literature-and-religion under Nathan Scott and others is to be understood as a reaction to the state of literature study under the influence of New Criticism. In 1961 William Empson criticized the tendency of this school to insist that 'a poem is a private self-subsisting world' (Wright 10; Eagleton refers to the fetishization of the poem according to this doctrine: poetry is effectively quarantined

---

[1]    One might note, as a legacy of the Tillichian approach, the 'public theology' of David Tracy, from Chicago. Tracy proposes 'mutually critical correlation' as the model for theology's interaction with culture and society, utilizing the notion of the 'classic' and of the 'religious classic' to describe expressions of transcendent meaning and experience that are publicly accessible (99–230).

from questions of religious belief, to the detriment of the latter). Critics who refused to abide by the *cordon sanitaire*, such as Empson (after 1951) and C.S. Lewis, atheist and believer respectively, ran into fierce opposition for their tactlessness (Wright 10). In the United States, as recorded by Harold Bloom and others, the New Critical hegemony in Yale, where obeisance to Eliot was mandatory, constituted 'an Anglo-Catholic nightmare' (Wright 10). The point to note here is that the New Critics' insistence on the disinterestedness of poetry with regard to religious or ideological commitment is hereby shown to be what existentialists decry as inauthentic bad faith. By contrast, Scott's call for a distinctively theological and Christian approach to literature, following Tillich's theology of culture, draws occluded religious presuppositions fully into the open, in such a way that the world of modernity could be properly and honestly engaged.

The contribution of Steiner, the other 'modernist', will be considered in detail below. In contrast to the modernist intensity of Scott and Steiner, Detweiler presents a more 'laid back' approach, interlacing profound seriousness with humour and iconoclasm, and with a deconstructive preference for the playful. This is of a piece with Detweiler's conviction that the study of literature and religion does not in fact constitute a 'discipline', and we should not demand a methodological coherence which it does not warrant. Instead, its practitioners are happy to work at the 'intersections and blurred edges of the traditional areas' (Detweiler, *Art/Literature/Religion* 1). Detweiler identifies three significant aspects of the literature-and-religion conversation: the curatorial (that is, countering the widespread religious illiteracy, including 'illiteracy' with respect to the Bible); the hermeneutical (reading religious traditions critically); and the existential (the shaping of one's life by means of critical choices).

Jasper, Detweiler's British collaborator, underwent a similar experience. In their co-edited *Reader in Religion and Literature* (2000), Detweiler and Jasper confirm their common journey 'from Modernism to Postmodernism' as 'the move from the rational and organized into the fear of chaos and disorder' (174). This disorder, in turn, brings 'fragmentation, deception, revelation, apocalypse, and irony' (174–8). Jasper makes explicit the presupposition of a mutual suspicion between 'official' theology and the 'suppressed' voices of the poet and mystic, voices which are in fact no less theological ('The Study' 29). Despite his pessimism with regard to 'systematic' theology in a postmodern age, Jasper sees hope in the religious 'return' in Eagleton's writing and in the attempts of some American theologians – such as David E. Klemm and William Schweiker – to advance a 'theological humanism' which affirms the 'both/and' of human flourishing and divine will. Previously Jasper had invoked the Chalcedonian

Ritter

formula of the human and divine natures of Christ, with literature as the 'human' and theology as the 'divine' components. Interestingly, in his 2011 essay he recognizes Chalcedon as one possible starting point (with Luther in the sixteenth century as another), but 'with the poets we are always in the present – by the willing suspension of disbelief – in a text where we believe ourselves to be' (Jasper, 'Interdisciplinarity in Impossible Times' 17).

However, as we shall see later with the three representative commentators, Frye, Kermode and Steiner, the liberating potential of chaos and indeterminacy is not something that has been universally or unequivocally welcomed. Jasper's co-editor of the *Handbook*, Elisabeth Jay, notes an interest in biblical themes among British novelists in the 1980s, such as Julian Barnes, Jeanette Winterson and Sara Maitland. Barnes in particular is cited for his assertion of a forward- rather than backward-looking appraisal of myth. In his own fictional appropriations of the Jonah and Noah stories, as well as modern, 'true-life' versions of these archetypes, he urges that 'myth will become reality, however sceptical we might be' (Jay 5).

The biblical turn, Jay suggests, may imply a hunger for simpler, more defined narrative moorings, in reaction to the shapelessness and aridity of much postmodern experimentation. A generation of scholars 'released from the bondage of the canon by a wave of critical theory, proceeded to lead their successors as students into a wilderness where texts replaced books, and hermeneutic and linguistic theories were preferred to contextual knowledge' (6). The Exodus motif cannot but remind us of Paul Ricoeur's dictum regarding 'second naiveté': 'beyond the desert of criticism, we wish to be called again' (*The Symbolism of Evil*, 351).

## Three Critics: Frye, Kermode, Steiner

The editors of the new-born journal *Literature and Theology* identified three leading critics as particularly representative of the new conversation between literature and theology: Frye, Kermode and Steiner. This section outlines the work of each, identifying their common approach, despite the striking divergence of their respective religious commitments. The Canadian scholar Northrop Frye is noted for his book on literature and the Bible, *The Great Code*. A companion volume, *Words with Power*, appeared in 1990. These volumes proceeded from his earlier critical work, above all from *An Anatomy of Criticism* (1957), which demonstrates Frye's interest in the nature of myth and narrative. Although the *Anatomy* is a defence of the autonomy of criticism, Frye asserted the proximity to religious concerns of the unified theory of criticism that he is espousing. He advocated a comprehensive, inductive approach which accommodated different critical methods. For such an approach to work, however, the barriers between the different methods needed to be broken down – hence the importance of archetypal or mythical criticism, which provided the appropriate, wide-angle lens. More explicitly, it was Frye's interest in William Blake, which issued in his classic 1947 study *Fearful Symmetry*, and his teaching of Milton, that led him ultimately to write on the Bible's importance for literature in *The Great Code* (Frye, *Great Code* xii).[2]

Frye's significance for the present discussion may be located in the *Anatomy*, which comprises a 'Polemical Introduction' and four essays of historical (modes), ethical (symbols), archetypal (myths) and rhetorical (genres) criticism. The 'Polemical Introduction' sets out his objections to the critical approaches, notably from those of the New Critical persuasion, which present 'objective' value judgements of writers, seemingly oblivious to the critics' own social and political selectivity. With regard to the essays themselves, the idea that literary texts can be read according to different levels of significance, literal, formal, mythical and anagogic, naturally opens up a link to scriptural hermeneutics in the patristic and medieval periods, and to the possibility of literature as an interconnected 'totality' of experience in analogy to that of biblical revelation (Frye, *Anatomy of Criticism* 115–28). It may be that the return to biblical myth as a means of structuring contemporary fiction, noted above in Barnes, Margaret Atwood and others (Jay 6), is an invitation to revisit Frye's rather grandiose encyclopaedic criticism.

Sir Frank Kermode was a well-regarded scholar in both Renaissance and modern literature, at first embracing modern theory in the 1960s before taking distance from its excesses. He shared Frye's concern that literature cannot be understood without some degree of biblical literacy, and in 1987 he edited, with Robert Alter, *The Literary Guide to the Bible*. Two other books, *The Sense of an Ending* (1966) and *The Genesis of Secrecy* (1979), explore the ways in which literary meanings, whether of sacred or secular texts, are crafted by deep-rooted assumptions and yearnings for, above all, inevitable or satisfying conclusions which bring an order and shape to both life and literature. *The Genesis of Secrecy* uses the motif of the 'Messianic secret' in Mark's gospel to show how we are 'hard-wired for meaning'; we examine a text with the assumption that it will prove to be intelligible, rather than the opposite – a massive and sometimes distorting

---

2    The Northrop Frye Centre at Victoria College, University of Toronto, indicates the continued interest in Frye's thought and work at its website ('Northrop Frye Centre').

presumption. Works of secular literature take on qualities once associated with religious texts. They are a combination of plain accessibility and 'secrecy', and invite us to ever further interpretation.[3]

Kermode was one of the first English critics to welcome continental theory, without being bewitched by it. His default position was a more genial, pipe-smoking English pragmatism:

> I don't at all think that the time we spent on Theory was wasted. One of the great benefits of seriously reading English is you're forced to read a lot of other things. You may not have a very deep acquaintance with Hegel but you need to know something about Hegel. Or Hobbes, or Aristotle, or Roland Barthes. We're all smatterers in a way, I suppose. But a certain amount of civilisation depends on intellectual smattering.[4] (Kermode, 'The Ideas Interview')

The same irenic spirit is manifest in the Prologue to *Essays on Fiction 1971–82*, published in 1983, in which Kermode gives a calm but devastating assessment of deconstructionism. He is respectful of Derrida but dismissive of the repetitive dullness of his acolytes. On the other hand, he distanced himself from its more strident critics (1–8). He regrets the absence of a mediating figure during a time of 'embattled vacuity and inaccessibility':

> We lack a great man who might, like Eliot, hold together the new and the traditional, catastrophe and continuity; unfortunately we do not lack doctrinaire and unconsidering people on both sides of the argument. My own inadequacy as a mediator has already been adequately demonstrated. There is a war on, and he who ventures into no-man's-land brandishing cigarettes and singing carols must expect to be shot at. (7)

Echoes of Hans Georg Gadamer's hermeneutics are to be found in Kermode's 'recuperative' view of criticism, as situating oneself within a tradition, rather than constantly seeking to overturn it – or to be more precise, frequently drawing attention to the fact that tradition is 'always already self-subverted' (5).

---

[3]   This affinity between the shape of secular and sacred literature parallels that of Erich Auerbach's *Mimesis* (1953), in which Auerbach highlights how certain capacities in Western literature for psychological and hermeneutical depth derive from biblical narratives, capacities which are beyond the capability of writers in classical antiquity.

[4]   The Collins German–English online dictionary renders 'a smattering of' as 'ein paar Broken' (a few scraps or chunks). I am not sure what we do with Kermode's coinage 'to smatter', or the substantive 'smatterers'!

His appeal to 'the kingdom of the larger existence' in the following quotation also hints at Gadamer's notion of *Bildung*, or formation as an expansion of horizons. Kermode was a non-believer who nevertheless retained 'a faint absenteeist affection' for the Church of England, and his default position at the close of the 1983 Prologue seems to reaffirm the compensatory (here 'surrogate') status of literature:

> There are those who argue that the history of criticism is a history of error; but if we stay within the tradition, rather than seek to overthrow it, we shall have to say rather that it is a history of accommodations, of attempts to earn the privilege of access to that kingdom of the larger existence which is in our time the secular surrogate of another Kingdom whose horizon is no longer within our range. (31–2)

Like Frye, therefore, Kermode finds in literature a shadow or analogy of religious fulfilment. Nevertheless, each is emphatic about 'policing' the border between the two related but autonomous disciplines. Frye cites the image at the conclusion of the *Purgatorio*, when Virgil entrusts Dante to Beatrice: the pagan poet can take the believer no further, and so bids him a courteous farewell.

By contrast, in the work of our third critic, George Steiner, the *cordon sanitaire* between religious and literary meaning seems to have been collapsed – most explicitly in the challenge set out in his 1986 *Real Presences*. The book is at once a refutation of postmodern trends in and outside the academy, thus far in broad agreement with Kermode, and, more intriguingly, a kind of aesthetic argument for the existence of God.

Steiner is what Frye would label as an 'Iliad' critic rather than an 'Odyssey' critic like Frye himself, drawn to comedy and romance. His preferential focus is on the restless, agonistic element of artistic creation, and on tragedy. He is also resolutely modernist, according to Wright's typology, sharing with Scott a resistance to deconstructionist theory.[5] Before *Real Presences*, a preoccupation bordering on obsession with linguistic themes runs through his work, the most salient of which are the nature and possibility of translation (Steiner himself is trilingual in English, French and German, and was a pioneer in the field of comparative literature), and the terrible and enigmatic complicity of language

---

[5]    Scott's appreciation is indicated in his co-editorship with R.A. Sharp of *Reading George Steiner* (1994), in which he has a chapter entitled 'Steiner on Interpretation'. Scott declares Steiner to be 'after Walter Benjamin, perhaps the only other major literary theorist since Coleridge whose literary reflections do in effect ask for completion by a metaphysical and theological project' (Scott 12).

in both the highest achievements of European civilization and its most brutal catastrophes, an ambiguity which dominates his 1967 collection, *Language and Silence: Essays 1958–1966*. His study of Heidegger (1978) probes, naturally, the sensitive questions regarding Heidegger's own existential and political commitments, while essays on Kafka and Schoenberg in this volume indicate his own identification, as a 'kind of survivor', with the middle-European Jewish culture which the National Socialist regime all but exterminated.

Throughout his *oeuvre*, Steiner has, like Scott, turned his back on the New Critical isolationism with regard to the poet and his/her creations. He insists instead on the ethical and even religious responsibility of art and of the artist – the modernist 'heroic' mode – reminding us that 'interpretation' in English can also refer to the total self-investment and 'answerability' of an actor or musician performing a script or a score.

This is not to imply that Steiner views the process of artistic creation as in any sense irenic, rather: 'it is radically agonistic. It is rival. In all substantive art-acts there beats an angry gaiety' (Steiner, *Real Presences* 204). The human maker is forever enraged at 'his coming *after*, at being, forever, second to the original and originating mystery of the forming of form' (204); his art is 'a thrust towards a rivalling totality' (204). Steiner wants to ask whether we can conceive of art without this wrestling. *Real Presences* is therefore a transcendental investigation, in the Kantian sense of examining the enabling condition of meaning in general, and aesthetic meaning in particular. Steiner proposes, in the face of deconstructionist hermeneutics, that 'any coherent understanding of what language is and how language performs, any coherent account of the capacity of human speech to communicate meaning and feeling is, in the final analysis, underwritten by the assumption of God's presence' (3). He argues that experience of aesthetic meaning especially requires the postulation of this 'real presence' as a 'necessary possibility' (3):

> What I affirm is the intuition that where God's presence is no longer a tenable supposition and where His absence is no longer a felt, indeed overwhelming weight, certain dimensions of thought and creativity are no longer attainable. And I would vary Yeats's axiom so as to say: no man can read fully, and answer answeringly to the aesthetic, whose 'nerve and blood' are at peace in sceptical rationality, are now at home in immanence and verification. We must read *as if*. (229)

This 'wager on the meaning of meaning', says Steiner, 'is the wager of Descartes, of Kant and of every poet, artist, composer of whom we have explicit record'.

His survey of those who know best – the poets, the artists – leads to the conclusion: 'I have found no deconstructionist among them' (227). The essay concludes with a powerful and – for a Jewish writer – astonishing coda, a meditation on the motif of the 'longest of days', Holy Saturday (230). Only here, says Steiner, are art and the consolation it brings possible. On Good Friday these are unbearable, on Easter Sunday they are unnecessary; but on our sabbatarian journey, they are indispensable: 'without them how could we be patient?' (232).[6]

However, the coda itself highlights the challenge and frustration that many feel in Steiner's work. Clearly, for the non-Christian and for the non-believer, the Paschal mystery of the crucified and risen Christ is being invoked in an analogical or metaphorical sense. But what then is the precise value of his religious affirmations of the transcendent, and what existential commitment do they entail, especially given Steiner's understandable Jewish refusal to engage in systematic theological argumentation? The lack of a coherent content is noted by a number of critics (for example, Kuschel 13–15), and the sense that Steiner seems to privilege the indirection of the creative arts over theological affirmation and yet have recourse to religious rhetoric at crucial moments, describing music, for example, as an 'unwritten theology' for those without formal creed, reaffirms the antagonistic relation of art and theology.

## Literature and Theology, 'Cheek by Jowl'

The three authors discussed above come from different faith backgrounds. Nevertheless each affirms the importance of the conversation between literary criticism and theology – though the ambiguity of Steiner's approach causes disquiet. They do so to such an extent that Jasper and his colleagues in 1987 can discern in their work a 'distinctively contemporary convergence' of the two disciplines. It is interesting to note, therefore, the apparent lack of progress in constructing the 'discipline' of literature-and-theology, despite their intense interaction over the previous 50 or 60 years. Scholars like Jasper and Detweiler, having opted for a 'postmodern' stance, seem unperturbed by this situation, and even suggest that they are quite happy to labour on the margins of the two disciplines, a far cry from the intentions expressed in the 1987 'manifesto' of *Literature and Theology*.

---

6    The Holy Saturday motif, powerfully and controversially revived for theology by Hans Urs von Balthasar, seems to have found its way to Steiner through the theology of George McKinnon. Another Cambridge theologian, Nicholas Lash, reflects upon this theme in 'Friday, Saturday, Sunday'.

It is clear that this hybrid discipline has not grown in a vacuum, but has been shaped contingently and markedly by the crisis of religious faith in Britain and the United States, which is for the most part a crisis of decline and stagnation (allowing for two very different cultural contexts). We have explored one example from either side of the Atlantic. The assertion by Eagleton that the study of literature blossomed as religion declined in nineteenth-century Britain inevitably renders the scholarly relationship between literature and theology as something of a 'turf war'. In the United States, on one reading at least, liberation from the strictures of the New Critics is a Reformation motif, a 'Protestant' gesture against an Anglo-Catholic domination pretending to scientific neutrality. Of course, many of the poets at the centre of the literature-and-religion canon, such as Milton, Blake and the Romantics, reinforce this gesture of nonconformist defiance – the religious allegiance of Shakespeare remains the exceptional enigma within this canon of dissent. Steiner, on the artist's 'loving rage' towards a totality which rivals that of God, and Bloom's 'anxiety of influence', are distinctive Jewish perspectives on this agonistic relationship.

A further problem is that, when the circumstances for a balanced conversation between literature and theology are less than favourable, there can be an intensification of the polarity within literature itself, its double function of 'instruction' and 'delight'. Theology, or a critical concern for transcendence, will pull towards the 'instructive' pole. By implication, the literary imagination *per se* is drawn towards promiscuous dispersal, leading to the 'division of labour' proposed by the theologian Paul Fiddes: 'Poetic metaphor and narratives rejoice in ambiguity and the opening up of multiple meaning; doctrine will always seek to reduce to concepts the images and stories upon which it draws – including those within its own scripture ... In short, literature tends to openness and doctrine to closure' (7).

If Fiddes is correct, and if Jasper and Detweiler are also correct in championing a postmodern 'turn' in the literature-and-theology conversation, then it is difficult to see how theology can remain an equal partner, since theology's very tendency to 'closure' is precisely what postmodernism on principle disallows. At best, theology and literature may have a shared life, necessary to each other because mutually corrective, but extrinsic to one another and implicitly resentful.

Is there a need here for a more sacramental, less dialectical articulation of the literature–theology relation? Jasper hints at this in his invocation of the Chalcedonian formula concerning the mysterious unity of Christ's human and divine natures, without separation, without confusion. In *Sacred and Secular Scriptures: A Catholic Approach to Literature* (2004), Nicholas Boyle is inspired by the French Dominican theologian Jean Marie-Dominique Chenu, who posits 'literature as the site of theology' (3). Such a site may serve as a place of mediation, because it is occupied by both sacred and secular scriptures: God, in revealing Godself, has, in Chenu's words, 'entered into association with a literary not a theological type of comprehensibility' (Boyle 4, 267). An acceptance of the Bible as literature, understood as a kind of *kenosis* or humbling, would bring about the elevation to a new dignity of literature itself. The Bible can in this way mediate between human culture and divine truth.

Upon this 'marvellous exchange' – the Bible as literature, and literature as Bible – Boyle wishes to construct a Catholic critical method of reading literature. In a chapter entitled 'Rewards and Fairies (I): The Idea of England', surveying what has been lost as a result of the Reformation, Boyle examines various appeals to a compensatory 'transcendence' in English national identity in Rudyard Kipling, Rupert Brook, J.R.R. Tolkien, and even in the James Bond films (221–47). Boyle remains clear, however, that the recovery project of a (Catholic) Christian humanism must not be a *reprise* of earlier hegemonic exercises. He distances himself, for example, from Balthasar's *Theological Aesthetics* and its colonization of literature by theology. There is no question of reinstating what Frye sardonically critiqued in Eliot and the New Critics as the 'Great Western Butterslide'.[7] This recovery project may be more a question of discerning, for example, what draws a thinker so far from Catholic commitment as the 'political theologian' Slavoj Žižek to the writings of G.K. Chesterton. Though an avowedly Marxist Lacanian, Žižek's injunction with regard to our cultural and political options may be cited here: 'Against today's onslaughts of New Age neo-paganism, it thus seems both theoretically productive and politically salient to stick to Judaeo-Christian logic' (107).

## Towards *eutrapelia*

Can the relationship between the two disciplines be revisited, so that a fruitful convergence may be discerned once more? Boyle argues for one such possibility in recovering a Catholic humanist perspective, echoed in Žižek. To push this further would require us to problematize the dichotomy set up by Paul Fiddes, and suggest a third position. This is the possibility that religious hope can be authentically conveyed with a lightness of touch, a delight which must always seem frivolous to more earnest temperaments. The German theologian Hugo

---

7   'The Great Western Butterslide, in which a large blob of Christian, Classical and Royalist butter melted down and congealed at last into *The Waste Land*' (Bloom ix).

Rahner, in his work entitled *Man at Play* (1965), expounds the Aristotelian virtue of *eutrapelia*, which denotes 'wittiness' or pleasantness in conversation; it represents the 'golden mean' between boorishness [ἀγροικία] and buffoonery [βωμολοχία] (2). Interestingly, what is extolled as a virtue in Aristotle later came to signify obscene or coarse jokes. The term makes only one biblical appearance, a negative one, in Ephesians 5:4: 'Let there be no filthiness, nor silly talk [*eutrapelia*], nor levity, which are not fitting' (Revised Standard Version).

I also wish to propose and explore the possibility that the tolerant Anglo-Saxon academic culture which produced the likes of Detweiler and Kermode – which, in short, enabled the practice of *eutrapelia* – is being largely swept away in the present culture war, in which a civilized conversation between believers and (new) atheists is becoming a rare event, and where rudeness and light-headedness too often seem to be default positions.

We shall return to this, but firstly a more theoretical exploration of what is at stake may be found in Steiner's essay, 'A Reading Against Shakespeare' (*No Passion Spent* 108–28). As noted above, all three of the chosen scholars, Frye, Kermode and Steiner, have engaged extensively with Shakespeare, but Steiner's essay is possibly the most intriguing. He notes various objections to the genius of Shakespeare, from Eliot, Shaw and Tolstoy; but it is the bewilderment of Ludwig Wittgenstein which forms the theoretical heart of the essay. Briefly, Wittgenstein declared that he 'cannot do anything with Shakespeare', nor avoid the impression that Shakespeare is praised because 'this is the thing to do', rather than out of genuine appreciation. According to Steiner, Wittgenstein's problem is that Shakespeare lacks the seriousness which we are to associate with the calling of the *Dichter*, the 'priest-poet'. This term is charged with philosophical significance as a result of Martin Heidegger tracing the mutual echoes of *dichten* (to create), *denken* (to think) and *danken* (to thank). Heidegger renders *Dichter* as the 'shepherd of Being', the one who is entrusted with 'responsibility for life', and with making good humanity's 'ostracism' from Being and from the gods. The speech of the poet re-enacts primordial creation. It is therefore, once again, an act of rivalry directed at the absent deities, one which invokes self-destruction. The example of Hölderlin, driven to mental breakdown by his obsession with his divine vocation, is key (Steiner, *Heidegger* 142–3).

In short, this is what *real* poets are for: this is what they are and what they do. The case 'against Shakespeare' that Steiner seeks to reconstruct is that his promiscuous imagination and his tragic-comic vision fall short of this intensity and this vocation. Shakespeare's drama yields no coherent and responsible world-view, no genuine 'answerability'. From such a perspective, the comic and bizarre interludes (for example, the doorkeeper in *Macbeth* and Gloucester's suicidal 'leap' from the Dover cliff-top in *King Lear*) can only appear grotesque and barbarous. Shakespeare's art does not, after all, take us to the heart of life, nor of the religious question it poses. Wittgenstein's puzzled verdict echoes those of Matthew Arnold, who argued that great art should demonstrate 'high seriousness', and of Eliot, that literary criticism and, by implication, the literature on which it comments 'should be completed by criticism from a definite ethical and theological standpoint' (97).

Not surprisingly, Steiner is uncomfortable with this judgement on Shakespeare, and seeks elsewhere to tune into hints of the divine to be found in Shakespearean drama. As indicated above, however, Steiner's project seems to founder on his own reticence to be more explicit about his own appeal to transcendence. There is also the concern, expressed by more than one commentator, that his insights are too hermetic and frankly too elitist to be helpful in the current debate.

It is interesting to contrast Steiner in this respect with Eagleton, whose own recent writings on literature-and-theology are vividly pugnacious. Eagleton's original commitment to Marxist-Catholic dialogue in the 1960s – he consistently acknowledges his indebtedness to the Dominican theologian Herbert McCabe – transformed in the subsequent decades into a vigorous resistance to postmodernist ideology, which he understands to be largely a despairing and compensatory gesture in the face of the post-1968 crisis of the left (Eagleton, *The Illusions of Postmodernism*). More recently, the theological dimension of the conversation has resurged. Much of Eagleton's writing in this vein has been a kind of negative or corrective theology. Above all, he protests vigorously against the grotesque and wilful misrepresentation of religion and of Christianity, which we find in the polemical literature of Richard Dawkins and Christopher Hitchens (Eagleton, *Reason, Faith, and Revolution*).

Eagleton is no less robust, however, in his dismissal of Alain de Botton's 'religion for atheists', according to which religious instincts and longings are to be catered for without any appeal to the transcendent. Such a project is merely the latest 'Arnoldian' attempt to colonize religion for cultural purposes; a conquest which, insofar as it immunizes against the prophetic-humanist demands of biblical faith, merely reinforces the stranglehold of late-capitalism on any kind of effective ethical or political protest (Eagleton, 'Religion for Atheists – review').

Eagleton's post-Marxist demotic offers a lively and sometimes bruising counterpart to Steiner's alleged 'mandarin' aloofness. They present very different commitments in the literature-and-theology debate, though in their reticence, even antipathy towards the postmodern turn, they have much in common. Both have focused on the question and possibility of 'tragedy'. From different perspectives, they address the seeming inability of our age to give authentic tragic form to our predicament and pathologies. In *Sweet Violence* (2003) Eagleton challenges Steiner's assertion that tragedy and Christianity are incompatible. The resurrection of Jesus does not annul the horror of Good Friday, and it is in his 'becoming sin' that Jesus truly enters into the predicament of the tragic persona (283). Graham Ward's exposition (2005) of Eagleton's book allows the difference with Steiner to be resolved. The tragic as a description of humanity's relation to God's 'intolerable presence' is not denied but nor is it allowed to have the last word, insofar as God in the abandoned and crucified Christ takes tragedy into himself.

## Conclusion

The critics fêted in *Literature and Theology* 25 years ago as the heralds of a new interdisciplinary convergence – Frye, Kermode and Steiner – shared the elusive conversational quality of *eutrapelia* which held promise of an overcoming of ancient barriers of mutual suspicion. This promise does not seem to have been fulfilled; at least, it has not issued in the formalized construction of (effectively) a new subject area, which the 1987 manifesto aspired to. The description by Jasper and others 20 years later is much scaled-down, as critics are content after all to work on the borders, and to see regeneration as coming from within each of the disciplines, rather than from their interaction as such. This implies a 'postmodern' suspicion of centres, as well as a recovery of silenced or marginalized voices. The mystic is at one with the poet in having a theological voice which is 'unauthorized' and unrecognized by the official doctrinal theologies, but is a voice nonetheless. What is evident in some of the critics we have considered, Jasper and Steiner, for example, is a pessimism about the capacity of formal religion either to reverse its general decline into irrelevance or to offer effective resistance to the magnetic pull towards extremism and fundamentalism. 'The best lack all conviction ...' (Yeats 294).

From the artists themselves, we can continue to discern interesting in-between spaces. There are, to be sure, prominent literary voices that have situated themselves firmly in the New Atheist camp, or at least have associated their work with the protest against religious fundamentalism and extremism. The controversy around Salman Rushdie's magical-realist *Satanic Verses* (1988) is, in this respect, iconic, while in the post-9/11 period the writings and commentary of Ian McEwan and Martin Amis suggest a kind of consensus among prominent writers and the intelligentsia.[8]

This is misleading, as the consensus is by no means overwhelming. The fiction of Margaret Atwood exemplifies the 'biblical' turn noted above, a gesture which is, strictly, a return to the potential of biblical myth. Atwood's own views express a tantalizing middle ground. Novels such as *The Handmaid's Tale* exemplify liberal abhorrence of religiously inspired totalitarianism, and yet her pronouncement in an interview on faith and religion that 'we cannot uproot the hunger for God without uprooting language' is a direct echo of George Steiner's theological aesthetic (Atwood, 'Margaret Atwood on Religion').

In the same interview, Atwood's acknowledgement that religious extremism seems to coincide with periods of social upheaval and uncertainty brings her close to the 'mimetic' analysis of the French American social anthropologist and literary critic, René Girard. She refers explicitly to the role of 'scapegoats' in maintaining order ('Margaret Atwood on Religion'). Girard's insights into 'violence and the sacred' have been gleaned from reading an immense variety of texts: mythical and anthropological testimonies, literary classics including Shakespeare, Dostoyevsky and Proust, and the Bible. He is explicit about the importance of the Christian revelation in enabling him to formulate these insights. Girard's is a distinctive and provocative voice within contemporary literary criticism, though not a mainstream one.

Or we might consider certain works of popular children's literature which have attracted theological commentary. The trilogy from Philip Pullman, *His Dark Materials*, and the Harry Potter books of J.K. Rowling are each the product of an indirect but real religious intent on the part of their author. Pullman expresses a desire to create a universe that will undermine Christian faith, while Rowling has become more explicit about her subtle affirmation of a Christian world-view, despite, it should be added, a lot of hysterical Christian antipathy towards her alleged celebration of witchcraft and paganism.

And yet, of the two authors, Pullman is more sophisticated in his dependence on literary-theological ideas. The ontology of *His Dark Materials* is familiar to anyone acquainted with Milton and Blake. Rowan Williams has commended Pullman's vitriolic attacks on theological totalitarianism as fully in line with what a purified, anti-idolatrous Christianity should be ready to profess.[9] Pullman has

---

[8]  See Tina Beattie, who includes these two novelists in her survey of *The New Atheists*. Beattie pays particular attention to McEwan's 2005 novel, *Saturday*.

[9]  See the discussion between Philip Pullman and Rowan Williams: 'The Dark Materials Debate: Life, God, the Universe ...' Williams himself is of course a noted commentator on the potential of literature for accessing theological themes.

in fact consented to the term 'theological' as a descriptor for his novels. It is ironic that his fiction, understood as a purification of false and idolatrous belief, might actually work more effectively in the cause of genuine religious commitment than Rowling's more discretely positive theological affirmation.[10]

If there is still a 'theological' voice in the literature-and-theology conversation, therefore, it is more likely to be heard from the site of unofficial or 'disguised theology'. Boyle's explicit espousal of a Christian humanist approach to literature is something of an exceptional voice.

At the close of *Real Presences*, Steiner indicts the deconstructionists with a lack of courtesy, in the brashness of their inquiry and their wilful refusal to acknowledge any first principles. Such a default scepticism is ultimately corrosive of understanding (230). It is precisely the stance of lovingly attentive courtesy which distinguishes the 'reader' from the 'critic'. The numinosity to which Steiner is appealing is not only 'present' in the work of art; it infuses the act of reading itself, our comportment of hospitality towards the text.

To return to the *eutrapelia* ideal, understood once again as the mean between two excesses: we appear to have survived (just) the irresponsible frivolity of postmodernity's theoretical excesses and the sheer tactlessness of its interrogations. The new threat to dialogue, it seems, comes from the other side of the balance, from a cultural allergy to religion, which, if not always boorish, certainly seems to lack sophistication and could do with 'lightening up'. Perhaps the tide is now turning, but the 'God debate' has been characterized by a deep joylessness on both sides, perhaps, but certainly among the so-called new atheist camp and its sloganizing campaigns.

Meanwhile, the 'Arnoldian' temptation to co-opt religious sentiment for the purposes of social and political stability is never far away. We have noted Alain de Botton's rendering of *Religion for Atheists*; however, the most breathtaking example would be A.C. Grayling's *The Good Book: A Secular Guide*, which is a rewriting of the Bible as a compendium of timeless philosophical and literary wisdom. Eagleton has taken both De Botton and Christopher Hitchens to task for precisely this strategy:

> I would simply point out that if we are to look to literature for our mode of
> transcendence, we are most certainly in deep trouble. This is not necessarily
> because we should look to religion instead. It is because, from Matthew Arnold
> and F.R. Leavis to I.A. Richards, new criticism, Northrop Frye and George

---

[10]    See, for example, a series of articles by Nikolaus Wandinger et al. ('Harry Potter and the Art of Theology') for an examination of Rowling's novels read theologically.

> Steiner, the campaign to convert literature into a pseudo-religion has ended up doing it considerable damage. Literature is both more and less important than that. (Eagleton, *Reason, Faith, and Revolution* 83–4)

The paragraph is, alas, nothing more than an aside in Eagleton's overall argument in this book. What, precisely, is the force of that hesitant but tantalizing 'necessarily'? And does Eagleton really mean to subsume these very different critics and styles under a single, dubious proselytizing enterprise? 'Campaign' suggests a conscious, strategic, co-operative effort, which sounds highly unlikely, given the diversity of the individuals named here. The need for vigilance is as strong as ever, requiring perhaps a clear and robustly positive relation between religion and literature and theology and literature, one that insists on neither being colonized by the other. But how is such a relation to be satisfactorily described? It seems as if the new conversation heralded in 1987 is still only just beginning.

## Works Cited

Atwood, Margaret. 'Margaret Atwood on Religion' 1/3. YouTube. 31 July 2006. Accessed 7 February 2014. <http://www.youtube.com/watch?v=VMrz_ivl8jo>.

Auerbach, Erich. *Mimesis: The Representation of Reality in Western Literature*. 1953. Princeton, NJ: Princeton University Press, 2003.

Beattie, Tina. *The New Atheists: The Twilight of Reason and the War on Religion*. London: Darton, Longman and Todd, 2007.

Bloom, Harold. 'Northrop Frye in Retrospect'. Foreword in Northrop Frye, *The Anatomy of Criticism*. 1957. Princeton, NJ: Princeton University Press, 2000, vii–xi.

Boyle, Nicholas. *Sacred and Secular Scriptures: A Catholic Approach to Literature*. London: Darton, Longman and Todd, 2004.

'The Dark Materials Debate: Life, God, the Universe ...' *The Telegraph*. 17 March 2004. Accessed 7 August 2013. <http://www.telegraph.co.uk/culture/3613962/The-Dark-Materials-debate-life-God-the-universe....html>.

—— ed. *Art/Literature/Religion: Life on the Borders*. Journal of American Academy of Religious Studies. Thematic Studies II (5–6) (1983).

Detweiler, Robert and David Jasper, eds. *Religion and Literature: A Reader*. [Great Britain]: Westminster John Knox Press, 2000.

Eagleton, Terry. *The Illusions of Postmodernism*. Oxford: Blackwell, 1996.

—— *Literary Theory: An Introduction*. Oxford: Blackwell, 1996.

—— *Reason, Faith, and Revolution: Reflections on the God Debate*. New Haven: Yale University Press, 2009.

—— 'Religion for Atheists by Alain de Botton – review'. *The Guardian*. 12 January 2012. Accessed 7 February 2014. <http://www.theguardian.com/books/2012/jan/12/religion-for-atheists-de-botton-review>.

—— *Sweet Violence: The Idea of the Tragic*. Oxford: Blackwell, 2003.

Eliot, T.S. 'Religion and Literature'. In *Selected Prose*. New York: Harcourt, 1975, 97–106.

Fiddes, Paul S. *The Promised End: Eschatology in Theology and Literature*. Oxford: Blackwell, 2000.

Frye, Northrop. *The Anatomy of Criticism*. 1957. Princeton, NJ: Princeton University Press, 2000.

—— *Fools of Time: Studies in Shakespearean Tragedy*. Toronto: University of Toronto Press, 1967.

—— *The Great Code: The Bible and Literature*. London: Routledge and Kegan Paul, 1982.

—— *The Myth of Deliverance: Reflections on Shakespeare's Problem Comedies*. Toronto: University of Toronto Press, 1983.

—— *A Natural Perspective: The Development of Shakespearean Comedy and Romance*. New York: Columbia University Press, 1965.

—— *Northrop Frye on Shakespeare*. Ed. Robert Sandler. New Haven: Yale University Press, 1986.

Grayling, Anthony C. *The Good Book: A Secular Guide*. London: Bloomsbury, 2011.

Hass, Andrew, David Jasper and Elisabeth Jay, eds. *The Oxford Handbook of English Literature and Theology*. Oxford: Oxford University Press, 2007.

Jasper, David. 'Interdisciplinarity in Impossible Times: Studying Religion through Literature and the Arts'. In *Literature and Theology: New Interdisciplinary Spaces*, ed. Heather Walton. Farnham: Ashgate, 2011, 5–18.

—— 'The Study of Literature and Theology'. In *The Oxford Handbook of English Literature and Theology*, ed. Andrew Hass, David Jasper and Elisabeth Jay. Oxford: Oxford University Press, 2007, 15–32.

Jasper, David et al. 'Editorial'. *Literature and Theology* 1.1 (March 1987): iii–v.

Jay, Elisabeth. 'Now and in England'. In *The Oxford Handbook of English Literature and Theology*, ed. Andrew Hass, David Jasper and Elisabeth Jay. Oxford: Oxford University Press, 2007, 3–14.

Kermode, Frank. *Essays on Fiction 1971–82*. London: Routledge and Kegan Paul, 1983.

——— *The Genesis of Secrecy: On the Interpretation of Narrative*. London: Harvard University Press, 1979.

——— 'The Ideas Interview: Frank Kermode'. *The Guardian*. 29 August 2006. Accessed 7 February 2014. <http://www.theguardian.com/education/2006/aug/29/highereducation.ideas>.

——— *The Sense of an Ending: Studies in the Theory of Fiction*. 1966. Oxford: Oxford University Press, 2000.

Kermode, Frank and Robert Alter, eds. *The Literary Guide to the Bible*. London: Collins and Sons, 1987.

Kuschel, Karl-Josef. 'Presence of God? Towards the Possibility of a Theological Aesthetic in an Analysis of George Steiner'. *Literature and Theology* 10.1 (March 1996): 1–19.

Lash, Nicholas. 'Friday, Saturday, Sunday'. *New Blackfriars* 71 (1990): 109–19.

'Northrop Frye Centre'. *Victoria College, University of Toronto*. Accessed 27 August 2013. <http://www.vic.utoronto.ca/academics/Research_Centres/fryecentre.htm>.

Pullman, Philip. *His Dark Materials*. New York: Knopf, 2007.

Rahner, Hugo. *Man at Play; or, Did You Ever Practise Eutrapelia?* London: Burns and Oates, 1965.

Ricoeur, Paul. *The Symbolism of Evil*. Boston: Beacon Press, 1969.

Scott, Nathan A., Jr. 'Steiner on Interpretation'. In *Reading George Steiner*, ed. Nathan A. Scott Jr and R.A. Sharp. Baltimore: Johns Hopkins University Press, 1994, 1–13.

Steiner, George. *The Death of Tragedy*. London: Faber and Faber, 1961.

——— *Heidegger*. London: Fontana, 1978.

——— *Language and Silence: Essays 1958–1966*. London: Faber and Faber, 1967.

——— *No Passion Spent: Essays 1978–1996*. London: Faber and Faber, 1996.

——— *Real Presences: Is There Anything in What We Say?* Chicago: University of Chicago Press, 1991.

Tracy, David. *The Analogical Imagination*. New York: Crossroad, 1981.

Walton, Heather. *Literature and Theology: New Interdisciplinary Spaces*. Farnham: Ashgate, 2011.

Wandinger, Nikolaus et al. 'Harry Potter and the Art of Theology 1'. *Milltown Studies* 52 (2003): 1–26.

——— 'Harry Potter and the Art of Theology 2'. *Milltown Studies* 53 (2003): 131–53.

—— 'Harry Potter and the Art of Theology Revisited'. *Milltown Studies* 61 (2008): 84–120.

Ward, Graham. 'Steiner and Eagleton: The Practice of Hope and the Idea of the Tragic'. *Literature and Theology* 19 (June 2005): 100–111.

Wright, Terry. 'Religion and Literature from the Modern to the Postmodern: Scott, Steiner and Detweiler'. *Literature and Theology* 19.1 (2005): 3–21.

Yeats, W.B. *Yeats's Poems, Edited and Annotated by A. Norman Jeffares with an Appendix by Warwick Gould.* London: Macmillan, 1989.

Žižek, Slavoj. *The Fragile Absolute: or, Why is the Christian Legacy Worth Fighting For?* London and New York: Verso, 2000.

Chapter 2

# Why Theologians Are Interested in Literature: Theological-Literary Hermeneutics in the Works of Guardini, Balthasar, Tillich and Kuschel

Georg Langenhorst

What makes literature interesting for theologians and why does an academically trained systematic theologian need poetry? This chapter will suggest four answers and four positions from a German perspective in order to throw light on the relationship between 'theology' and 'literature'. The first answer to these questions is that the poetic word 'always serves to make an experience or a thing – or perhaps human destiny – more meaningful and more clear' (Guardini, *Elegies* 303). More specifically, particularly in a poem, a reader takes a new stance towards existence, 'deeper than an everyday stance and more alive than a philosopher's stance' because 'words that offer a deeper understanding of the world have more power than those of custom and are more original than the speech of an intellectual' (Guardini, *Sprache* 154).[1]

The writer of these lines, Romano Guardini (1885–1968), is considered to be one of the greatest theological interpreters of literature of the twentieth century. From the outset he combined his vocation as a theologian with his interest in and love of literature, the arts and philosophy. In his childhood he was an avid reader. If he could have chosen his career freely and independently of his family's wishes and the contemporary socio-political context, he would have 'probably studied philology and literature', as he says in his autobiographical writings (*Berichte* 65).

What role, then, did poetry actually play in Guardini's life and thinking? What is the significance of Guardini's interpretations of literary works for theology, or more specifically theology and literature? To start with, let us look

---

[1] All the following direct quotations that are not available in English have been translated by Georg Langenhorst.

at the situation that Guardini encountered when he first started thinking about the relationship between the two. How did contemporary theologians deal with poetry at that time? More precisely, was any hermeneutical significance granted to literature by theology? Obviously theologians have always read fiction and poetry in their leisure time. But did they normally integrate these private literary experiences with their theological thinking and writing?[2]

## Theology and Literature in the Pre-Modern Period

To talk about 'religion' on the one hand and 'literature' on the other as two distinct endeavours has not been the norm in European thought. Notwithstanding their differences, in the pre-modern period these two areas, it can be claimed, belonged together. The emancipation of the arts from Christianity only took place in the seventeenth century. It then quickly took hold. The idea that the arts in general and literature in particular were 'autonomous' prevailed and became widely accepted on account of the secularization of culture at the beginning of the nineteenth century.

Their autonomy did not exclude connections between them. On the contrary, it was only after the coexistence between the Christian churches and the production of literature had been broken that independent, creative and challenging literary works emerged and looked afresh and impartially at the Christian tradition. Prior to this separation, an important aspect of literature had been that of embellishing, illustrating and affirming religious doctrines. The tension between theology and literature today has been rewarding for both. Theology is able to reassess itself and develop by considering the reflections and provocations to be found in literature. Literature, on the other hand, can grow artistically through its continual involvement with traditional religions, religious experience and theological contemplation.

In German-speaking countries the first theological reflections on this new relationship between theology and literature occurred when the term 'Christian literature' was used in contrast to 'secular literature', a distinction which hitherto had not been invoked. The expression was first applied by the Romantic August Wilhelm Schlegel (1767–1845), who, together with his contemporaries Joseph Freiherr von Eichendorff, Clemens Brentano and Annette von Droste-Hülshoff, attempted to heal the breach between literature and religion. The expression

---

[2]    For more information on this, see Langenhorst, *Theologie*: <www.theologie-und-literatur.de>.

'Christian literature' was a direct response to secularization. However, in the following decades the term and concept 'Christian literature' remained only loosely defined.

To this day, the best definition of the expression is that of Gisbert Kranz, the most influential advocate of Christian literature. In 1961, in his *Christliche Literatur in der Gegenwart* ('Christian Literature Today'), he stated that he was merely presenting 'works of world literature' which 'display Christianity from a faithful Christian perspective' (7), without opposition or objections to this definition. In the years that followed, Kranz proposed a more precise understanding in his monumental *Lexikon der Christlichen Weltliteratur* ('Encyclopaedia of Christian World Literature'): 'Christian literature is a type of literature – no matter the genre or subject – which has been produced with a Christian understanding of God, human kind and the world around us. As a result, it cannot be adequately interpreted without such a Christian understanding' (4).

In the 1950s and 1960s attempts were made to reinvigorate the concept of Christian literature. But why were academics interested in this term? What motivation or interest in it can be discerned today? It is revealing that this debate concentrated mainly on contemporary writers who were part of the *renouveau catholique*, an international movement of writers which promoted a Catholic view of the world and tried to revive Catholic aesthetics. The word *renouveau* indicated the conservative nature of the movement. Though it is hazardous to generalize, given the wide range of authors, styles, intentions and literary texts that it included, the movement as a whole refused to come to terms with modernity. As a reaction to the crises of modernity and their repercussions, it promulgated a return to a safe, religious, Christian, denominational perception of the world as a closed reality.

In particular, the use of both the literary forms and the content of the pre-modern era, adherence to a rigid, pre-secular world-view, and the refusal to accept modern developments and changes marked the first wave of academic discourse in the field of 'theology and literature' in Germany. This was exactly the way in which theology considered poetry and the climate that Guardini encountered when he published his interpretation of literature. So what did Guardini learn from his predecessors and what was novel about his contribution?

## Poets as Prophets of Our Time: Romano Guardini

Awe and surprise are the natural reactions to the scale and scope of Guardini's interpretations. Apart from his shorter studies of Dante, Goethe, Shakespeare,

Hopkins, Wilhelm Raabe and Mörike, he published three monographs on major literary figures: Dostoyevsky (1932), Hölderlin (1939) and Rilke (1953). Let us look more closely at what inspired his interest in literature, an interest that went far beyond common enthusiasm for poetry. As he writes in his introductory remarks to his interpretation of Wilhelm Raabe's 'Stopfkuchen', Guardini did not 'so much want to talk in general terms about the book as really to interpret it' (*Sprache* 87). What does he mean by 'really interpret it'? What does it mean for him as a theologian and philosopher? Why was he so fascinated by these three particular authors? How did he interpret the fictitious worlds of these writers to his readers?

Guardini's passionate involvement with literature was inspired by the philosopher Max Scheler (1874–1928). When Guardini was appointed to the chair of 'Philosophy of Religion and Catholic *Weltanschaung*' in Berlin, one that had been created especially for him, he did not know at the start exactly how to structure his programme of study. During what was for Guardini a 'very momentous talk', Scheler, who was eleven years his senior, recommended, as he later noted, the following: 'You have to make real the content of the word *Weltanschaung*: to contemplate the world, things, human kind and their works with the eyes – and here lies your personal expertise – of a responsible Christian. Then you have to talk about all the things you see in an academic form of discourse.' Scheler also gave him additional advice: 'For example, examine Dostoyevsky's texts. Then discuss them from your Christian perspective in order to shed light on the text and its contextual starting-point' (*Stationen* 19–20). Guardini followed this advice and would always remember his colleague with gratitude.

Scheler's recommendations were, of course, only an external cause of Guardini's interest in the interpretation of literature. Two inner convictions defined his study of literature. In his momentous work *Das Ende der Neuzeit* ('The End of the Modern World'), published in 1950, he formulated a fundamental critique of rational technological expediency in modernity on which he blamed the catastrophes of the world wars and the Nazi regime. All Guardini's works emphasize the intellectual potential of Christianity to act as a true spiritual guideline in the post-war era. It was by referring to the great poetic-religious thinkers in history that he developed this spiritual concept. In this context, it is essential to know what kind of Christianity he wanted to strengthen as a spiritual counter-weight. It was neither the rigid system of pre-modern theology, which he linked to the concept of neo-scholasticism, nor the hierarchical, inflexible forms of the current regime in the Roman Catholic Church, with its fossilized liturgical routine. For Guardini, returning to pre-modern times was not an option. He was convinced that Christianity had to prove its worth and find a new form and conception of itself appropriate to modernity.

To manifest such a living spirituality, one that would push against current boundaries, and to demonstrate its profound impact, Guardini needed witnesses. For that reason he looked to the writings of the great authors, in both philosophy and literature. Guardini, who was both a theologian and a philosopher, had his own 'private canon of poetry' firmly rooted in the 'tradition of the seers and the prophets' (Kuschel, 'Modernismuskrise' 174). According to Karl-Josef Kuschel, the texts which Guardini interpreted stood as an 'intellectual and spiritual counterbalance' to, on the one hand, 'the *Zeitgeist* of rational, technological expediency' and 'a narrow ecclesiastical understanding of revelation on the other' ('Modernismuskrise' 174).

For this reason, it is hardly surprising that Guardini did not turn to explicitly Christian thinkers who did no more than re-emphasize traditional beliefs. Instead he grouped his chosen authors into a category called 'seers'. For him, they all have the gift of acting as visionary prophets. This is the essential trait which made his authors religious witnesses: the ability to see and express truth more clear-sightedly, profoundly and sharply. Guardini's way of introducing Hölderlin will serve as an example. In contrast with other poets' work, Hölderlin's does not spring from 'the strength of an author which can be determined by authenticity of experience, a clarity of the eye, a power of style or exactness'. Instead, for Guardini the distinctive feature of Hölderlin was 'his vision and restlessness as a seer'. The origin of his works 'lies in a more inward and higher order', with the result that it is 'in the service of a calling' that cannot be ignored without 'resisting a power which transcends the being and desire of the individual' (Guardini, *Hölderlin* 11–12). Consequently, in Hölderlin the reader not only encountered 'the voice of a brilliant human being' but also experienced the divine voice.

## As Much Contact as Possible with the Actual Texts

Guardini's comments on Hölderlin's style are typical of the authors and texts that he chose to interpret. Dostoyevsky's novels capture his interest because they offer the possibility of demonstrating the religious sentiments of outstanding characters in literature. These characters were 'exposed to their fate and to divine powers in a particular way' (Guardini, *Der Mensch* 11). Writers' visionary powers help to pave the way to a deeper understanding of the human soul. Guardini was interested in seekers, disturbed and disturbing visionaries, or people torn between divergent ideals and styles of life. To him they were kindred spirits standing as witnesses to 'the end of the modern era'. It was in relation to these authors and their texts that a new spirituality, a new firmly grounded view of the world, had to prove its worth.

This was why Guardini focused on Rilke, who, in his words, was 'the most sensitive and subtle German poet of modern times' (*Elegies* 9). With no other poet's work did Guardini struggle so much as with Rilke's; no other poet both fascinated and repulsed him as much. For him, Rilke – like Hölderlin – had 'a mediating disposition' (*Elegies* 9) because he saw himself 'in the situation of a seer' and was 'convinced that he was the bearer of a message which had been "dictated" to him from a source which could only be described as "religious"' (*Elegies* 13). According to Guardini, Rilke saw himself as 'a prophet – an inspired vessel filled with the divine voice which spoke through him. Rilke himself had to listen to his own words and "penetrate" them gradually' (*Elegies* 14). His impulse to provoke led him to present these religious elements in ways that were 'in deliberate contrast' to the Christian world-view (*Elegies* 14).

Guardini was in contact with numerous writers of his time. He was friendly with many, often inviting them to his lectures, and exchanged letters and read their works. Remarkably, however, at no point did he offer public interpretations of works published in his own day. This was a significant and probably deliberate policy. Literary criticism entailed analysing the complete oeuvre of an author. Nor did he want to taint his interpretations with personal acquaintance or with ties of friendship. It was not writers as witnesses to the present but a theological conception of literary texts and their spiritual-intellectual worlds that absorbed him.

Guardini's emphasis on a personal appropriation and spiritual interpretation of literary texts is evident in the way that he approached them. He describes his technique in the preface to his book on Hölderlin: 'I tried to get into close contact with the texts themselves' (*Hölderlin* 17). Generally, he did not focus on an academic analysis of a literary work but deliberately preferred an individual style of reading guided by 'philosophical intentions' (*Hölderlin* 23). He said, almost jokingly, that he did not read secondary sources, not even important ones: 'I intentionally abstained from the expertise of each different discipline ... I rather preferred to follow my instincts' (*Berichte* 47). He deliberately limited the secondary literature he read in advance 'to a minimum which was essential in order to be informed about the main facts' (*Hölderlin* 17). In his autobiographical notes he claims to have developed a method by which he could 'gain an understanding – on the basis of an exact interpretation of the text – of the whole thoughts and personality' and thereby 'extract the Christian content from all the dilutions and blendings' brought on by 'modern relativism' (*Berichte* 46).

Guardini's method of a close reading of original texts and his struggle with message, meaning and truth are intriguing but they came at a cost. Though still worth reading, his interpretations lack academic respectability. Nevertheless, there can be no doubt that his interpretations are important milestones on the road of the theological reception of literature in that he incorporated literature within a theological-spiritual framework. Guardini said in retrospect that he had aimed to focus on 'an encounter', 'a look from one discipline to another', an approach that ultimately 'wants to be neither literary studies nor theology' (*Stationen* 299–300). In this he underestimated how much of a theologian he remained when interpreting literature. Calling poets 'seers' and regarding works of poetry as witnesses in the service of a divine calling or even as a form of revelation resulted in a radically theological interpretation of literature.

Subsequent initiatives promoting dialogue between literature and theology criticized his approach and asked whether Guardini had neglected the autonomy of aesthetic objects with respect to theology. Theodore Ziolkowski – to take only one example – praised Guardini's literary interpretations because of their 'sensible combination of careful textual analysis and Christian hermeneutics' (Ziolkowski 115), but proved, through an interpretation of Mörike, that Guardini forced 'his own belief and his own expectations at a key position in the text' (119) and that he found religious elements where he wanted. Today this criticism seems justified.

Let us now compare Guardini's ways of interpreting literature to those of another great Catholic twentieth-century interpreter of literature, the Swiss theologian Hans Urs von Balthasar (1905–88), who, as a student, attended a series of lectures on Kierkegaard given by Guardini in Berlin. 'There was only one man in his right mind', he wrote about his 'horrid' time in Berlin, 'Romano Guardini' (quoted in Lochbrunner, *Hans Urs von Balthasar* 277). In 1970 von Balthasar published the first comprehensive monograph, written with great respect, on his teacher Guardini who was 20 years his senior.

## Hans Urs von Balthasar: Withdrawal into the Unity of Pre-Modernity

During his lifetime, Balthasar would call himself 'a scholar of German literature by training' ('Geist und Feuer' 73). Before entering the Society of Jesus in 1929 and completing a degree in theology, he had obtained a PhD in philology. In 1937–39 he published a three-volume work, *Die Apokalypse der deutschen Seele* ('The Apocalypse of the German Soul'), a wide-ranging history of modern German intellectual life, which included the main findings of his thesis. While

Guardini's biographical-intellectual path had led him from theology to literature, Balthasar's path was the reverse, 'from literature to theology' (Lochbrunner, 'Romano Guardini' 169).

Like Guardini, Balthasar was aware of the intellectual changes taking place in his time and sought a new synthesis in the history of ideas. Long before most of his contemporaries, he had seen clearly the renewals and awakenings and the abysses of modernity. In contrast to later proponents of the collective 'Christian movement', Balthasar faced contemporary challenges with equanimity. First, he did not view the theology of his time as a promising starting-point that led to the resolution of contemporary issues. On the contrary, the discipline bored him. In search of inspiration, he stumbled upon the much broader field of literature and this would become the starting point for his confrontation with modernity. In his book about Bernanos, published in 1954, Balthasar openly admits: 'In the great Catholic literary figures we find more originality and vibrancy of thought – an intellectual life thriving superbly in a free and open landscape – than we do in the somewhat broken-winded theology of our time' (*Bernanos* 17).

Balthasar turned to modernity because he was looking for an 'intellectual life', but, surprisingly, he became taken up almost exclusively with Christian literature. In contrast to Guardini, he drew mainly upon contemporary literature, though not to the exclusion of Goethe, Rilke and Dostoyevsky. He published monographs on Paul Claudel, Charles Péguy, Georges Bernanos and Gerard Manley Hopkins. In his roles as translator, editor and interpreter, he continued to serve as an important guide to the *renouveau catholique* for the German-speaking world today (Kapp 397–412). In the field of literature, he became particularly interested in one author, Reinhold Schneider.

Balthasar's initial trajectory was similar to that of Guardini. Even though he was familiar with the various forms of literary criticism, he interpreted Schneider's work exclusively by examining its content and its historical-intellectual context. In contrast to most interpretations of Christian literature, he openly stated that he was leaving aside 'biographical or aesthetic evaluation' (*Reinhold Schneider* 11). Literature was to be 'used to examine historical problems without any special regard for its aesthetic qualities' (*Geschichte des eschatologischen Problems* 9). Since he focused narrowly on presenting a standardized picture of a life and contemporary world-view of 'Christian existence', he did not need to engage in either biographical or philological-aesthetic discussion. Spirituality, testimony, recurring images and figures, and typology were the important elements. He remained unconcerned with literary form, the author or his or her background.

The German scholar Sabine Haupt accurately called this method a variant of a 'metaphysically radical form of text-interpretation based on the history of ideas' (41). She recognized Balthasar's hermeneutics as a 'general de-historicization and de-rationalization of the history of ideas' worked out with a 'decidedly projective method' (52). Balthasar repeatedly practised a 'decontextualization' (Haupt 55) of quotations to blur the original meanings and to align them with his own ideas.[3] As a consequence, he generally 'flattens and distorts' the 'poetic potential' of the text because he ignored the text's intrinsic aesthetic values (Haupt 57).

A central point should be noted, namely, that Balthasar's hermeneutics serve a particular agenda in terms of his general concept of theology. Although he recognized the changes introduced by modernity more clear-sightedly than many, in his confrontations with modernity he insisted on the cohesion of content and an aesthetics that belong to a pre-modern age. This perspective continues to be Balthasar's great appeal today: the creation of an impressive theological-aesthetic system of thought which explores comprehensively the tradition of the history of ideas, but which leads back to the cohesiveness of a pre-modern world-view. In particular, the transcendental-aesthetic works *Herrlichkeit* (*The Glory of the Lord: A Theological Aesthetics*) of 1961–69 and *Theodramatik* (*Theo-Drama*) – a corpus of twelve volumes – are nothing less than a new conception of systematic theology from an aesthetic-philosophical perspective.

Balthasar used a great number of primary sources and secondary literature, yet he created a closed oeuvre with a predetermined system of theological thought. In this he did not need literature except as an inspiration in terms of form and an affirmation of ideas that had already been part of his theological world-view from the start. His approach has elicited various reactions. Manfred Lochbrunner, an admirer of Balthasar, emphasized that these works 'sent out a very strong message to contemporary theology' that it should 'restructure' itself by adopting 'the principle of the dramatic' (*Hans Urs von Balthasar* 292–3). The Swiss scholar Stefan Bodo Würffel, on the other hand, came to the conclusion that Balthasar practised an 'interpretation of literature with *a priori* assumptions in mind' and did not focus on 'texts or literature' (73). From the outset he forced predetermined meanings onto poetry, irrespective of the actual content of the texts. Hence the Catholic theologian Peter Hofmann, in an exemplary study of Goethe's reception, concluded that 'this gives the impression that Balthasar, when talking ... about Goethe, ultimately seems to

---

3    Würffel even identifies 'manipulated citations' (63–82).

be talking about von Balthasar himself' (95). Further, as Karl-Josef Kuschel noted, 'von Balthasar's theology is not dialogical in the sense of finding truth in solidarity with non-theological and non-Christian witnesses'. 'The aesthetic gives von Balthasar's theology shape and form, but the faith of the Church alone provides the substance' ('Theologen' 112–13).

Another perspective corroborates this evaluation. Lochbrunner included 'theological literary criticism' among Balthasar's idea of 'layers of interpretation' ('Romano Guardini' 174–5). Genuine dialogue, however, requires that a 'literary criticism of theology' should also necessarily be part of it. However, this was emphatically not the role that poetry played in Balthasar's interpretation of the relationship between theology and literature. In the last count, Balthasar was mainly interested in a wide-ranging affirmation through literature of his own convictions or in stimulating a rhetorically very creative but, content-wise, repetitive reformulation of a pre-modern, closed theological world-view.

## Guardini and Balthasar: Similarities and Differences in the Reception of Literature

What did Balthasar's and Romano Guardini's theological interpretations of literature have in common?

1. In contrast to the ways of handling 'Christian texts' prevailing in their day, both were concerned with original literary texts and less interested in biographies or the authors themselves. They integrated their understanding of texts into a world-view dominated by theology. This approach led them to draw only incidentally on biographical, cultural-contextual or philological secondary literature.
2. Both theologians, independently of each other, interpreted in great detail the work of four writers: Goethe, Rilke, Dostoyevsky and Hopkins.
3. Through literature, both theologians developed a language, authenticity and contemporary relevance not found in the publications of other theologians of the time. Both individuated a 'prophetic' power in their four great authors, without implying that this power was of the same kind as prophecy as described in the Bible.
4. Both were keenly aware of the cultural changes taking place in their times. They felt that they were witnesses to a process in which a

religiously defined pre-modernity was increasingly becoming ousted by a modernity defined by new philosophical, economic, political and social contours. They proposed their theological reading of literature to meet these challenges.

So much for the similarities. There are also important differences.

1. While Guardini employed close reading when interpreting texts, Balthasar focused on formulating an intellectual profile, one that included a stylized version of the poet's personality or the 'poet's soul'.

2. Guardini based his conclusions on a reading of the complete oeuvre of an author's works, a procedure that could only be applied to authors who were no longer living. Balthasar, on the other hand, offered interpretations of contemporary and emerging literary projects. Balthasar thus ran the risk that his interpretations might become awkward or untenable when authors changed their literary style or the focus of their work. An example was Reinhold Schneider (Langenhorst, 'Reinhold Schneider' 1–30). The 'intellectual profiles' created by Balthasar were norms which, as he implied, were normative even for the authors themselves.

3. In the eyes of Balthasar, Christianity was well oriented and focused when it concentrated on an established and proven system of beliefs. This system, it was true, needed to be reformulated but not substantially changed. Guardini was more adventurous. While he did not engage in a true dialogue with literature or countenance that literature was in a position to criticize or question theology, he admitted that Christianity in modernity had to create new paradigms and have the courage to redefine itself. Ultimately, Balthasar's theology remained pre-modern; Guardini's dared to step into the unfamiliar to find an answer.

4. Their different approaches led them to study different works of literature. Balthasar analysed works which, in his view, confirmed the main tenets of Christianity. He concentrated mainly on works of the *renouveau catholique*. On the other hand, he consulted dramatic texts because he was looking for alternative literary forms that might help re-express the meanings of Christianity. Guardini, by contrast, explored literary works that went beyond the boundaries of Christianity, addressing the challenges of his time. His Christian interpretations of literature struggled with these texts in terms of both form and content in search of new solutions.

Guardini's and Balthasar's concepts of 'theology and literature' were independent systems of thought steeped in Catholicism and closely linked to their intellectual systems of thought. Neither was concerned about creating a new hermeneutics or establishing his own 'school'. To date, their approaches have not stimulated productive debates, ones that might encourage the further exploration of their concepts and ideas.[4] The few academic attempts to interpret their ideas systematically have not inspired original theological-literary concepts.

## Paul Tillich: Correlation

From today's perspective, Guardini's and Balthasar's interpretations of literature mark the moment when the dialogue between theology and literature assumed the status of a discipline, 'theology and literature'. Both thinkers examined works that were not overtly Christian. Neither, however, had a long-lasting influence on the development of the discipline. Instead, the developments that did take place were shaped by Tillich's 'theology of culture' and his method of 'correlation'. It was Tillich's work, not that of Guardini and Balthasar, that gave rise to later independent hermeneutical approaches – theses, anthologies, articles and essays – which continue today.

Through his method of correlation, Tillich discovered a new understanding of the relationship between culture and religion, one that sought to relate, rather than harmonize or integrate, the two. He defined 'correlation' as follows: 'The method of correlation explains the content of Christian faith through existential questions and theological answers in mutual interdependence' (Tillich 60). For theologians, this method has two consequences: 'Theology formulates the questions implied in human existence', and at the same time it 'formulates the answers implied in divine self-manifestation under the guidance of the questions implied in human existence' (61). This poses the following problem: how do we arrive at a formulation of these 'questions implied in human existence'? It was obvious for Tillich that 'pictures, poems and music' (13) could be the objects of investigation for theology. 'The analysis of the human situation employs materials made available by man's creative self-interpretation in all realms of culture. Philosophy makes a contribution' and – as he explicitly mentions– 'so do poetry, drama, the novel' (63). For that

---

[4]    In Latin America especially we find attempts to practise 'literary theology' in the spirit of Balthasar (see, for example, de Palumbo).

reason, literature is 'primarily ... [a part of man's] creative self-interpretation' (13–14). As such it is an object for theological analysis, because it helps to illuminate the human situation in its existential dimensions by asking important questions to which the Christian message can give reliable answers.

In the years that followed, Tillich's students developed this approach. Even today it is still perceived as the productive way of thinking about the relationship between theology and literature. Although Tillich himself never undertook a systematic interpretation of contemporary literature (Kucharz 292–332), his approach provided the basis for later theological-literary analyses, which developed largely independently from each other in Germany, England and the USA. Here are some examples:

- Hans Jürgen Baden, Friedrich Hahn, Dorothee Sölle, Henning Schröer and other Protestant theologians created various theological-literary systems of interpretation along the lines laid down by Tillich.
- Amos Niven Wilder, Nathan Scott and Robert Detweiler, who established the study of theology and literature in the USA from the 1950s onwards, took Tillich's work as their starting point.
- David Jasper and Terry Wright, probably the most important figures in the foundation of the academic discipline of theology and literature in Great Britain, based their diverging concepts of the discipline on Tillich's approach.

Four distinctive features of theological-literary approaches in the tradition of Tillich may be noted. First, modernity is accepted unreservedly as a fact. Within the framework of this new cultural paradigm, theology needed to be re-expressed. Second, the method of correlation provided the means. Cultural artefacts, including literature, were to be set in a relationship of tension with works of theology. Literature posed questions; theology addressed them. Third, the works of Christian literature were to be ignored because they usually did no more than reaffirm an already familiar way of thinking. Looking at works of art that were ideologically and aesthetically independent would provoke fruitful debate. Fourth, since Tillich's approach was mainly about challenge, inspiration and dialogue, content rather than style must be the focus. The following questions were fundamental: which modern literary texts identify issues that could also be found, *mutatis mutandis*, in the Christian tradition? In what ways should Christian theology be reshaped or its world-view adapted in order to face these challenges productively?

## Karl-Josef Kuschel: Theology and Literature in the Name of Dialogue

The fact that 'autonomous' literary texts can have their own value for theology and the Church was affirmed publicly for the first time by the Roman Catholic Church at the Second Vatican Council. The Pastoral Constitution *Gaudium et Spes* stated in Chapter 62, under the subtitle 'Proper Harmony between Culture and Christian Formation':

> In their own way literature and art are very important in the life of the Church. They seek to give expression to man's nature, his problems and his experience in an effort to discover and perfect man himself and the world in which he lives; they try to discover his place in history and in the universe, to throw light on his suffering and his joy, his needs and his potentialities, and to outline a happy destiny in store for him. Hence they can elevate human life, which they express under many forms according to various times and places. (Flannery 966–7)

Here literature is said to have the following roles: to explore human nature; to consider humankind's problems and experience; to improve humankind and the world in which humans live; to shed light on humanity's place in history and in the universe (notably not 'creation' in this context); and to focus on human suffering and joy, human needs and potentialities.

This was an exceptional and comprehensive affirmation of the value of literature for theology. Without narrowing the focus to overtly Christian literature, it announced a new appreciation of something that had not previously been expressed with such clarity. For the first time, a truly dialogical understanding was under way.

During the same period, independent academic reflection on theology and literature established itself in German-speaking countries. Kuschel (born 1948) entered the field in 1978 with his well-received dissertation *Jesus in der deutschsprachigen Gegenwartsliteratur* ('Jesus in Contemporary German-Speaking Literature'). He emphasized the dialogical character of his approach from the beginning. The focus of this work was that 'it deals with literary studies and theology at the same time' (Kuschel, *Jesus* 3). Several central themes in Kuschel's oeuvre, which continues to provoke debate to this day, are already evident in this monograph.

Essentially, Kuschel is interested in 'a mutual challenge' (*Jesus* 4). But how could this new dialogical paradigm of mutual challenge be defined with regard to content? The answer was that both areas could act as a 'critical corrective' to each other. Literature could become a critical corrective 'for a theological language which often disguises human reality with empty language that claims truth and invariability, instead of illuminating it' (*Jesus* 4). And theology could be a corrective because it challenged literature to 'keep the quest open, the quest for genuine humanity, the quest for reality as it is, the quest for hope' (*Jesus* 5). Kuschel notes that Tillich's model had begun to tackle the problems addressed by modernity but that in his model the dialogue between literature remained one-sided; literature posed the question, theology answered it. He developed his own approach further in the 1980s, emphasizing the importance of dialogue by concentrating on mutual questioning and challenging.

The following features characterize Kuschel's interpretation of how literature and theology might fruitfully interact, one that remains an accepted model in German-speaking countries. First, modernity is recognized as a reality with which theology must come to terms in the tradition of the Second Vatican Council. Second, three guiding principles inform the relationship of theology and literature: the acceptance of literary works as autonomous works of art, the recognition that literary works challenge theological thinking and the construction of a dialogue between literature and theology. Third, the interpretation of texts is paramount, meaning in practice that an interpreter should analyse primary texts in conjunction with secondary literature. Fourth, studies focused on theological subject matter, themes, characters and other literary motifs should aim to or contribute to the findings of systematic theology. In addition, such studies should concentrate on the work of authors whose oeuvre is characterized by the incorporation of religious elements. These interpretations should eschew idealized stylization or standardization of the kind of literary work worthy of study. Fifth, emphasis should be placed on interpreting literature, whether contemporary or canonical, that speaks of the advent, the crisis and the transformations of modernity rather than explicitly Christian literature. Works of German-Jewish literature offer particularly important texts in this respect. Sixth, theoretical reflection of a purely academic kind concerning literature is of secondary relevance. Seventh, in contrast to approaches that focus exclusively on the text, all methods that contribute to the understanding of a text are valid, examples being the methods of literary criticism, the analysis of socio-historical contexts, biography, comparative thematic studies and the history of ideas.

Kuschel's general hermeneutical approach was set out in the volume *'Vielleicht hält Gott sich einige Dichter ...'* ('Perhaps God Cares for Some Poets') published in 1991. In this monograph he develops ten 'literary-theological portraits', which he then sums up and comments on in a detailed and programmatic final chapter entitled 'Towards a Theo-Poetics'. Kuschel begins by presenting two models that had previously been used to describe the relationship between theology and literature. The 'confrontational model' assumes an 'antithetical position of a theology of revelation' which is of necessity 'different from the religiousness of the authors and their products' (Kuschel, *'Vielleicht'* 380–1). This model can be found in theological approaches that consider culture as something essentially bad. In the second model, the 'model of correlation' in the tradition of Paul Tillich and the Second Vatican Council, literature is taken seriously 'as an expression of authentic, contemporary human experience'. In this perspective, 'the vision of a different religiousness' is not felt as a threat but as an enrichment 'which may lead to a self-critical questioning of one's own Christian heritage' and to an interest in opening up 'a dialogue'. But this type of dialogue still leads to the conclusion that literature merely bears a hint, a trace and the beginnings of an understanding of a deeper truth, 'which can of course only be fully understood by a correctly practised Christian theology' (*'Vielleicht'* 382–3).

Kuschel's main aim is to sketch out an original approach which he calls 'the method of structural analogy'. By that he means a double perspective of 'correspondences and contradictions'. He writes: 'Looking for correspondences' does not serve to instrumentalize literature. 'Thinking in structural analogies means to perceive correspondences between one's own thinking and that of someone else' (*'Vielleicht'* 385). This also applies in reverse: 'Contradictions of Christian explanations of reality' in literature must be clearly recognized and named because 'only in this way does the relationship between theology and literature turn into a relationship of tension, dialogue and struggle for truth' (*'Vielleicht'* 385). What, then, is the special, new, quality of this model that would inspire dialogue? If Christian theology takes literary works seriously, it can definitely no longer claim to be the 'answer to every existential question' (*'Vielleicht'* 385). 'The aim is a theology with a different style' (*'Vielleicht'* 386). Kuschel's statement here summarizes the obligation that theology would face when confronted with a challenging – in a positive sense – body of literature.

In this context it is interesting to see that Kuschel, in contrast with most parts of the English-language discourse on this topic, remains firmly within the paradigm of modernity with all its hermeneutical prerequisites. He continues to have a steadfast belief in meaning and in meaningful interpretation leading to knowledge, in the existence of an objective value system, in a literary canon that includes important and enduringly significant works of literature, and in the possibility of a dialogical theology which accepts the challenges of modernity and supplies convincing answers. All of these assumptions, rooted deeply in the history of ideas, are part of the approach that has been adopted by the majority of theses in the academic discipline of theology and literature written in German over the last 30 years.

In theological discussions of literature today, the task of demonstrating a full appreciation of literature's autonomy is seen to be so necessary and can take up so much space that a convincing theological response tends to remain undeveloped. Beyond Guardini and Balthasar, no fully developed concept of a theology supported and inspired by literature has come to the fore. Other concepts barely progress beyond the first steps of, for example, formulating questions for or challenges to contemporary theological thinking and writing. I suggest, therefore, that one of the most provoking lines of thought in Guardini's and von Balthasar's interpretation of literature might well provide us with the key question for postmodernity. The question is this: How can theology, on the one hand, take literature seriously and appreciate its autonomous content, and, on the other hand, create an independent Christian interpretation of being by using these same texts in an effort, both appreciative and challenging, that paves the way for future discourse?

## Works Cited

Balthasar, Hans Urs von. *Bernanos: An Ecclesial Existence*. San Francisco: Ignatius, 1996.

—— 'Geist und Feuer. Ein Gespräch mit Michael Albus'. *Herder Korrespondenz* 30 (1976): 72–82.

—— *Geschichte des eschatologischen Problems in der modernen deutschen Literatur*. Freiburg and Einsiedeln: Johannes, 1988.

—— *Reinhold Schneider: Sein Weg und sein Werk*. Cologne and Olten: Hegner, 1953.

Flannery, Austin, ed. *Vatican Council II. The Conciliar and Post Conciliar Documents*. Dublin: Dominican Publications St Saviour's, 1975.

Guardini, Romano. *Berichte über mein Leben: Autobiographische Aufzeichnungen*. Ed. Franz Henrich. Düsseldorf: Patmos, 1984.

—— *Der Mensch und der Glaube: Versuche über die religiöse Existenz in Dostojewskijs großen Romanen*. Leipzig: Hegner, 1932.

—— *Hölderlin. Weltbild und Frömmigkeit*. Leipzig: Hegner, 1939.

—— *Rilke's Duino Elegies: An Interpretation*. Trans. K.G. Knight. London: Darwen Finlayson, 1961.

—— *Sprache–Dichtung–Deutung. Gegenwart und Geheimnis*. Mainz: Matthias-Grünewald, 1992.

—— *Stationen und Rückblicke*. Würzburg: Werkbund, 1965.

Hallensleben, Barbara and Guido Vergauwen, eds. *Letzte Haltungen: Hans Urs von Balthasars 'Apokalypse der deutschen Seele' – neu gelesen*. Fribourg: Academic Press, 2006.

Haupt, Sabine. 'Vom Geist zur Seele: Hans Urs von Balthasars theologisierte Geistesgeschichte im Kontext der zeitgenössischen Germanistik und am Beispiel seiner Novalis-Auslegung'. In *Letzte Haltungen*, ed. Hallensleben and Vergauwen, 2006, 40–62.

Hofmann, Peter. 'Balthasar liest Goethe: *Die Apokalypse der deutschen Seele* als theologische *divina comedia*'. In *Letzte Haltungen*, ed. Hallenslebenand and Vergauwen, 2006, 83–100.

Kapp, Volker. 'Die katholischen Dichter in Frankreich und das deutsche Geistesleben. Hans Urs von Balthasar als Deuter und Mittler des *Renouveau catholique*'. In *Moderne und Antimoderne. Der* Renouveau catholique *und die deutsche Literatur*, ed. Wilhelm Kühlmann and Roman Luckscheiter. Freiburg, Berlin and Vienna: Rombach, 2008, 397–412.

Kranz, Gisbert. *Christliche Literatur der Gegenwart*. Aschaffenburg: Pattloch, 1961.

—— *Lexikon der Christlichen Weltliteratur*. Freiburg: Herder, 1978.

Krenski, Thomas. *Hans Urs von Balthasars Literaturtheologie*. Hamburg: Kovac, 2007.

Kucharz, Thomas. *Theologen und ihre Dichter: Literatur, Kultur und Kunst bei Karl Barth, Rudolf Bultmann und Paul Tillich*. Mainz: Matthias-Grünewald, 1995.

Kuschel, Karl-Josef. *Jesus in der deutschsprachigen Gegenwartsliteratur*. Munich and Zürich: Piper, 1987.

—— 'Theologen und ihre Dichter: Analysen zur Funktion der Literatur bei Rudolf Bultmann und Hans Urs von Balthasar'. *Theologische Quartalschrift* 172 (1992): 98–116.

—— *'Vielleicht hält Gott sich einige Dichter ...': Literarisch-Theologische Porträts*. Mainz: Matthias-Grünewald, 1991.

—— 'Zwischen Modernismuskrise und Modernekritik: Romano Guardini'. *Theologische Quartalschrift* 184 (2004): 158–84.

Langenhorst, Georg. *'Ich gönne mir das Wort Gott.' Annäherungen an Gott in der Gegenwartsliteratur*. Freiburg: Herder, 2009.

—— 'Reinhold Schneider heute lesen? Theologisch-literarische Annäherungen'. In *Wege zu Reinhold Schneider: Zum 50. Todestag des Dichters*, ed. Friedrich Emde and Ralf Schuster. Passau: Schuster, 2008, 1–30.

—— 'Theologie und Literatur: Aktuelle Tendenzen'. *Theologische Revue* 109 (2013): 355–72.

—— *Theologie und Literatur: Ein Handbuch*. Darmstadt: Wissenschaftliche Buchgesellschaft, 2005.

—— ed. 'Theologie und Literatur'. *Theologie und Literatur*. <www.theologie-und-literatur.de>.

Lochbrunner, Manfred. *Hans Urs von Balthasar und seine Literatenfreunde: Neun Korrespondenzen*. Würzburg: Echter, 2007.

—— 'Romano Guardini und Hans Urs von Balthasar: Integration von Theologie und Literatur'. *Internationale Katholische Zeitschrift Communio* 34 (2005): 169–85.

Palumbo, Cecilia Inés Avenatti de. *La Literatura en la Estética de Hans Urs von Balthasar: Figura, Drama y Verdad*. Salamanca: Secretariado Trinitario, 2002.

Tillich, Paul. *Systematic Theology*. Vol. 1. Chicago: University of Chicago Press, 1951.

Würffel, Stefan Bodo. 'Endzeit-Philologie. Hans Urs von Balthasars germanistische Anfänge'. In *Letzte Haltungen*, ed. Hallensleben and Vergauwen, 2006, 63–82.

Ziolkowski, Theodore. 'Theologie und Literatur: Eine polemische Stellungnahme zu literaturwissenschaftlichen Problemen'. In *Theologie und Literatur: Zum Stand des Dialogs*, ed. Walter Jens, Hans Küng and Karl-Josef Kuschel. Munich: Kindler, 1986.

# PART II
# The Religious Imagination: From Thomas Aquinas to Wallace Stevens

# Chapter 3
# Identifying a Religious Imagination

Michael Paul Gallagher SJ

On the theme of imagination, my favourite line comes from Emily Dickinson, who wrote with her typical mixture of subtlety and simplicity that 'the possible's slow fuse is lit by imagination' (689). Here she herself fuses two horizons. Imagination carries us to thresholds of possibility but it becomes transformative when its fuse catches fire and causes an explosion of new perception. Another poet from the same continent, Margaret Avison, of Toronto, suggested that if we are 'boxed, bottled, barrelled / in rows', then imagination has the power to unbox us, offering both 'a jail-break and re-creation' (69, 97). Here lies a battlefield of our freedom. Although culture can kidnap us into smallness, imagination can offer a transfiguration, and Avison saw this as applying not only to poets but also to scientists and explorers of all kinds when they emerge from passivity into exciting insight.

Such positive claims are not always the order of the day. In everyday parlance we still use the term with a pejorative slant: 'you are only imagining it' or 'it's mere imagination'. Through the centuries imagination has had many critics, both religious and philosophical, accusing it of being a source of falsity or dangerous fantasy. St Basil the Great claimed that imagination was only an empty affection coming from the unreasoning part of the soul. In a revealing moment of his *Saint Joan*, George Bernard Shaw has the following interchange between the heroine and a sceptical nobleman:

> Joan: I hear voices telling me what to do. They come from God.
> Robert: They come from your imagination.
> Joan: Of course. That is how the messages of God come to us. (11)

Even when it was not being attacked, imagination was not always highly valued. Thinkers such as Locke and Hume saw it as mainly passive, a filter of impressions. Kant would later see it as a dynamic and unifying power. But before him came another voice that turned out to be prophetic. In 1715 in Naples, Giambattista

Vico published his *Nuova Scienza* proposing that imagination or *fantasia* offers a different poetic logic, as a primordial power of human beings.

With these opening remarks, I gesture towards complex philosophical horizons which will have to remain in the background. I want to divide this essay into two main sections, first of all telling a story, and then asking a question. The story echoes the Cinderella fairy tale and tells of the emergence of imagination into renewed admiration over a century or more. Then I ask, as in the title of this work, about ways of identifying a religious imagination. In both parts I will call various writers to the 'witness stand', as witnesses for the defence of imagination in the first half, and then various experts who can fine tune our debate about the nature of religious imagination.

## The Emergence of Cinderella

What I am calling the Cinderella narrative tells us how the one-sided rationality of modernity, like an ugly sibling, bullied imagination and kept her confined to a kitchen in the basement. As long as this narrow logic reigned supreme in philosophy, in industrial society, in the dominant utilitarian culture, and even in theology, imagination as Cinderella remained underground and was seldom visited, except by some eccentrics like poets or marginal thinkers.

But, to overwork our analogy, when the fairy godmother of late- or postmodernity appears on the cultural scene, she allows Cinderella to emerge from her kitchen, and to come well dressed to the ball where her beauty is recognized. Thus imagination was restored to her rightful place in human knowing, including, as will be seen, a key role in religious faith.

### From Newman to Nussbaum

Who were some of the courageous visitors to Cinderella in her kitchen days? To begin with, John Henry Newman was an original thinker concerning imagination, and in particular, the religious imagination. It was at the heart of a series of letters to *The Times* in 1841 where he attacked a speech of Sir Robert Peel. Opening a new public library at Tamworth, this leading politician, who was twice prime minister, had suggested that the ethical fruits of religion could now be acquired through education in literature and science. The idea horrified the future cardinal because it was so contrary not only to his sense of the uniqueness of religious truth but also to his whole anthropology. In reply Newman passionately defended the human person as more than a 'reasoning animal', as made for action and moved by feeling. In this context he claimed that 'the heart is commonly reached, not through the reason, but through the imagination' (92). Nearly 30 years later Newman quoted these sections of his critique of Peel in the *Grammar of Assent* (at the end of chapter 4), and he went on (at the beginning of chapter 5) to argue that faith needs to be 'discerned, rested in, and appropriated as a reality, by the religious imagination' (98). His carefully chosen words imply that imagination recognizes religious realities, that it invites us to a certain spiritual receptivity, and that it also carries faith towards personal commitment. He added that 'the theology of a religious imagination' has 'a living hold on truths' and therefore opens the door towards 'habits of personal religion'(117). The sentence 'There is a God', Newman argues, can work 'a revolution in the mind' only when the imagination is 'kindled' and 'hearts inflamed' (126).

There seem to be three areas where Newman's unsystematic insights on this topic were prophetic. First of all, imagination for him was a key mediator of faith's credibility, because if God is not 'realized' in the imagination, faith will simply remain unreal or unexistential. Secondly, the presence of imagination fosters participatory knowing, in other words an enlarged rationality that acknowledges the pre-rational. Thirdly, what Newman meant by imagination is close to what theologians of today are retrieving as the affective or aesthetic dimensions of religion, aspects that were neglected as long as faith was interpreted in terms of cognition rather than a deeply transforming relationship.

If we change context and come to the late twentieth century, we find that leading thinkers such as Paul Ricoeur, Charles Taylor and Martha Nussbaum have explored imagination as an essential gateway to both meaning and commitment. Nussbaum, working mainly in the field of ethics, has explored various literary works, ranging from Proust to Henry James, as embodiments of moral discernment, and insists that ethical perception is diminished when we 'cultivate calculative intellect' alone (81). Although she does not describe herself as a religious thinker, and diagnoses a certain escapism in claims to transcendence through literature, she argues that not only do affectivity and imagination play an essential role in our major decisions, but that some forms of knowledge are accessible only through love.

## Two Recent Philosophers: Taylor and Ricoeur

As a philosopher and historian of culture, Charles Taylor is also notable for stressing the role of imagination in the changes of sensibility associated with modernity. In various books he seeks to deepen the agenda from the history of ideas or the world of concepts to the more hidden world of our 'social imaginary'. This expression refers to our ways of imaging our lives, before theory comes along to analyse or explain. It points to a 'largely unstructured and inarticulate understanding of our whole situation' (Taylor 25). Thus, from diverse horizons, both Nussbaum and Taylor recognize imagination as a theatre where the drama of meaning and values are played out today.

A third witness to a crucial role for imagination, in the context of his development of a critical hermeneutics, is Paul Ricoeur. Like many others he sees it as a key threshold towards embracing new possibilities, including the possibility of God and faith. Through imagination we can focus our questioning openness and even transfigure experience. To understand imagination, Ricoeur suggests starting with the ordinary surprise of a metaphor, in poetry or in ordinary discourse, which connects one zone with another and extends our rationality. But imagination is here also a vehicle of identity, of conversion, and a spur towards action. In this sense it has a 'projective function' and is part of the 'dynamism of action' (Ricoeur, *Du texte à l'action* 224).

If imagination has the power to transform our narrative identity, religious horizons are not far away. In Ricoeur's view biblical texts invite imagination to be re-formed by an encounter with divine meaning. Thus reading the Bible can be a 'creative operation' with 'the power of redescribing reality' (Ricoeur, *Figuring the Sacred* 144–5). Prayer is where our small imagination meets a larger imagination of love. On one occasion, in an interview with the *Manhattan Review*, Ricoeur offered some hints towards discerning what was genuinely religious, and hence some pointers of particular relevance to our present theme. In Rilke, for example, our imagination is beautifully enlarged, but is this its whole potential scope? Without self-transcendence, imagination can remain aesthetic and not attain its possible role as a mediator of religious transformation. For imagination to serve 'religious experience', the French philosopher suggests three conditions: 1) opening to a dimension of commitment; 2) belonging to a definite community; and 3) connecting to a social or ethical stance. Ricoeur concludes that 'there is an element of promise and commitment in the religious attitude which is different from the pure play through imagination' that some poetry offers (Valdés 455).

Thus, religious imagination invites us beyond the magnificence of the verbal into trusting a promise, a revelation, a call. As such, it is more likely to bring prophetic rupture than to reaffirm our existing reality. Through religious imagination we move from an unchanging ego sameness (*idem*-identity) into the adventure of shaping a genuine selfhood (*ipse*-identity). Thus, in Ricoeur's own words we can experience 'redemption through imagination' because, in 'imagining possibilities, we can act as a prophets of our own existence' (*History and Truth* 127).

## Two Jesuits: Lonergan and Lynch

We may draw a brief parallel from a more theological thinker, the Canadian Bernard Lonergan; one of his key proposals was that theology of faith requires an experiential foundation which he locates in the adventure of 'affective conversion' (*A Third Collection* 179), through love. On his way to this discovery there is a fascinating shift of vocabulary in one particular section of *Insight*, a passage where he recognizes imagination as a crucial zone of human liberation. Here, Lonergan changes his discourse from aloof intellectualism to a sense of existential drama. What is really needed to change our history from tragedy to salvation? He answers that 'images' can be 'so charged with affects' that they guide and propel us to 'action'. Here he is close to Ricoeur. Our 'sensitivity needs symbols that unlock its transforming dynamism', and hence religious faith can become a healing therapy in history if it can 'nourish imagination ... [and] release affectivity' (Lonergan, *Insight* 744).

So far the witnesses called to testify in defence of imagination have offered optimistic theories about its role. We have heard little about imagination as a key ambiguous battleground in our culture. So I want to call another witness, so to speak, the American Jesuit William Lynch, author of several books on imagination, who died in 1987. As early as the 1950s, with his eye on the mass media of that decade, he became concerned about 'techniques for the fixation of imagination' and proposed that artists and religious thinkers needed one another in the struggle for freedom of imagination (Lynch, *The Image Industries* 20). Imagination had become a battle zone because, if this precious dimension is misused, people become alienated from reality and go in quest of addictive substitutes.

In later years, and having experienced and then studied mental breakdown, he came to see another fixation of images as an unfreedom at the core of psychological illness. In his *Images of Hope*, being trapped in some tyrannical absolute is typical of neurotic hopelessness, but 'to have the image of oneself as human is the beginning of hope' (181). In other words, imagination which can be an obsessive tyrant may, with sensitive help, become a source of psychological healing, because hope involves re-imagining life and being saved from narcissism.

Lynch was suspicious of any Romantic identifying of imagination with special artistic creativity. For him, imagination is incarnational: it is our ordinary way of shaping our lives, and of discovering images that are worthy of us and of

God. So he had little patience with what he described as 'angelic' or 'gnostic' imagination, which could cultivate a world of fantasy in flight from the finite. Instead Lynch developed a positive theology of images, claiming that Hebraic-Christian faith can be a 'prime imaginer of the world' (*Images of Faith* 14). In his view, Christ can be seen as the Lord of the imagination who 'subverted the whole order of the old imagination' (*Christ and Apollo* 192). Here Lynch begins to sound like René Girard, and indeed for both of them imagination is the theatre both of our darkness and of our light. In Lynch's words, 'if the right people do not imagine the world, somebody else always will ... The religious imagination ... tries literally to imagine things with God' (*Christ and Prometheus* 23). Faith in this light involves a new imagination of who we are and who God is, of what we are doing here and what God is trying to do in our lives. Lynch insisted that we need to experience faith as a movement through the ordinary, as the transformation of our images, through various moments of a life story. That conversion of self-images can come from contemplating Christ's imagination, which is ironic or subversive of the dominant images around us.

From all these various thinkers, what have we learned? We have been reminded that imagination is both perception and interpretation, both preconceptual and cognitive. It allows us to gather our scattered experiences and to shape our possibilities. It is a bearer of truth, because images think and put us in touch with the drama of existing more powerfully than do mere ideas. Thus, it can be a vital carrier of religious experience. It can be a source of therapy or transfiguration.

In this respect we can recall a moving moment in Shakespeare's *King Lear* when the king, in his madness, thinks that his old friend Gloucester is a pharmacist who could sell him a precious perfume: 'Give me an ounce of civet, good apothecary, to sweeten my imagination' (IV, vi). Here the term 'imagination' stands for his state of heart, his whole outlook. It has nothing to do with daydreams about some 'airy nothing', as Shakespeare says elsewhere. Lear's imagination here is the opposite of escapist. It is his way of coping with terrifying reality. His is an incarnate imagination collapsing under the weight of incredible pain. It is also the location for his amazing transformation of attitude – from the dictatorial pride of his all-or-nothing absolutism to the gentleness and humility of his later, if tragic, wisdom. Through his imagination, Lear's vision moves through darkness into something of light, but it moves downwards, not upwards, into the finite drama of his life, not soaring dishonestly above it. This masterpiece of Shakespeare, like all genuine art, moves us out of temptingly easy dreaming into a complex reality, and it helps us to endure that movement. Something of the same healing ministry can be mediated by what we call the religious imagination.

## Criteria for a Religious Imagination

From this narrative of the re-emergence of imagination as a source of special truthfulness, we have some foundations for the second part of this essay: how can we identify the religious imagination? Here a key question is to what extent we want the adjective 'religious' to be wide-ranging, or else stricter in its application. As a passionate plea for a wide-ranging or inclusive approach, we can recall George Steiner's famous book, *Real Presences*, where he advocates a 'wager on transcendence' (214), insisting that our encounter with art involves a 'transformative summons' (143). Great art and literature, he claims, are born from an impulse of the human spirit to explore the unknown, beyond easily visible realms. If literature begins 'in immanence', it does 'not stop there' (227), hence a completely 'secular poetics' (223) seems impossible. In Steiner's eloquent expression, 'where God's presence is no longer a tenable supposition' or God's absence an 'overwhelming weight ... certain dimensions of ... creativity are no longer attainable' (229). In other words, not only has religious imagination been omnipresent in art and artists, through different ages and even when religious themes were not central, but a totally secular imagination would signal cultural impoverishment, a tragic shrinking of the range of human exploration.

### Which Form of Transcendence?

If Steiner invites us to cherish thematic richness, gesturing towards mystery, as a characteristic of religious imagination, other authors would have us look at the spiritual dispositions awoken by art in its audience. Perhaps what we call religious imagination is a double reality, not only a matter of art as content or vision, but also involving a quality of receptivity that it requires and fosters. Here I draw on William Desmond, the distinguished Irish philosopher based in Louvain, who points to a certain reverence in imagination as the key to connecting religion, philosophy and science. Without reverence there can be no real openness to otherness as gift. This is what makes the difference of attitude between a self-transcendence that can be caught up in its own achievement and the threshold of *the* Transcendent as gift or promise. This is where imagination as a 'possibilizing power' (Desmond, 'Religious Imagination' 291) bows down before the possibility of grace. Here imagination opts to be more icon than idol (to echo Jean-Luc Marion). An iconic sensibility receives with a certain humility and so enters into the flow of the art work. The idol approach is addicted to control through analysis and interpretation, or what Newman would call intense self-contemplation, and hence the stance remains that of a shielded observer, a judge rather than a recipient.

Desmond speaks of 'the majestic sacramental imagination of pre-modern religiousness' ('Religious Imagination' 282) as involving a 'threshold power' (305) that we need to recover. But threshold of what? Where the adventure of transcendence in Steiner was slow to commit itself to definite religious horizons, Desmond is more daring. 'I mean the transcendence of God', he writes, adding that a genuinely religious imagination 'points beyond itself to an otherness of the divine not reducible' to 'immanent otherness' (300). This is a transcendence of promise and gift that dismantles any closed logic of human achieving. When reverence takes us beyond ourselves as merely autonomous knowers, we encounter a 'fullness impossible to … master' (Desmond, 'On the Betrayals of Reverence' 215). Indeed, if we remain shy like Steiner about naming God, we may easily exaggerate imagination as almighty and salvific, instead of recognizing it as a privileged mediator of dispositions of readiness. As Hamlet said, 'the readiness is all'. In brief, for William Desmond, religious imagination is marked by this different reverence, where we may glimpse gratefully that there is more than ourselves. In this way imagination, Desmond tells us, involves 'the birth of mindful being … open to the other as other' ('Religious Imagination' 284). It becomes a crucial vehicle to liberate us from narrowly rational versions of truth and to open doors to the divine. Why? Simply because love 'is at home in imaginative discourse' (Desmond, *God and the Between* 264) and because imagination realizes that God is 'gift prior to [our] construction' (Desmond, *The Intimate Strangeness of Being* 288).

In summary, it is clear that there can be many kinds of religious imagination, in the wide sense of capturing thresholds of wonder, and, in a more focused sense, certain artistic expressions seek to be more definitely 'religious', pointing to some encounter with God. Even if we do not limit the religious imagination only to this second variety, how crucial is this tension between self-transcending moments of wonder and thresholds of the Transcendent as gift?

## Theological Tensions and Two Works of Art

Facing this question could, or would, lead us into hidden theological minefields. Let me suggest three theological tendencies that are not at ease with one another on this issue. One school likes to speak of God as ultimate mystery; let us label it the transcendence school with Rahner as its patron. Another, more insistently Christian, stresses the definiteness of God revealed in human drama; let us call it the incarnational school, with Balthasar as its key figure. And a third, more socially conscious, seeks to discern the Spirit's presence, or performance of interruption, in the struggles of history; let us call it the transformation school with Lonergan or Dorothee Sölle as different models of this approach.

We could spend a long time discussing the different presuppositions of these three stances. For our present purpose it seems more fruitful to imagine how they could evaluate two recent art works, from totally different genres. I am thinking of Terrence Malick's film *The Tree of Life* and the St John's Bible Project, a seven-volume hand-written illuminated manuscript designed by the British calligrapher Donald Jackson and a team of artists for St John's Benedictine Abbey at Collegeville in the United States. Both are large and ambitious works with openly religious intentions.

The beautiful production of the St John's Bible is a contemporary retrieval of an ancient tradition, using an experimental style of art and motifs from recent history to illustrate the sacred text. Judging from reports from various exhibitions of this Bible, the impact on many of its viewers seems to be one of awe and amazement. Indeed, the spiritual ambition behind this work was to awaken a dormant sense of transcendence in its viewers and in this way to point to a possible encounter with the divine. Obviously the St John's Bible is more explicitly and directly religious than the film, which nevertheless begins with a quotation from Chapter 38 of the Book of Job: 'Where were you when I laid the foundations of the earth ... When the morning stars sang in chorus and all the sons of God shouted for joy?' With this background the film voices three central questions. Is the 'way of nature' the whole story, where life is random and unhappy, where self-pleasing is everything, and you have to fight in a world dominated by rivalry? Or is there a 'way of grace', meaning that we can learn to grow in wisdom, gentleness and forgiveness, even in this world? But faced with the shadows and tragedies of life, God's silence is interrogated: 'what are we to you?' In the spirit of the Book of Job, the film dares to situate our vulnerable human journey within a huge cosmic story. At one stage there is a challenging sermon in church on Job and about how we cannot protect ourselves from disaster because there is 'no hiding place from sorrow'. Thus the film seeks to portray the vastness of God and the fragility of struggling religious faith in a situation of family tragedy and the seeming absence of God. Side by side with stunning visual images, the film is studded with moments of shy, whispered prayer, usually in the voice of a child: 'I search for you ... I want to know who you are ... Are you watching me? ... I want to see what you see ... I didn't notice the glory ... You spoke to me through her voice ... Keep us. Guide us.' *The Tree of Life* is also an anthology of music, much of it classical (Bach, Mozart, Brahms, Mahler, Holst, Taverner and others). The film is one of overwhelming beauty, in both vision and sound, but it grounds its gesturing towards the sacred in the quotidian tensions and joys of a family.

The first few moments of the film show Mrs O'Brien as a young girl, who has been taught by the Sisters (the church scenes are largely but not clearly Catholic) to follow the way of grace. Her voice-over says 'I will be true to you whatever comes', but immediately we have the arrival, years later, of the telegram with the news of the death of her son. After a series of powerful evocations of the grief of both parents, the questions 'Lord why? Where were you?' introduce the amazing 20-minute sequence of astrophysical effects, portraying the creation of the universe, a mixture of calm beauty and volcanic energy, of soaring music and silence.

Clearly this is an exceptional film, where Malick breaks with a linear narrative and seeks to evoke a sensibility in his audience that goes beyond the usual formula of psychological realism or social irony. His film moves in a wavelength of spiritual and metaphysical poetry, while doing justice to the secular realities of the O'Brien household in Texas, a family full of loves and tensions, joys and questions. Among many other horizons, it is about parenting and sonship, bereavement and its healing, and how childhood reactions echo into adulthood. In many ways the film can be seen as a series of memories by Jack, the eldest son of the family, now an architect in Houston. This role is played by Sean Penn as a middle-aged man and brilliantly by Hunter McCracken as a boy of about 13. The adult Jack still suffers from the (unexplained) death of his younger brother at the age of 19. He lights a candle in blue glass in his memory, as if on his anniversary, and all day at work he is distracted by moments from the past and with some flashes of mountain or beach scenes that will become the final sequence of the film.

Even during the creation images, we hear some voice-over quasi-prayers such as 'what are we to you?', 'answer me', 'we cry to you' and 'I search for you, my child'. After this whole sequence, the film returns to a delicate celebration of human life with the birth of Jack and the early years of the three sons. Fear and tension enters the scene with the relationship between Jack as early adolescent and his father (Brad Pitt). As in Malick's *The Thin Red Line*, there is a constant counterpointing of two philosophies, between seeing life as survival of the toughest or as something of a larger miracle. The father is a subtle combination of tense authority and tenderness, of frustration in a functional job and the musical talents that could have given him a different life. He seems to represent the way of nature, at least as a philosophy of the cynical toughness needed to get on in this world. This is in stark contrast with another wavelength, embodied in the mother (Jessica Chastain), for whom a way of grace is possible because 'unless you love, your life will flash by'. 'Mother. Father. Always you wrestle inside me', says Jack, the eldest son, as an adult. Meanwhile the younger Jack, the central figure of the three boys, runs into mortality, sexuality, confused emotions ('she only loves me', he says about his mother to his father, but later he says 'I'm more like you than her'). There is a marvellous moment of murderous temptation against his father, and also a series of quick interactions with his younger brother, a musician and gentle soul, where Jack swings from affection to bullying, from guilt to forgiveness.

Taking the film overall, one finds a double imagination at work, swinging between the transcendence of the sacral and the immanence of the anthropological. It suggests that these two stories of vast and small worlds can connect one with the other and ultimately perhaps that there can be a tree of life, as in the Book of Revelation, that produces fruits of reconciliation each month of the year. At one moment the family plants a tree, and frequently trees are shown as opening to the sky. In its closing sequence, accompanied by the Agnus Dei of Berlioz's *Requiem*, the film evokes a possible transcendence of loss and lostness for Jack. After climbing a rocky ledge, he enters a new landscape led by his younger self. He goes through a door and comes to a beach-like scene where he is reunited with all of his family and others. As the Agnus Dei comes to its final amen, Mrs O'Brien raises her hands and the voice says 'I give him to you, my son'. The film ends with a rapid series of images such as sunflowers, of the older Jack seeming to smile in his office, and once again a mysterious wavering flame that had appeared at various points of the film. Beyond the usual realism, evocation is everything for Malick. As a director, he will no doubt be accused by some critics of excess, of ambiguity, even of self-indulgent pretentiousness. This film divides audiences and critics. But I think it can at least claim to be the most provocatively beautiful variation on the Book of Job in the history of cinema, a hymn to love, loss and ultimate healing.

One should add that Malick followed up in 2012 with another highly spiritual film entitled *To the Wonder*. Although it had less success with the critics, it is if anything more explicitly religious. It even has a Catholic priest as one of the three main characters, someone who serves the poor but remains somewhat desolate in his own faith. He preaches that love is transformative, prays 'Where are you leading me? Teach me to see you', but remains low in spirits: 'All I see is destruction and ruin.' The other narrative has to do with a couple who swing in moods from exaltation to painful distance. A central theme is the instability of love as experienced. Is there some healing for our pain? Again and again its magnificent visual art evokes another kind of light. At the end the woman (without name) for an instant goes towards the light of Mont St Michel and the voice-over says 'Love that loves us. Thank you.'

Both the St John's Bible Project and Malick's films challenge our quality of attentiveness to religious horizons, in other words our receptive dispositions. If viewed in a superficial spirit of tourism, neither will have much impact, but when an audience gives permission for the stream of images to reach us slowly, both reveal their riches as creative crossroads between the Word of God and religious imagination.

So what of our three theological families faced with these works? The St John's Bible Project would surely get high praise from the transcendence and incarnational schools, as a significant attempt to surprise people into wonder and as a powerful embodiment of the biblical narrative in contemporary form. Possibly the transformation school would have more reservations about its ability to provoke conversion of consciousness or action. More differences between the three approaches would come to light over Terrence Malick. The incarnational school might praise the portrayal of family fragility and reconciliation, but would be less enthusiastic about the potentially gnostic style of its cosmic and extraterrestrial explorations. By contrast, the transcendence school would probably rate it highly, rejoicing in a film that powerfully gestures towards mystery and ultimate reconciliation beyond death. The transformation school would also be impressed by cinema that puts us in touch with larger horizons of ourselves, or of grace, and even of all of creation. But it might worry that in some visionary moments the film rhetoric is more blurred and misty than it needs to be.

So which criterion is crucial? Does any school deserve a casting vote? I think not, because the docking manoeuvre between theological stances and artistic embodiments is too delicate for facile evaluations. If I had to decide what constitutes a genuinely religious imagination, perhaps I would go beyond the labels of transcendence and incarnation and recall a famous poem by Rilke that evokes the power of a broken torso in the Louvre and ends with 'you must change your life'. Such art-provoked transformation may not be total or life-long, any more than the daily and unsteady erosion of the ego in prayer, but to echo D.H. Lawrence, religious imagination can lead into new places the flow of our sympathetic consciousness. The St John's Bible and *The Tree of Life*, for all their dissimilarity, invite us towards such thresholds of transformed sensibility. And that is surely one basic way of identifying the religious imagination. By its fruits we will know the roots.

**Towards a Conclusion, with Poetry**

Before concluding, I want to mention an impressive book that I discovered only as I was preparing this essay. Malcolm Guite's *Faith, Hope and Poetry: Theology and the Poetic Imagination* draws at length on Seamus Heaney, citing him on poetry's ability to provide 'a draught of the clear water of transformed understanding' (18). I propose looking at a Heaney poem not treated by Guite, one which captures an experience of secular transcendence but which could surely also be described as a form of non-explicit religious imagination. In this piece, from his 1991 book *Seeing Things*, Heaney evokes a moment of intense excitement in children who have made for themselves a slide of black ice: they let go 'into a sheerness that was its own reward' and reach 'a pitch beyond our usual hold upon ourselves' (86). With that typically exact word 'pitch', with its echoes of music, the poem identifies a kind of ecstasy beyond the securities of the everyday. Here nothing is 'sure' and all is 'sheer'. And thus the reader too is drawn into a transcendence or movement towards a mysterious 'ring of light'.

Finally, on the question of movement towards, let me mention a major advocate of the religious imagination, St Ignatius of Loyola. Like Newman, he saw imagination as a praxis of 'realization', where the Gospels, for instance, could be re-enacted in prayer. But more pertinent to our question of identifying a religious imagination is Ignatius's account of consolation as essentially an 'interior movement' towards a fire of love or faith or hope (348). In this light we can see that for imagination to be genuinely religious does not require the inner movement to be explicitly religious. Sometimes yes, sometimes no. On the more explicit side there is George Herbert or Dante or T.S. Eliot. On the other side there is Seamus Heaney or Yeats or Wallace Stevens. Some poetry asks us, through the very performance of words, to relish an act of perception or intense awareness. Some poetry is more transparent of specifically religious transcendence and of an enlarged awareness close to prayerfulness. Indeed, there is a strangeness about art that is parallel to the strangeness of praying. In both encounters we are asked for a quality of slow attentiveness. Both require a readiness for wonder but the fruits remain unpredictable, without guarantees. In both, we surrender our solitude in order to enter a space of surprising gift.

## Works Cited

Avison, Margaret. *Always Now: Collected Poems*. Erin, Ontario: Porcupine's Quill, 2003.

Chesterton, G.K. *Orthodoxy*. London: Hodder and Stoughton, 1996.

Desmond, William. *God and the Between*. Oxford: Blackwell, 2008.

—— *The Intimate Strangeness of Being: Metaphysics after Dialectic*. Washington DC: Catholic University of America Press, 2012.

—— 'On the Betrayals of Reverence'. *Irish Theological Quarterly* 65 (2000): 211–30.

—— 'Religious Imagination and the Counterfeit Doubles of God'. *Louvain Studies* 27 (2002): 280–305.

Dickinson, Emily. *The Complete Poems*. Ed. T.H. Johnson. Boston: Little Brown, 1960.

Guite, Malcolm. *Faith, Hope and Poetry: Theology and the Poetic Imagination*. Farnham: Ashgate, 2010.

Heaney, Seamus. *Seeing Things*. London: Faber and Faber, 1991.

Ignatius of Loyola. *Personal Writings*. Ed. J.A. Munitiz and P. Endean. London: Penguin Books, 1996.

Lonergan, Bernard. *Insight: A Study of Human Understanding*. Ed. F. Crowe and R. Doran. Toronto: University of Toronto Press, 1992.

—— *A Third Collection*. New York: Paulist Press, 1985.

Lynch, William F. *Christ and Apollo: The Dimensions of the Literary Imagination*. Notre Dame, IN: University of Notre Dame Press, 1960.

—— *Christ and Prometheus: A New Image of the Secular*. Notre Dame, IN: University of Notre Dame Press, 1970.

—— *The Image Industries*. New York: Sheed and Ward, 1959.

—— *Images of Faith: An Exploration of the Ironic Imagination*. Notre Dame, IN: University of Notre Dame Press, 1973.

—— *Images of Hope: Imagination as Healer of the Hopeless*. New York: New American Library, 1966.

Malick, Terrence, dir. *The Tree of Life*. Twentieth Century Fox, 2011. DVD.

—— *To the Wonder*. Studiocanal Ltd., 2012. DVD.

Newman, John Henry. *An Essay in Aid of a Grammar of Assent*. London: Longman, 1909.

Nussbaum, Martha. *Love's Knowledge: Essays on Philosophy and Literature*. Oxford: Oxford University Press, 1990.

Ricoeur, Paul. *Du texte à l'action. Essais d'herméneutique II*. Paris: Seuil, 1986.

—— *Figuring the Sacred: Religion, Narrative and Imagination*. Minneapolis, MN: Fortress Press, 1995.

—— *History and Truth*. Evanston, IL: Northwestern University Press, 1965.

Shaw, George Bernard. *Saint Joan*. London: Constable, 1924.

Steiner, George. *Real Presences: Is There Anything in What We Say?* London: Faber and Faber, 1989.

Taylor, Charles. *Modern Social Imaginaries*. Durham, NC: Duke University Press, 2004.

Valdés, Mario, ed. *A Ricoeur Reader*. Toronto: University of Toronto Press, 1991.

# Chapter 4

# Religious Imagination and Poetic Audacity in Thomas Aquinas[1]

## Olivier-Thomas Venard OP

Scholastic thought is often presented as indifferent to poetry, or even in opposition to the search for an aesthetics of linguistic expression. Thomas Aquinas, at first sight, seems quite severe in this respect. Even if it has a place within his hierarchy of the sciences, he reminds us that poetry is a profane science, a human invention, and that *poetae theologi*[2] have often proved misleading.[3] However, we need to put this resistance to poetics in its historical context where, as Curtius explains, in the rediscovered work of Aristotle, poetics was not simply a question of art but was also associated with doctrines which, for Thomas, were incompatible with Christianity (Curtius vol. 1, 348–9, 357–8).

The fact that Thomas Aquinas himself composed poems demonstrates that the search for beauty in language was important to him. He wrote a new liturgy for the Feast of Corpus Christi, and, as several commentators have shown (Michel, *In hymnis et canticis* 223–33; Gourmont 308), the poems which form part of it, *Tantum ergo*, *Lauda Sion* and *Pange lingua*, have been used and loved by the Church for many centuries. And yet their author is still too often presented only as someone who developed the great systematic philosophical expression of the Catholic faith, in which the few pejorative references to poetry have been taken to define his position on the subject. Since, however, he did not formulate a theory of poetry or literary discourse, to understand his attitude to language we need to begin by examining his *poetica utens*. In fact, several authors

[1]    Many kindly thanks to my friend, Robert Pelik, for our conversations on God, the world and beauty, and for his translation of this essay.
[2]    'Apud graecos primi famosi in scientia fuerunt quidam poëtae theologi, sic dicti, quia de divinis carmina faciebant … Isti autem poëtae quibusdam aenigmatibus fabularum aliquid de rerum natura tractaverunt' (*Sententia super Metaphysicam*, lib. 1, lectio 4 n.15). For information about the editions of Thomas's works quoted in this chapter, see Emery.
[3]    'Sed poetae non solum in hoc, sed in multis aliis mentiuntur' (*Sententia super Metaphysicam*, lib. 1, lectio 3, n. 12).

such as Klaus Müller and Tanner have shown that Thomas's praxis in dealing with language and poetics is often more interesting than his theories about them. In my own detailed study of the poetics of Thomistic theology,[4] I proposed an insight into the nature of language which I shall summarize in this chapter.

## Thomas's Theoretical Approach to Beauty and Language

### *Thomas on Beauty*[5]

Curtius comments that Aquinas always appears to 'touch on the subject of aesthetics by accident' and 'the answers he gives to these questions seem like appendages. They do not arise from a lack of interest, but rather the opposite: a vision of the world in terms of beauty was for him so spontaneous and natural that it is present as the underlying tonality of his sensibility and religious vision' (vol. 1, 357). Moreover:

> When Scholasticism speaks of beauty, the word is used to indicate an attribute of God. The metaphysics of beauty (for example, in Plotinus) and theories of art have nothing whatever to do with each other. 'Modern' man immeasurably over-values art because he has lost the sense of intelligible beauty that Neoplatonism and the Middle Ages possessed. (357)

To this, Curtius adds the words that St Augustine addressed to God: 'Sero te amavi pulchritudo tam antiqua et tam nova, sero te amavi' ('Late have I loved you, beauty so old and so new: late have I loved you') (*Confessions* X, 27, 38, in Curtius vol. 1, 357). Thus, as Umberto Eco writes, 'paradoxically, it is not that the mediaeval age did not have an aesthetics, but that modern aesthetics is excessively narrow' (19–20; my translation).

---

[4]    I am following in the footsteps of several authors who have dealt with Thomas from different perspectives. For example, his biography: Torrell, *Initiation*; the history of culture: Boyle; art history: Panofsky, De Bruyne and Eco; the history of the theory of language and speculative grammar: Schoot and Rosier-Catach; the history of rhetoric: Mongeau; the history of poetics: Wielockx, 'Poetry and Theology'.

[5]    Thomas's conception of the beautiful is well researched: see Vallet; Maritain; Kovach; Gilson (*Introduction* and *Matières et formes*); Czapiewski; Eco; L. Müller. Nevertheless, to put it in Dasseleer's words: 'vouloir saisir l'esthétique thomasienne d'un strict point de vue historique, relève de l'illusion' (335).

Beyond the *quod visu placet* ('that which is pleasing to the eye'), which is what modern aesthetic subjectivism tends to reduce to, the medieval world offered objective metaphysical categories in order to describe beauty. Thomas Aquinas sums it up in three famous lines: 'Three things are needed for beauty. Firstly, wholeness or perfection, because what is lacking in this respect cannot be truly worthy; then harmony between the parts which make up the whole; and finally, radiance, which explains why a brilliant colour may be described as beautiful' (*Summa theologiae* 1, 39, 8 contra; cf. *Summa* 2–2, 145, 2 contra, and 2–2, 180, 2 ad 3). For Thomas, therefore, *integritas*, *claritas* and *proportio* are the three characteristics essential to beauty. They do not constitute a simple objectivist aesthetics, because *proportio*, for example, designates the belonging together of the subject and object in a created world constructed from a fundamental musical harmony.

The full perception of beauty is only possible in the mind of God. As Eco states in his book on the subject, the 'Thomistic aesthetic system' affirms 'that natural substances are ontologically prior to artificial forms, divine creation prior to human productions. Thus, human productions are beautiful only in a superficial sense; their aesthetic value is deficient, as it were, in ontological density' (Eco 203). So, how do we appreciate the *integritas*, *proportio* and *claritas* of divine creation (Eco 212)?

Because God is transcendent, a complete appreciation of beauty, Eco concludes, is not possible for human beings (210). To grasp fully the *integritas* of a created thing, for example, it would be necessary for the human intellect to judge it against the eternal idea of its essence in the mind of God, which precedes any manifestation: 'the kind of knowledge that is needed for aesthetic experience is just this substantial knowledge, this creator's knowledge' (Eco 210). Similarly, the *proportio* between subject and object is problematic when related to God. How do we establish the necessary harmony, when the object contemplated is God Himself? The task, says Eco, is impossible (211).

*Beauty as a Task to Accomplish*

Eco is quite right to describe knowledge aimed at as a 'substantial knowledge'. However, his pessimism about the possibility of obtaining it is connected to the loss of his faith, about which he writes in the preface to the latest edition of his study. That attitude inevitably involves a reduction of Thomas's work to merely logical discourse, which he even compares to a computer (Eco 202).

In fact it is the intuition belonging to faith that gives Thomas the confidence to try to approach this divine vision: 'datum non ambigitur' ('Given with certainty'), says the *Lauda Sion*. He believes that his intelligence receives the impression of divine thought in the course of the practices which give expression to that faith (*Summa* 1, 1, 3, ad 2). *Lectio* (or prayerful reading infused by the desire for inspiration) and liturgical celebration actualize the performativity of Holy Scripture. Flowing in the midst of *doctrina sacra*, the practice of theology – encompassing reading, lecturing, dictating or writing – permits one to approach the divine knowledge of the world and to glimpse beauty in its transcendental fullness.

We all know that famous remark that Thomas made to his secretary when he decided to write no more: 'I cannot continue, Reginald, everything I have written seems to me as straw in comparison with what I have seen' (Torrell, *Initiation* 424). Does that not suggest that Thomas wrote in order to see? I have already shown elsewhere (Venard, *Thomas d'Aquin*, vol. 2, especially 299–300) that the mind's detour through the words of reasoning in order to reach the intuition of truth is for Thomas a 'deferred regard' (*regard différé*).[6] In short, truth and beauty appear in his work as a 'task', almost in the Kantian sense of that term. The principal instrument used to accomplish that task is language.

## Thomas on Language

For Thomas, language functions as an instrument of vision, pointing beyond representation. The way in which he uses language is governed by its referential function: for him, language is fundamentally a way of showing, a *deixis*, rather than the system of representation and expression that it is nowadays usually taken to be. What is remarkable in his work, and somewhat shocking to our present rhetorical timidity, is that the awareness of the ineffable transcendence of the divine produces not silence but abundance. Combining the apophaticism of the mystics with the metaphysical and linguistic disciplines of his time, and practising both humility and boldness, Thomas elaborates a language which enables the expression of truths about God beyond what we can fully understand. He frequently uses, for example, the modes of *significatio* or *suppositio*; he has recourse to the *intentio* or *usus loquentium* of what would later be dubbed 'speculative grammar', in ways which can easily match in refinement the pragmatic, semantic and syntactical analyses of modern linguistics.

---

[6]  Chrétien (130), quoting *Summa* 1, 67, 1, contra, and commenting on *Summa contra gentiles* 1, 57 *in fine*: 'Quae enim ratiocinando scimus non sunt secundum se nobis nuda et aperta, sed ratione aperiuntur et nudantur'; *Summa* 2–2, 49, 5, ad 2: 'Certitudo rationis est ex intellectu, sed necessitas rationis est ex defectu intellectus: illa enim in quibus vis intellectiva plenarie viget ratione non indigent, sed suo simplici intuitu veritatem comprehendunt, sicut Deus et angeli'.

I have described elsewhere at some length the ways in which the *Summa theologiae* puts into practice this performative conception of language and beauty (Venard, *Thomas d'Aquin*, vol. 1, 169–85). In the *Summa*, Thomas uses poetics that unfolds around several principles: *eruditio* (which etymologically refers to 'rough-hewing' and is the opposite of accumulation), *determinatio*, *clarificatio* and causality, including the specifically mediaeval type of 'etymology' which straddles both words and things (Venard, *Thomas d'Aquin*, vol. 1, 147–67). The beauty that this poetics radiates is not the product of embellishment but of the search for a maximal *manifestatio*. This domination of the practical over semantics translates, in terms of the human poetic impulse, into a 'metaphysics of being as act' rather than concept, and it is this which characterizes Thomas's thought. Contrary to the caricature of scholasticism which has sometimes been presented, Thomas shows no linguistic naivety: he is fully aware of the irreducibility of language for human thought.

The first principle in his thought is not the principle of identity (contrary to what neo-Thomism has long maintained) but that of non-contradiction, which therefore includes concrete language, because if nothing is said (*dicere*) nothing can be contradicted (*contra dicere*), as Courtès concluded. Nevertheless, Thomas is scarcely concerned by what seems to us today to be 'the problem of language', namely, the fact of the union of the material word and meaning, the dialectic of signifier and signified in the sign. Both this fact and this dialectic constitute the linguistic manifestation of the fundamental noetic problem of the bridge between the senses and the intellect.

In order to resolve this dialectic tension, as we must necessarily do if we want to affirm anything as true, we have a tendency today to eliminate one of the terms. Modernism ignores language, while postmodernism considers everything to be language. Thomas does not try to oversimplify the problem. He juxtaposes an ideal conception of language – as pure transfer of information – with a more prosaic view of language as a set of material signs. On the one hand, Thomas sees language as the 'face of pure intelligibility', the *Logos* with which it is directly united. This *Logos* was, in mediaeval theology, an infinitely creative subjectivity: 'the intelligible face of the sign is always turned towards the Word and face of God' (Derrida 25–6). On the other hand, Thomas does not claim to be able 'to abstract meaning, truth, being, etc. from the gesture of signification' (Derrida 26), to which his recourse to the sophisticated analyses provided by grammarians bears witness. He does not try, however, to demonstrate how to overcome the problem of the dialectic of the sign, not because it is insoluble, but, on the contrary, because it has already been resolved.

Thomas founds his trust in language as mediation for truth on the theoretical and practical relationship to God. The problem of the dialectic of the sign is immediately resolved in a conception of the world as creation, which means that the world can be read as a *'pansemiosis'*. By his creative Word, God gives to ontology a latent semiotics, and to semiotics an ontological depth.

Thomas's faith in language relies on a subtle noetics, developed from his understanding of the Trinity. He elaborates a theory of 'the mental word' in the double dialectic between, on the one hand, the expressed exterior word and the inner mental word, and, on the other, the human word and the divine *Logos* (Venard, *Thomas d'Aquin*, vol. 2, chapter 9). Thus, he finds a firm foundation for confidence, both in the possibility of representative knowledge and in the realism of metaphysical discourse. But it should be noted that it is a theological foundation, and in no way 'foundationalist'.

The belief that everything was created through the Word comes from biblical revelation, which provides the third pillar supporting Thomas Aquinas's confidence in language: it becomes a whole way of life, linked to Holy Scripture, sustaining his vision of the world and understanding of the Word. The traditional way of receiving Scripture consists in, first of all, believing: an action leading to a new experience, rather than a simple recognition of certain facts. In 'La résurrection dans le langage du Nouveau Testament', Delorme writes:

> The language of faith is not the simple reflection of experience. In a sense, it makes experience happen. Without the language of faith, would experience happen in the precise form in which it is described? Because the language of faith eludes verification while at the same time allowing itself to be put to the test, it relaunches experience and renews it. Which comes first, my hope or that at the heart of which I learn to hope? My act of faith or the faith into which I have been initiated? (172; editor's translation)[7]

To believe in Scripture is to put it into practice, which means to enact its performative quality in life beyond the text. In the sacred context of the mediaeval university, the word of the master who teaches was seen to be situated, so to speak, midway between ordinary conversation and liturgical language, where the divine Word comes to inhabit the human voice, making

---

[7]    'Le langage de la foi n'est pas le simple reflet de l'expérience. En un sens, il la fait advenir. Sans lui, serait-elle faite sous la forme précise qu'il énonce? Parce qu'il échappe à la vérification tout en se laissant éprouver, il relance l'expérience et la renouvelle. Qu'est-ce qui est premier: mon espérance, ou celle à l'intérieur de laquelle j'ai appris à espérer? Mon acte de foi, ou la foi à laquelle j'ai été initié?' (Delorme 172).

it into a continuation of the experience of Scripture. Present in *lectio*, in *lectura* and in preaching, the word incites to action, for example, to devotion before the Crucifix, sacramental ritual, indeed to a whole way of life which is entirely what Lindbeck refers to as 'intratextual'.

At the heart of the celebration of the sacraments is the transfiguration involved in giving a name to matter, which brings to birth a living response to the *aporias* of signification by the actual presence of the Word of God united with human words, as Catherine Pickstock points out. Therefore someone who assents to the belief that the incarnate Word, because it has been spoken, is present in the Eucharistic bread no longer needs to ask about the origin of meaning, or doubt the possible ontological reality of the union of signifier and signified. 'Nothing is more true than the Word of truth', wrote Thomas in the poem we shall examine later: the frequentation of this sacrament is the concrete resolution of the problem of the dialectic of the sign.

More generally, from the viewpoint of literary deconstruction, the work of Thomas contains a Christological foundation for language, which Etienne Gilson invoked in a letter to Jacques Maritain, on 6 April 1953, when he wrote of 'the amazing words of St Thomas, that language is an analogue of the Incarnation of the Word' (Prouvost 187). Gilson was referring to, for example, *Summa theologiae* 1, 27 or *Summa contra gentiles* 4, 11. Schoot explores this analogy at some length. The analogy with the Incarnation concerns first of all the structure of language, combining sound and meaning. Although a champion of Christological apophaticism, Thomas nevertheless proposes an approximation between the hypostatic union and language, for example, in the union of meaning and sound in speech.[8] Christ is 'the way, the truth and the life', that is to say, the signifier, the signified and the referent. *Logos* means not only Jesus' own word but also the word about Jesus and Jesus himself. This is wonderfully embedded in the enunciative structure of the Gospel itself which, as I have shown elsewhere, is the structure of a Möbius strip (*Thomas d'Aquin*, vol. 3, chapter 4, section 1).

This structural analogy unfolds in the functioning of language. There is in Thomas a 'static' analogy between the mystery of the Incarnation and the functioning of words when we talk about God. As Schoot points out, Thomas's doctrine of the hypostatic union rests upon 'a fundamental analogy between the human mode of signification on the one hand and the personal union of Christ on the other' (110). He also deploys a 'dynamic' analogy between the knowledge that man can have of God and the mystery of the self-understanding

---

[8]    *Summa* 3, 6, 6, 3 ad 3 (on the incarnation); 3, 62, 4 ad 1 (on grace); 3, 60, 6 contra (on the overall fittingness of these mysteries with anthropology).

and revelation of God himself. The union of sound and meaning, of word and idea, is as enigmatic as the mysterious union of the Word of God and human knowledge of Him in Jesus, the relationship between Christ and the Old Testament or the relationship between the suffering Christ and the Eucharistic species. The Incarnation tells us something about language, in the same way as language prefigures the mystery of the Incarnation. Circular as it may be, such reasoning is enlightening. As Schoot puts it, 'reasoning which employs analogy is normally thought of as a weak, but nevertheless valid means of proving something to be the case' (187). Thus, when language has Christ himself as its object, it is as though, in a sublime moment, the river had returned to its source.

## Thomas's Actual Poetry

Let us now see what we can learn from looking at one of his actual poems, the famous *Adoro te Devote*:[9]

> Adoro te devote, latens veritas,
> Te que sub his formis vere latitas.
> Tibi se cor meum totum subicit
> Quia te contemplans totum deficit.
>
> Visus, tactus, gustus, in te fallitur,
> Sed auditu solo tute creditur,
> Credo quicquid dixit dei filius,
> Nichil veritatis verbo verius.
>
> In cruce latebat sola deitas,
> Sed hic latet simul et humanitas.
> Ambo vere credens atque confitens,
> Peto quod petivit latro penitens.
>
> Plagas sicut Thomas non intueor,
> Deum tamen meum te confiteor.
> Fac me tibi semper magis credere,
> In te spem habere, te diligere.

---

[9]	For a general history of the reception of the poem, see Wielockx, *'Adoro te devote'* 118–23.

O memoriale mortis Domini,
Panis vivus vitam prestans homini.
Presta michi semper de te vivere,
Et te michi semper dulce sapere.

Pie pellicane, Ihesu Domine,
Me immundum munda tuo sanguine,
Cuius una stilla salvum facere
Totum mundum posset omni scelere!

Ihesu, quem velatum nunc aspicio,
Quando fiet illud quod tam sicio?
Ut te revelata cernens facie,
Visu sim beatus tue glorie.

[I adore You devoutly, Truth that hides,
You who are truly there, hidden beneath these forms
To You my heart submits itself completely
Because in contemplating you it entirely falls short:

Sight, touch, taste, all fail in You;
Only by hearing is it all believed!
I believe what the Son of God said:
Nothing is more true than the Word of truth.

On the cross was hidden the divinity alone
But here at the same time hides the humanity.
Truly believing and professing both,
I plead for what the good thief pleaded.

Like Thomas, I do not see the wounds
Nevertheless I confess that you are my God!
Make me believe in You,
Hope in You, love You always more!

O memorial of the death of the Lord!
Living bread giving life to man,
Make me always live through you
And to savour your sweetness always.

Kind pelican, Jesus Lord
Purify impure me by your blood
Of which one drop could save
The entire world from every sin.

Jesus whom I now see veiled,
When will that which I thirst for come?
When, discovering you with unveiled face,
Will I be blessed by the vision of your glory][10]

Here we will simply address two questions: what kind of language do we find in this poem? What is the nature of the Eucharistic beauty that it celebrates?

## The Language of the Theological Poet

The search for *claritas* requires Thomas to use the language of *deixis*. As the prayer of the priest after the consecration, the poem *Adoro* is entirely a designation of 'this' (as the celebrating priest says, 'this is my body'). The performative theological language of the adoring 'I' of the poet uses Scripture, Aristotelian philosophy and an Augustinian lyricism. Let us begin with the last mentioned.

### Augustinian Lyricism

Thomas Aquinas's biographers claim that the *Sacerdos* Office represents a turning-point in his work, in which a quite new emphasis is placed on affectivity. *Suavitas* and *dulcedo*, which are absent from Thomas's commentary on the *Sentences*, but repeated in *Sacerdos*, also reappear in the *Summa theologiae*: 'quaedam actualis refectio spiritualis dulcedinis' (*Summa* 3, 79, 8).

From the very beginning of the poem, he speaks in the first person: *adoro*. Like Augustine of Hippo, Thomas sees in praise the only response 'proportional' to the ineffability of God. Human speech about God evolves between two asymptotes: *tibi silet laus, Deus* ('praise to thee is speechless, O God), and *tibi reddetur votum* ('a vow shall be paid to thee'). Since the essence of God is incomprehensible and indescribable, one can only love and praise Him. Michel

---

[10]   I am grateful to Fr Terence Crotty OP for his (yet unpublished) translation of this poem and to Sr Marie (Geneviève) Trainar OP, who co-authored with me *Thomas d'Aquin*, *Adoro, petit traité de la présence de Dieu à trois voix dominicaines*. In the following paragraphs, I borrow several passages from this booklet.

and Borde explain: 'The aim of praise is not communication ... which is rendered unnecessary by the fact of God's omniscience, but communion which is a self-abandonment to a never-ending movement reaching towards the divine: praise, expressed outwardly in words and inwardly in thought, which carries one forever farther' (No. 6, 5–6). In our poem, the personal nature of this relationship with God is revealed in the play between the first and second person singular. It is the élan of desire which this poem expresses, the desire to understand, to see, to enjoy the beatific vision.

## The Language of Scripture

Thomas Aquinas is attached to the literal meaning of the Scriptures, although it is also important to recognize that he did not understand that expression in the historicist way that is familiar to us (Venard, 'Problematique' 293–354). The literal meaning is the foundation of the whole poem. In fact faith in the real presence was not a dogma of the Church before the controversies of the Reformation. For Thomas, as for nearly all his contemporaries, it was the result of a serious reading of Scripture; 'I adore You devoutly, hidden Truth / You are truly there, hidden beneath these appearances' (*Adoro*, lines 1–2).

'Faith in the real presence consists in faith in the words of Christ in the institution: the words of the priest in the celebration of the Eucharist, like those of Jesus during the Last Supper must be taken literally' (Roguet 367). We need to read the image of the Pelican in that context, as well as the refusal of a *concetto* about the possibility for God to redeem mankind without any drop of blood in lines 23–4. Similarly, the description of the sacrament as a 'memorial' in line 17 shows respect for the passage of Scripture (Luke 22:19; 1 Cor. 11:25), quoting Jesus' words during the Last Supper, used in the liturgy.

However, the words of Scripture are not only respected by the theologian as a memorial of a past event: they also embody a present experience. The idea that everything proceeds from the heart is profoundly biblical. Under the appearance of bread, *this* is his Body, the Incarnate Word who died and rose again. How could the mind not fail before this surreal reality? That is why this knowledge springs from the heart in a poetic gesture of adoration: *cor meum* ('To You my entire heart submits itself / Because in contemplating you it entirely falls short' [*Adoro*, lines 3–4]).

Naturally the poem is also formed by the literary genre of the liturgical hymn. But, above all, it is a response to the God who looks at the heart when humans look at the outward appearance (1 Sam. 16:7), the response of a humble man who feels the presence of something infinitely beyond anything that he could conceive and therefore even ask for (Eph. 3:20). Yes, for in God alone is our refuge, or, as the Vulgate says: *Deo subjecta erit anima mea* (Ps. 62 (61):2).

This desire for intimacy with God is characteristic of the expression of the ancient prophets (and of Jesus himself). The magnificent symmetrical phrases in line 15, *me tibi semper* ('Make me always believe more in You'), and line 20, *te michi semper* ('Make me always live through you), are literary echoes of the Vulgate version of Hosea 2:19: 'Sponsabo te mihi in sempiternum' (New Revised Standard Version: 'And I will take you for my wife for ever'). Thomas is the only one of his time to quote this passage of Hosea to describe union with God by faith.[11] In so doing, he discreetly affirms the place of the ordinary believer in the story of the marriage between God and his people.

Nevertheless, Thomas does not only speak from the heart. Following a biblical anthropology, profoundly rooted in the hours spent each morning commenting on the *pagina sacra*, he proceeds from the heart (line 3) to the inadequacy of sensory perception (line 5) to the purity of faith alone (line 7). The emphasis placed on faith leads the mediaeval Thomas to imitate Thomas the Apostle, expressing the full intensity of the experience:

> The wounds which Thomas saw I do not see;
> Nevertheless I confess that you are my God!
> Make me always believe more in You,
> Hope in You, love You! (lines 13–16)

'You said to Thomas "blessed are those who have not seen and yet have come to believe"' (John 20:29). Thirteen hundred years later: 'Here I am: I see nothing but these modest appearances in which I believe you to be present, Lord; I love You and I believe in You!' This stanza devoted to the apostle Thomas is the centre of the poem, and thus emphasizes the patristic theme: 'he saw a man and he confessed him as his God'. The model of Saint Thomas the Apostle can probably be seen as a discrete signature by Thomas Aquinas himself, who had a strong devotion to his patron saint, as Torrell suggests (*Saint Thomas d'Aquin* 7).[12]

An insistence on speech is the correlative to this emphasis placed on faith: 'Only by hearing is it all believed.' Did Luther realize how close he was to Thomas when he proposed that one nourish oneself on that which appears nowhere

---

[11]    See *Scriptum super libros Sententiarum Petri Lombardi* in IV, d. 39, q. unica, 6, 2; and *Sermo in Symbolum Apostolorum*.

[12]    In the same place Torrell quotes *Lectura super Ioannem* 20, lect. 6, n. 2562: 'Statim factus est Thomas bonus theologus veram fidem confitendo'.

except in the clue provided by the hearing of the Word? Both men related their faith to the experience of Israel. And in fact the importance of hearing is eminently biblical, as can be seen, for example, in 'Hear, O Israel' (Deut. 6:4), and in Paul's words, 'So faith comes from what is heard' (Rom. 10:17; cf. Mark 10:46–52). This is anchored in the most ancient experience of Israel, a people born when they learnt in Sinai to see God in sounds (Exod. 20:18): 'for no-one may see me and live'. But one can *hear* him. Paradoxically, faith sees by means of hearing the word.

In discovering the presence of God through the words which invoke him, Thomas reaffirms the tradition of Israel's ancient liturgies, for which God lives in the praise of his people (Ps. 22:3), which constitutes an agreeable sacrifice (Hos. 14:3). Christ is truly present in the community of his faithful and in their praise (Matt. 18:19). In the case of Eucharistic poetry, the divine habitation in human speech clothes itself in a sublime realism. As Michel and Borde point out, 'there is a profound analogy between praise and Christ: both are mediators between the human and the divine. But there is another reason arising from the very nature of the Eucharist' (No. 6, 5–6), where Christ is present in person.

Thus the Church continues the adventure of the chosen people. She also receives, to help her across the desert, manna, the bread of heaven. The writer of the Scriptures described in detail the appearance of this manna. But what it truly was, no one, not even Moses, could say. And the question itself provided its name: *manna* derives from the Hebrew *man-hu?* ('What is it?') The question remained unanswered. Subsequently, the manna disappeared from the Ark of the Covenant, where it had been piously kept, and it was forgotten, as was the question. But on the evening when Jesus took the bread and, after giving thanks and praise, broke it, saying 'This is my body that is for you' (1 Cor. 11:23–4), the true nature of the manna was finally revealed. Like Adam, who gave names to all the creatures of Paradise, Jesus revealed the true substance of the bread of heaven, and, like God on the first day of creation, he spoke and it was so (Gen. 1:3, 9).

What is it (*man-hu*)? The words which give manna provoke wonder, a true metaphysical awe at the action of the Lord in the cosmos. Thomas, lost in amazement, spent his life trying to understand this *mysterion*. Thus it is from Scripture itself that Thomas draws his metaphysical curiosity: Aristotle and the entire philosophical tradition are used in the service of the comprehension of the God who reveals himself. Contrary to widely held but, in fact, superficial beliefs about oppositions between Hebrew and Greek thought, the Bible and philosophy meet in this very wonderment, as the Jewish Greek adaptation and supplementation of the scriptural theophanies translated in Alexandria show.

*The Language of Philosophy*

Rooted in realist sensory experience, the philosophy of Aristotle permits the development and deepening of the questions provoked by the Eucharistic performativity of Scripture. The second stanza reads:

> Sight, touch, taste, all fail in You;
> Only by hearing is it all believed!
> I believe what the Son of God said:
> Nothing is more true than the Word of truth.

The first line of this stanza apparently contradicts Aristotelian philosophy. The Aristotelian tradition is clear: the senses are never mistaken about their objects.[13] Worse still, this line contradicts Thomas's own writings, which clearly reject any idea of fiction or illusion.[14] Neither the emotion of poetry nor devotion should have led Thomas to take such a licence.[15] But here again, the interpreters tend to reify words into doctrine, whereas their truth is to be found in the gesture of reaching towards the infinite. Let us examine this idea further.

*Videtur quod* ... As we have just seen, the senses can be mistaken. Intelligence cannot extract the meaning of the Eucharist from sight or touch or taste. Thomas draws our attention to this fact in his hymn *Pange lingua*: 'Et si sensus deficit' ('even if sense is deficient'). *Sed contra* ... the words of the Gospels which the priest repeats at the altar before the congregation are clear: this is my body, this is my blood. *Responsio dicendum quod* ... The object of sensory perception, which is here and now, is mentioned in lines 2 and 10 in the form of a demonstrative adjective first of all and then an adverb: *his formis* ('these forms'); *hic latet* ('lies here'), as Wielockx points out in 'Poetry and Theology in the *Adoro te devote*' (158). Nevertheless, what Thomas speaks of

---

[13]   'Sensus ... propriorum semper verus est' (Aristotle, *De anima* 427b 11–12; 428b 18–20, translated by William of Moerbeke).

[14]   'In hoc sacramento non est aliqua deceptio neque fictio' (*Scriptum super libros Sententiarum Petri Lombardi* IV, d.11, q.1 a.1 qc. 2 ad 1); 'In hoc sacramento nulla est deceptio' (*Summa* 3, 75, 5 ad 2; also 3, 76, 8; *Summa* 3, 77, 2 and 7; *Summa contra gentiles* 4, 62 s).

[15]   *Sacerdos*, in the second reading of Matins, has, for example: 'Accidentia enim sine subiecto in eodem existunt, ut fides locum habeat dum visibile invisibiliter sumitur, aliena specie occultatum, et sensus a deceptione immunes reddantur, qui de accidentibus iudicant sibi notis.'

when he invokes the weakness of the senses is not their object but that which it signifies: 'in te fallitur' ('it fails in you'). Here the theologian addresses Christ, not the consecrated bread and wine. In the bread, the eyes see something pale, the hands touch a crust which encloses a kind of sponge, the tongue tastes something bland. But it is the intelligence which sees the bread, sees what is hidden under the appearance, which we call its substance, and, *a fortiori*, the transubstantiation of Christ. Thus, as Wielockx goes on to argue, Thomas does not enclose himself within the noetic. He remains Aristotelian, believing that the senses are not mistaken in their object (169). But the senses cannot go beyond that object. *Adoro* does not say that the senses are mistaken, but that reality is fully manifest only to one of them, namely,  hearing (*auditus*). The judgement by the other senses is somewhat corrected by the *auditus*. The synthesis of the data of the senses belongs to the *sensus communis*, which will be governed here by the hearing (*Summa* 1, 78, 4).

There is more. Normally, the appearances correspond to the thing that they reveal, but here, that is not at all the case. Although the substance has changed, the appearances of bread and wine remain. Therefore there is a kind of second miracle in the Eucharist: the substance has not been destroyed but transformed and contains the very substance of the Body of Christ. Is not that already the world beyond revealed by the prophets: 'God all in all' – a world which Aristotelian language allows us to recognize and admire in the process of becoming on the altar? Far from going against biblical inspiration, Aristotle's metaphysics allows a deepening of wonder at the dynamic relation between God and his creation first revealed in Exodus.

## The Nature of the Beauty Celebrated: *Proportio, Integritas, Claritas*

Concerning *proportio*, the poem starkly presents the inequality of the relationship between man and God. The comparison between human weakness and God's power is perfectly depicted in the inversions in lines 3–4 and 23–4: 'Tibi se cor meum totum subicit / quia ... totum deficit' ['To You my entire heart submits itself / Because in contemplating you it entirely falls short']; 'una stilla salvum facere / totum mundum posset omni scelere' ('Of which one drop could save / the entire world from its sentence').

These lines contrast the impotence of everything which is most intimate to the believer (his whole heart) with the omnipotence of the smallest portion of the exteriority of Christ: one drop of blood. This proportionality also illustrates a fundamental principle of the Dionysian hierarchy: the smallest degree of a higher level is more powerful than the highest degree of the inferior one.[16]

This *proportio* is not just witnessed from the exterior, but is constructed within the poem. As Michel and Borde argue, 'everything is action in this poem; from which originates the proud words [of the *Lauda Sion*] (which could describe the ambition of Gothic art): "Quantum potes, tantum aude" ['Dare as much as you can']. It is the courage which comes from faith which establishes the relationship between finite humanity and infinite divinity. It knows its place and its limits in the order of grades, but dares nevertheless to desire perfection. It therefore reaches towards moral beauty, in the spiritual splendour of the *honestum*' (No. 7, 2). Out of that arise the petitions present throughout the poem:

> Make me always believe more in You,
> Hope in You, love You.
> Make me always live through you
> And to savour your sweetness.
> Purify impure me by your blood.
> When will that which I thirst for come?

The poetics which demands action in order to be made manifest is what is involved in the Christian vision of holiness and arises from the ancient Ciceronian, moral ideal of *honestas*. This provides the context for the poetic deed, which is first of all the concrete action in the life of any believer: prayer, praise and sanctification.

With regard to *integritas*, this quality is found fully expressed in the object. As in Pseudo-Dionysius (and it is worth noting that Thomas copied by hand Albert the Great's commentary on his *Celestial Hierarchy*), Thomas considers the Eucharist as the perfection of the whole sacramental order, because it contains not only Christ's action and power, as in the other sacraments, but Christ himself (*In Io.* 6, 7, 181; *Summa* 3, 65, 3). According to his biographers, the *Office of Corpus Christi* marks a turning point in his spiritual evolution: he centres everything not simply in the body and blood of Christ, but in a profound understanding of Christ himself present in this sacrament: *Christus/ Deus sumitur* (*Summa* 3, 73, 1 ad 3).

---

[16] *Super librum Dionysii De divinis nominibus* 2,1. See also *Summa* 1, 7, 1–2: 'Jesus' unicity is not that of an individual among other individuals: it is the infinite individuality, with no restriction whatsoever.'

In terms of the subject, *integritas*, like *proportio*, is something to be actively created. It appears as a totality of faith, hope and charity (lines 15–16), in other words, of life (line 19), to be achieved over time in individual and collective history, and yet transcending them. The mystery, when celebrated, is turned equally to the past (Jesus as the historical person who instituted it), to the present (the consecrated bread, taken and eaten, revivifying the community of the Church through the mystical communion with the glorified Christ) and to the future (the Eucharist as a support in our pilgrimage towards the heavenly banquet which it represents). This eschatological tension in Eucharistic doctrine is peculiar to Thomas among his contemporaries, as Gy has shown ('Le texte original' and 'La relation au Christ').

The poem also describes the noetic progress of humanity: from natural sensory vision to the beatific vision by way of faith. A whole theology of faith runs through and is illustrated and enacted in the poem itself, as Wielockx has shown. In 'Poetry and Theology in the *Adoro te devote*' he lists the main causalities of the act of faith included in the poem as: instrumental (lines 1–6, 'auditu solo'; lines 9 and 10, 'hic'); material (line 7, 'quicquid dixit'); formal (line 8, 'dei filius veritatis verbum'); efficient (line 15, 'fac me tibi semper magis credere'); final (lines 19 and 20, 'de te vivere sapere'). This faith is only the beginning of the story, not yet the perfection of joy, the eternal life which God will give definitively and completely in the beatific vision.

On the two occasions on which the word *visus* is used (lines 5 and 28), it describes the whole journey from our present sensory nature to the realization of the fullness of our human integrity in the Resurrection: 'Sight, touch, taste, all fail in You' and 'When will I be blessed to see your glory?' It is therefore the pilgrimage to the full achievement of our *integritas* that the poem describes. Michel and Borde (quoting *Summa* 2–2, 85, 1) comment that: 'If there is a fullness to be achieved it can only be in a continual movement towards God' (5). Hence the lines:

> Jesus whom I now see veiled,
> When will that which I thirst for come?
> When, discovering you with unveiled face,
> Will I be blessed to see your glory?

To paraphrase it in our words: 'Jesus, it is really you whom I see when the priest, after having consecrated the host, raises it up to show me [*aspicere*]. But you remain covered by this modest veil, and I would love to see you face-to-face as when talking with a friend.'

*Claritas*, the object of which is the real presence of God, is also revealed more powerfully as the poem develops. The literary devices mimic the spiritual actions. The first half, lines 1–14, which uses masculine rhymes, is centred on the concrete, physical experience of Eucharistic adoration: the limits of sensation are suggested by the consonantal ending of each line. The second half, lines 15–28, using feminine rhymes, is devoted to the expression of the nature of Eucharistic faith, which opens out on to eschatological vision, and it is that openness which the feminine rhymes evoke.

One could also mention the Christological sense of the consonant 't', as Lucia Treanor proposed in an extremely original recent study, as yet unpublished. She suggests that the 't' represents the cross of Jesus, and even the three crosses of Golgotha, all through the poem which celebrates its memorial. The use of singing is also relevant since it infuses the enunciation of the words with a radiant clarity. Michel and Borde argue: 'Saint Thomas defines praise as an "act of religion" and we need to hear the word "act" with its full poetic resonance' (5; cf. *Summa* 2–2, 82 *incipit*).

Inversely, the whole poem is marked by the fact that there is nothing, or almost nothing, to see except to the eyes of faith. It is as if the words of the hymn 'present something without any support'[17] – except for the bread and wine, but they are only signs. It is as if the hymn was itself its own proof, since the object of contemplation, by (non-)definition, is beyond any sensory experience.

In thus paying full attention to language itself in the work of Thomas, we discover theological writing consubstantial with prayer. What we have found present in concentrated form in the sublime poetry of *Adoro te devote* is also there in the *Summa* itself, written with confidence in the grace of God (*Summa* 1, Prologue *in fine*). It is through and in words that their object can be experienced, as it is through and in the liturgy that faith is born and grows. In this manner beauty becomes a sacrament of the divine; poetry carries the grace of theology into the soul of the person who is touched by its beauty. As act which is knowledge, and knowledge which is act, the Eucharist allows us to approach the 'substantial knowledge' which Eco considers necessary for the experience of transcendent beauty.

## Conclusion

Let us conclude with one circumstantial point and one question. There is an ongoing debate on the authenticity of the hymn *Adoro te devote*, a surprisingly

---

[17] See John of the Cross, 114: 'mi alma se ve ya sin arrimo y con arrimo'.

lyrical piece in Thomas's work, which apparently contains an Aristotelian heresy (*visus tactus gustus fallitur*). The history of the handwritten transmission shows a gap between 1264, when Thomas could have composed the poem, and its first written witness in 1323 (de Tocco, fasc. 58, 380–1). According to the most recent editor of the early life of Thomas, it is authentic.[18] And expert contemporary scholars such as Gauthier and Torrell (Torrell, *Recherches thomasiennes* 369–70) have decided in favour of its authenticity, even though the Leonine Commission has not formally pronounced on the subject. In the dispute about this poem, theologians and historians assume conscious or unconscious positions regarding theology, poetry, science, language and prayer. Concentrating on the poetic ambition and method of this piece, more than on its themes, the meditation presented here has uncovered within it, at very least, several typically 'Thomistic' theological features embedded in its very poetry.

Let us end with a question which our poet invites us to pose. Eucharistic poetry continues and intensifies the historical experience of revelation. As Michel and Borde have said:

> Having reached its greatest degree of intensity, it becomes prayer which transcends the power of words; instead of celebrating beauty with beauty, it enters into a direct relationship with ... the beauty of God. It is this which puts into question the idea of a work of art [as] personal expression. That becomes sublimated [and superseded]: literary devices are abandoned; the poetry becomes that which it celebrates ... The poetry is a monstrance which displays God to the faithful ... [It] is thus not only a work of art but also an object of worship, humbly participating in the life of the divinity which it reveals. (No. 7, 10–11)

The question is: does this experience, which Thomas expresses in his poems, have a place in the literary world of today?

Thomas is not a 'visionary' writer in the sense of certain Romantics. As has been suggested elsewhere (Venard, *Thomas d'Aquin*, vol. 1, 225–61), he is closer to the *voyant* of Rimbaud, whose programme he accomplishes in advance, while reversing the means. By a rational submission to the incarnate Word, and not in an alchemical revolt against Christ as the 'thief of energy', he transcends speech without denying reason. Singing of Christ substantially present under the veil of the visible bread is not yet quite seeing, but it points towards a real possibility of seeing. In his fascination with the Eucharist, Thomas, poet and theologian, gives back to Western culture the forgotten foundation of its ancient confidence

---

[18]   For an up-to-date account of the *status quaestionis*, see Murray.

in language for which it retains a nostalgia – if one follows Yves Bonnefoy or George Steiner.

## Works Cited

Boyle, Leonard E. 'The Setting of the *Summa Theologiae* of Saint Thomas'. In *The Gilson Lectures on Thomas Aquinas* 5, ed. James P. Reilly. Toronto: PIMS, 1982, 19–45.

Bruyne, Edgar de *Études d'esthétique médiévale* and *L'Esthétique du Moyen Âge*. 3 vols. Bruges: De Temple, 1946.

Chrétien, Jean-Louis. 'La connaissance angélique'. In *Le regard de l'amour*. Paris: Minuit, 2000, 125–39.

Courtès, Pierre-Ceslas. *L'être et le non être selon saint Thomas d'Aquin*. Paris: Téqui, 1998.

Curtius, Ernst Robert. *La littérature européenne et le Moyen Âge latin*. Trans. Jean Bréjoux. 2 vols. Paris: Presses Universitaires de France, 1956; second edition: Agora, 1986.

Czapiewski, Winfried. *Das Schöne bei Thomas von Aquin*. Freiburg: Herder, 1964.

Dasseleer, Pascal. 'Esthétique "thomiste" ou esthétique "thomasienne"?' *Revue philosophique de Louvain* 2 (May 1999): 312–35.

Delorme, Jean. 'La résurrection dans le langage du Nouveau Testament'. In *Le langage de la foi dans l'Ecriture*, ed. Jean Delorme. Paris: Cerf, 1972, 101–82.

Derrida, Jacques. *De la grammatologie*. Paris: Minuit, 1967.

Eco, Umberto. *Le problème esthétique chez Thomas d'Aquin*. Trans. M. Javion. Paris: Presses Universitaires de France, 1993.

Emery, Gilles. 'Bref catalogue des œuvres de saint Thomas'. In *Initiation à saint Thomas d'Aquin, sa personne et son œuvre*, ed. Jean-Pierre Torrell. Paris: Cerf, 1993, 483–525.

Gilson, Étienne. *Introduction aux arts du beau: Essais d'art et de philosophie*. Paris: Vrin, 1963.

—— *Matières et formes*. Paris: Vrin, 1964.

Gourmont, Remy de. *Le Latin mystique*. Monaco: Rocher, 1990.

Gy, Pierre-Marie. 'Le texte original de la *Tertia pars* de la *Somme Théologique* de S. Thomas d'Aquin dans l'apparat de l'Edition Léonine: le cas de l'eucharistie'. *Revue des sciences philosophiques et théologiques* 65 (1981): 608–16.

—— 'La relation au Christ dans l'Eucharistie selon S. Bonaventure et S. Thomas d'Aquin'. In *Sacrements de Jésus-Christ*, ed. J. Doré. Paris: Desclée, 1983.

John of the Cross. 'A lo Divino'. In *The Poems of Saint John of the Cross*, ed. and trans. Kathleen Jones. London: Continuum, 2001.

Kovach, Francis J. *Die Ästhetik des Thomas von Aquin: Eine Genetische und Systematische Analyse*. Berlin: De Gruyter, 1961.

Lindbeck, George. *The Nature of Doctrine: Religion and Theology in a Postliberal Age*. Philadelphia: Westminster Press, 1984.

Maritain, Jacques. *Art et scholastique*. Paris: Rouart, 1935.

Michel, Alain. *In hymnis et canticis, culture et beauté dans l'hymnique chrétienne latine*. Paris and Louvain: Peeters, 1976.

Michel, Alain and Pascale Borde. 'A propos du *Lauda Sion*: poésie et théologie chez saint Thomas d'Aquin'. *Gregoriana* 6–7 (Le Mesnil-Saint Martin) (1987): 5–6; 2–11. (The translation is mine.)

Millet-Gérard, Dominique. *Claudel thomiste?* Paris: Honoré Champion, 1999.

Mongeau, Gilles. 'The Spiritual Pedagogy of the *Summa*'. *Nova et Vetera* (English edition) 2.1 (2004): 91–114.

Müller, Klaus. *Thomas von Aquins Theorie und Praxis der Analogie. Der Streit um das rechte Vorurteil und die Analyse einer aufschlußreichen Diskrepanz in der* Summa Theologiae. New York: P. Lang, 1983.

Müller, L. 'Das Schöne im Denken des Thomas von Aquin'. *Theologie und Philosophie* 57 (1982): 413–24.

Murray, Paul. *Aquinas at Prayer: The Bible, Mysticism and Poetry*. London: Bloomsbury-Continuum, 2013.

Panofsky, Erwin. *Architecture gothique et pensée scolastique*. Trans. Pierre Bourdieu. Paris: Minuit, 1967.

Pickstock, Catherine. 'Thomas Aquinas and the Quest for the Eucharist'. *Modern Theology* 15 (April 1999): 159–80.

Prouvost, Géry, ed. *Etienne Gilson et Jacques Maritain: Deux approches de l'être. Correspondance 1923–1971*. Paris: Vrin, 1991.

Roguet, A.-M. Appendice II in Thomas d'Aquin, *Somme théologique*. Edition de la Revue des Jeunes, *Les sacrements*. Paris: Cerf, 1951.

Rosier-Catach, Irene. *La parole comme acte: Sur la grammaire et la sémantique du XIIIe siècle*. Paris: Vrin, 1994.

—— *La parole efficace: Signes, pratiques sacrées, institutions*. Paris: Seuil, 2004.

Schoot, Henk J.M. *Christ the Name of God: Thomas Aquinas on Naming Christ*. Leuven: Peeters, 1993.

Tanner, Kathryn. *God and Creation in Christian Theology: Tyranny or Empowerment?* Oxford: Blackwell, 1988.

Thomas Aquinas. [The works are quoted from the most common editions listed in Emery. The texts are also available at: <http://www.corpusthomisticum.org/>]

——— *Lectura super Ioannem* (1270–72).

——— *Sacerdos: Officium de festo Corporis Christi ad mandatum Urbani Papae* (1264).

——— *Scriptum super libros Sententiarum Petri Lombardi*, I–IV (1252–56 and 1265–66).

——— *Sententia super Metaphysicam* (1270–72).

——— *Summa contra gentiles* (1260–65).

——— *Summa theologiae* (1265–73).

——— *Super librum Dionysii De divinis nominibus* (1261–68).

Tocco, Guillaume de. 'Vita S. Thomae Aquinatis'. In *Ystoria sancti Thome de Aquino' de Guillaume de Tocco (1323)*, ed. Claire Lebrun-Gouanvic. Toronto: PIMS, 1996.

Torrell, Jean-Pierre. *Initiation à saint Thomas d'Aquin, sa personne et son œuvre.* Paris: Cerf, 1993.

——— *Recherches thomasiennes: études revues et augmentées.* Paris: Vrin, 2000.

——— *Saint Thomas d'Aquin, maître spirituel: Initiation 2.* Paris: Cerf, 1996.

Treanor, Lucia. 'The Palindromic Structure of Aquinas's *Adoro te devote*'. 43rd International Congress on Medieval Studies, 8–11 May 2008 (I should like to thank the author for sending me a copy of her paper).

Vallet, Pierre. *L'idée de beau dans la philosophie de S. Thomas d'Aquin.* Paris: Chernovitz, 1883.

Venard, Olivier-Thomas. 'Problématique du sens littéral'. In *Le sens littéral des Écritures*, ed. Olivier-Thomas Venard. Paris: Cerf, 2009, 293–353.

——— *Thomas d'Aquin, poète-théologien, vol. 1: Littérature et théologie: une saison en enfer.* Geneva: Ad Solem, 2002.

——— *Thomas d'Aquin, poète-théologien, vol. 2: La langue de l'ineffable, essai sur le fondement théologique de la métaphysique.* Geneva: Ad Solem, 2004.

——— *Thomas d'Aquin, poète-théologien, vol. 3: Pagina sacra: le passage de l'Écriture sainte à l'écriture théologique illustré par l'exemple de saint Thomas d'Aquin.* Paris: Cerf, 2010.

Venard, Olivier-Thomas and Sr Marie (Geneviève) Trainar. *Thomas d'Aquin, Adoro, petit traité de la présence de Dieu à trois voix dominicaines.* Geneva: Ad Solem, 2005.

Wielockx, Robert. '*Adoro te devote*: Zur Losung Einer Alter Crux'. *Annales Theologici* 21 (2007): 101–38.

—— 'Poetry and Theology in the *Adoro te devote*: Thomas Aquinas on the Eucharist and Christ's Uniqueness'. In *Christ among the Medieval Dominicans: Representations of Christ in the Texts and Images of the Order of Preachers*, ed. Kent Emery and Joseph Peter Wawrykow. Notre Dame, IN: University of Notre Dame Press, 1998.

# Chapter 5

# Dante and the Indispensability of the Image

## John Took

p 95

Dante, it hardly needs to be said, is a larger-than-life figure in our tradition, the range and depth of his intuition in the areas of natural and moral philosophy, theology and literary aesthetics being as impressive as the great ocean of being – the 'gran mar de l'essere' – of which he speaks in the first canto of the *Paradiso*. Neither is it necessary to stress how his struggle for resolution on the plane of ideas is at the same time a struggle for resolution on the plane of art and of artistic integrity, the act of understanding at every stage involving him in an interrogation of his own expressive means. Sensitive as I am, then, to the scale of the question here, but above all to its moral and ontological seriousness (its 'serietà terribile', as the Italian philologist Gianfranco Contini used to say),[1] I shall in what follows take the line of least resistance, providing just a few preliminary remarks on Dante's imagery generally (with special reference to his particular brand of historical symbolism) and a couple of examples by way of illustration.

The *Commedia*, completed by Dante in the year of his death (1321), offers an account of the soul's journey into God as the beginning and end of all journeying, a journey explored in the poem by way of his progress through the three realms of the afterlife – hell, purgatory and paradise – as contained by the divine mind as the encompassing, as the whereabouts of everything that was, is and ever shall be in consequence of the original and abiding *fiat*. First, and as the necessary condition of everything coming next by way of renewal and resurrection, comes the moment of descent, the nothing if not painful business of self-confrontation and self-recognition in the depths. This, then, is the infernal phase of the journey, famous, certainly, for its inventiveness as an essay in divine retribution, but, on any more thoughtful reading of the poem, pervaded by an infinite sadness, the

---

[1] 'Mai in lui un sospetto di scetticismo. Ci sono scherzi anche nella sua opera, ma remotissimi dai centri dell'ispirazione. In fondo, una serietà terribile ...' (Contini x).

sadness of self as lost to the properly deiform substance of its humanity, to the possibility of its being in, through and for God as the final cause of its every significant inflexion of the spirit. Next, as the fruit of self-recognition thus understood, of the soul's knowing itself in its power to self-annihilation and in the guilt thereof, comes the moment of sorrowing, the moment in which, by way of what Bernard used to call an 'assiduity of tears',[2] the soul embarks on the gathering in of self to self on the plane of loving, on a bringing home of the kind of love engendered by the world round about to the kind of love given with the act itself of existence and making at last for communion with God as the beginning and end of all loving. This, then, is the purgatorial phase of the journey, a phase having about it very little of the legalism tending in other circumstances to bring the whole idea of purgatory into disrepute – in the words of *The Book of Common Prayer*, a 'fond thing, vainly imagined, and grounded upon no warranty of Scripture, but rather repugnant to the word of God'[3] – but bearing now on something altogether more intimate, on the reshaping of the soul itself, no less, in its affective structure. With this, the soul is ready to embark on the final phase of its journey into God, on an opening out of self upon its rapturous finality. Sphere by sphere, then, and spirit by spirit (Thomas Aquinas, Bonaventure, Benedict, Bernard, Peter, James and John), the pilgrim enters at last into the immediate presence of his maker, there to behold, impressed upon the simple light of divine being – simple in the degree to which it comprehends in its undifferentiation the endlessly differentiated character of its showing forth in the world – our likeness ('la nostra effige'), evidence, were evidence required, of its centrality to the very life of the Godhead itself. The geometry of it, however, is all too much for the pilgrim poet, the wings of his mind (the 'ali' of Alighieri) being unequal to the conceiving, let alone to the imaging, of what he now sees before him. Conceiving and imaging alike give way in the forum of consciousness to the ultimate irreducible in human experience, to the love which moves the sun and the other stars as both the first and the final cause of that movement:

> A l'alta fantasia qui mancò possa;
> ma già volgeva il mio disio e 'l velle,
> sì come rota ch'igualmente è mossa,
>     l'amor che move il sole e l'altre stelle.

---

[2]   '... oculorum vero concupiscentiam superet studium compunctionis, et assiduitas lacrymarum' (Bernard of Clairvaux 290).

[3]   *The Book of Common Prayer*, *Articles of Religion* XXII.

[Here power failed the lofty phantasy; but already my desire and my will were revolved, like a wheel that is evenly moved, by the love which moves the sun and the other stars. (*Paradiso* XXXIII 142–5)]

Now in the course of this imaginary journey into God, as yet in the flesh rather than out of it, Dante touches on all the main areas of high-scholastic theological discourse. Turning, for example, in *Paradiso* VII to the question of atonement and to the how and why of God's replying in quite the way he did to the catastrophe of Eden, he settles on a sense of God's work in Christ as a matter, not only of expiation and of propitiation, but of enabling man by way of his power to self-determination to participate in his own resurrection (the 'per far l'uom sufficiente a rilevarsi' of line 116) – a sense of that work as transparent to the love-substance generally of his dealings with man, love, properly understood, being nothing other than the letting it be of a thing in the fullness of that being. And what applies in the area of atonement theology applies also in the area of election theology, where it is a question of what to say about those who, through no fault of their own, know not the Christ either as yet to come or else as now present to us – about the noble pagans of antiquity nonetheless cherished by Dante as decisive for his coming about both as a poet and as a philosopher. Are they lost for ever? At an early stage of the *Commedia* Dante had done his best for them by locating them in a twilight world not so much of suffering as of sighing, of a kind of hopeless yearning – the Dantean limbo situated on the upper and outer edge of hell. But in the *Paradiso*, where each successive emphasis in the areas of theological and dogmatic awareness is subject to a review in the light of its innermost reasons, it is a question, not of exclusion, but of inclusion, of, as Dante himself puts it, God's vulnerability in respect of each and every authentic movement of the spirit on the plane of properly human loving, God's vulnerability on the plane of loving being the mark of his victory as a lover:

> *Regnum celorum* vïolenza pate
> da caldo amore e da viva speranza,
> che vince la divina volontate:
>     non a guisa che l'omo a l'om sobranza,
> ma vince lei perché vuole esser vinta,
> e, vinta, vince con sua beninanza.

[The kingdom of heaven suffers violence from fervent love and from living hope which vanquishes the divine will: not as man overcomes man, but vanquishes it because it wills to be vanquished, and vanquished, vanquishes with its own kindness. (*Paradiso* XX 94–9)]

The courage to rethink positions, therefore, in the light of their innermost reasons (where, by the expression 'their innermost reasons', we mean, as Dante himself did, their innermost affective reasons) is not lacking, which is why, attuned as he is, not only to the philosophy, but to the phenomenology of existence, to the mood of being in the moment of its positive living out, we are nonetheless in the presence here of a genuinely speculative spirit, of one who both cherished the idea and rejoiced in its careful elaboration.

But – and this now is what matters – for all the speculative substance of the text, Dante is inclined to proceed by way, not of the idea in and for itself, but rather of the one to whom it is present either (in its espousal) as a principle of self-affirmation or (in its eschewal) as a principle of self-annihilation, at which point the image, in all its power not only to confirm but also to engender the idea pure and simple, comes fully into its own as a way of pursuing the theological enterprise. As far, then, as the first of these things is concerned – Dante's commitment less to the idea pure and simple than to the predicament of the one to whom it is present as a principle of self-actualization – we may take the very first lines of the *Commedia*, secure in their sense of the I-self, of the first-person protagonist of the poem, as the *across which* of theological awareness and the whereabouts of its verification as a principle of new life:

> Nel mezzo del cammin di nostra vita
> mi ritrovai per una selva oscura,
> ché la diritta via era smarrita.
>     Ahi quanto a dir qual era è cosa dura
> esta selva selvaggia e aspra e forte
> che nel pensier rinova la paura!

[Midway in the journey of our life I found myself in a dark wood, for the straight way was lost. Ah, how hard it is to say how that wood was, wild, rugged, harsh; the very thought of it renews my fear! (*Inferno* I 1–6)]

Dispensing with the propaedeutics of sacred science as envisaged by, say, Thomas as among the most cherished of his *auctores*, with the substance and methodology, that is to say, of theology over against philosophy as a discipline of the spirit, Dante begins with the predicament of the one who says 'I', of the individual as ranged over against self at the point of fundamental willing, and thus as overwhelmed by a sense of the fear, of the inexplicability, of the self-forgetfulness and, as the boundary condition of all these things, of the despair of it all (the 'ch'io perdei la speranza de l'altezza' of line 54).[4] The dialectical, in short, gives way to the dramatic as the means of inaugurating the theological project and of ensuring its centrality to human experience in the positive living-out of that experience. The idea, to be sure, subsists from beforehand as a structuring principle of the narrative as a whole, the narrative as a whole turning precisely on the notion of lostness both from self and from God as the truth of this or that instance of specifically human being, on the reliving in each and every individual of the catastrophe of Eden as a given of theological consciousness. But this is not where Dante begins. Rather, he begins with the mood or sensation of being in its far-wandering, this being the province, not of the idea in the notional purity of the idea, but of the image in all its endless power to summon up the *how it is* with self in its estrangement, the felt-condition of existence in its *longe peregrinare*.

Prominent among the imaginative procedures of the *Commedia* is Dante's recourse to the historical figure as the embodiment or positive instantiation of the leading idea, as at once unprecedented and unparalleled in the uniqueness of his or her humanity and yet at the same time exemplifying a universal possibility – in short, his particular brand of historical symbolism. Take, for example, the case of Francesca among the lustful and adulterous in *Inferno* V, where, as Dante himself says, it is a question of her having submitted reason to desire as the ground of her condemnation (the 'Intesi ch'a così fatto tormento / enno dannati i peccator carnali, / che la ragion sommettono al talento' of line 37).[5] Now here we need to be careful, for never, in Dante, is it a question of his proscribing or prohibiting the love of the sensitive soul in favour of something more spiritual, of the love of the rational soul as that whereby the individual reaches out for communion with God as the beginning and end of all loving. Rather, it is a question of the rational soul as gathering in the legitimate but proximate yearning of the sensitive soul to its ultimately ecstatic finality, of its bringing home the one to the other by way of the capacity for free choice whereby man most resembles God and is most cherished by him.[6] In the degree, therefore, to which the individual brings home the love-impulses of the sensitive soul to

---

[4]    '... that I lost hope of the height'.

[5]    'I understood that to such torment are condemned the carnal sinners, who subject reason to desire'.

[6]    On free will as the principle in man of Godlikeness and as that whereby he is most cherished by God, see the 'maggior don' of *Paradiso* V 19–22: 'Lo maggior don che Dio per sua larghezza / fesse creando, e a la sua bontate / più conformato, e quel ch'e' più apprezza / fu de la volontà la libertate' ('The greatest gift which God in his bounty bestowed in creating,

those of the rational soul, he knows himself in a consummate act of properly human existence, in an act of existence wholly at one with itself at the point of fundamental willing. In the degree, by contrast, to which he fails in this, settling instead for the waywardness of sensitive in respect of rational loving, he knows himself only in the broken and thus the tragic substance of his presence in the world, in the infinite sadness of being as ranged over against itself in the forum of conscience. This, then, is the situation with Francesca and with the intemperate souls generally of this second circle of the pit, for, called like everyone else to be in, through and for God as the first and final cause of all spiritual striving, she has instead, and in full consciousness of the catastrophic consequences of it all, loved indiscriminately, in a manner making less for being than for non-being, less for life than for lifelessness, as the truth of her existence. But for all the decisiveness of the idea thus understood for any interpretation of this, the first genuinely tragic episode of the *Commedia*, it is not by way of the idea that Dante chooses to proceed, his instead being a summoning up of personality in the round as the whereabouts of its contemplation, at which point the image once again takes over as the means of Dante's discourse in the poem and as the guarantee of its particular kind of truthfulness. First, then, and in response to the pilgrim poet's plea that he might speak with those borne like gossamer on the wings of the wind (the 'Poeta, volontieri / parlerei a quei due che 'nsieme vanno, / e paion sì al vento esser leggieri' of lines 73–5),[7] comes the greeting, the *captatio benevolentiae* gracious beyond words but testimony already to the kind of sweet acquiescence opening out in one and the same instant upon both the divine and the demonic:

> O animal grazïoso e benigno
> che visitando vai per l'aere perso
> noi che tignemmo il mondo di sanguigno,
>     se fosse amico il re de l'universo,
> noi pregheremmo lui de la tua pace,
> poi c'hai pietà del nostro mal perverso.
>     Di quel che udire e che parlar vi piace,
> noi udiremo e parleremo a voi,
> mentre che 'l vento, come fa, ci tace.

---

and the most conformed to his own goodness and that which he most prizes, was the freedom of the will').

7    "Poet", I began, "willingly would I speak with those two that go together and seem to be so light upon the wind."

[O living creature, gracious and benign, that goes through the black air visiting us
who stained the world with blood, if the king of the universe were friendly to us,
we would pray him for your peace, since you have pity on our perverse ill. Of that
which pleases you to hear and to speak, we will hear and we will speak with you,
while the wind, as now, is silent for us. (*Inferno* V 88–96)]

But then, quite as eloquent in respect of the anxiety and indeed of the agony of
being under the aspect of denial and thus of estrangement, comes the moment
of self-evasion, the moment in which, reluctant to take into self the guilt of that
denial, the soul seeks to redistribute responsibility, to lay it at the door of a third
party – to, in short, mythologize it away. Caught up, in other words, in a crisis
of conscience, but firm in her contritionlessness, Francesca looks the other way,
*away* from self rather than *into* self as the agent of her suffering:

> 'Amor, ch'al cor gentil ratto s'apprende,
> prese costui de la bella persona
> che mi fu tolta; e 'l modo ancor m'offende.
>    Amor, ch' a nullo amato amar perdona,
> mi prese del costui piacer sì forte,
> che, come vedi, ancor non m'abbandona.
>    Amor condusse noi ad una morte.
> Caina attende chi a vita ci spense.'

['Love, which is quickly kindled in a noble heart, seized this one for the fair form
that was taken from me; and the way of it afflicts me still. Love, which absolves no
loved one from loving, seized me so strongly with delight in him that, as you see,
it does not leave me even now. Love brought us to one death. Caina awaits him
who quenched our life.' (*Inferno* V 100–108)]

The strategy is everywhere discernible in this first canticle of the *Inferno*, the
soul in its obduracy, in its refusal to take into self the guilt of self, having no
other means of softening the contradiction at the core of its existence, the
contradiction implicit in both willing and not willing its own high calling.
It has, therefore, no alternative but to sidestep the truth of its own being, to
countenance that truth, even for an instant, to stare yet again into the face of its
own unintelligibility, its dereliction as a creature of orderly self-structuring. But
Dante, busy as he is at the point of disclosure, of seeing through the strategies
of self-deception, will have none of this. Deftly, then, he has his protagonist ask
after the crucial moment of delivery, the moment of sweet sighing decisive for

the now eternal destiny of the spirit, a manoeuvre which, contrary to her every inclination, leaves Francesca nowhere else to look other than into the recesses of her existence, no alternative but to live out again – and again and again – the critical moment of self-abandonment and of ontological undoing:

> 'Ma dimmi: al tempo d'i dolci sospiri,
> a che e come concedette amore
> che conosceste i dubbiosi disiri?'
>     E quella a me: 'Nessun maggior dolore
> che ricordarsi del tempo felice
> ne la miseria; e ciò sa 'l tuo dottore.
>     Ma s'a conoscer la prima radice
> del nostro amor tu hai cotanto affetto,
> dirò come colui che piange e dice.
>     Noi leggiavamo un giorno per diletto
> di Lancialotto come amor lo strinse;
> soli eravamo e sanza alcun sospetto.
>     Per più fïate li occhi ci sospinse
> quella lettura, e scolorocci il viso;
> ma solo un punto fu quel che ci vinse.
>     Quando leggemmo il disïato riso
> esser basciato da cotanto amante,
> questi, che mai da me non fia diviso,
> la bocca mi basciò tutto tremante.
>     Galeotto fu 'l libro e chi lo scrisse:
> quel giorno più non vi leggemmo avante.'

['But tell me, in the time of the sweet sighs, by what and how did love grant you to know the dubious desires?' And she to me: 'There is no greater sorrow than to recall, in wretchedness, the happy time, and this your teacher knows. But if you have such great desire to know the first root of our love, I will tell as one who weeps and tells. One day, for pastime, we read of Lancelot, how love constrained him. We were alone, suspecting nothing. Several times that reading urged our eyes to meet, and took the colour from our faces, but one moment alone was it that overcame us. When we read how the longed-for smile was kissed by so great a lover, this one, who never shall be parted from me, kissed my mouth all trembling. A Gallehaut was the book, and he who wrote it; that day we read no farther in it.' (*Inferno* V 118–38)]

The exposition, as always in Dante, is consummate, but consummate in respect, not only, nor indeed primarily, of the idea pure and simple, the idea of hell as a matter of submitting reason to desire (the 'peccator carnali, / che la ragion sommettono al talento' of *Inferno* V 39),[8] but, more than this, of the infinite sadness of it all, of the grief everywhere attendant upon loving awry, of delivering the greater to the lesser on the plane of properly human affectivity. And it is at this point that image takes over from the idea, indeed in a certain sense engenders the idea; for the idea, though in one sense preceding and precipitating the catastrophe of existence, is in another sense but the distillation of that catastrophe, a subsequent rationalization of the event unequal, however, either to its substance or intensity.

As a further example of the indispensability of the image to the theological enterprise, we may take the case of Piccarda in *Paradiso* III, antiphonal, we might say, in respect of that of Francesca in *Inferno* V; for here it is a question, not of denial and self-evasion as the way of easing the contradiction at the core of existence, but rather of the soul's living out the substance of its high calling in and through a mutual indwelling of human and divine intentionality. This, then, is the leading idea hereabouts in the text, Dante's, when it comes to defining the relationship between human and divine purposing in man, being a countenancing – indeed an accommodation – of the one by and with the other within the economy of the whole. But here again he proceeds not so much dialectically as dramatically, by way of the radiant presence of Piccarda Donati – party, clearly, to a tender companionship in times gone by – as the embodiment of this, in truth, resplendent notion. First, then, comes the preliminary encounter in the heaven of the moon, nicely attuned by way of its apparently passing reference to Narcissus (but nothing, in Dante, is 'apparently passing') to what matters about this canto:

> Quali per vetri trasparenti e tersi,
>  o ver per acque nitide e tranquille,
>  non sì profonde che i fondi sien persi,
>    tornan d'i nostri visi le postille
>  debili sì, che perla in bianca fronte
>  non vien men forte a le nostre pupille;
>    tali vid' io più facce a parlar pronte;
>  per ch'io dentro a l'error contrario corsi
>  a quel ch'accese amor tra l'omo e 'l fonte.

---

[8]   'the carnal sinners, who subject reason to desire'.

[As through smooth and transparent glass, or through clear and tranquil waters,
yet not so deep that the bottom be lost, the outlines of our faces return so faint,
that a pearl on a white brow comes not less boldly to our eyes, so did I behold
many a countenance eager to speak; wherefore I fell into the contrary error to
that which kindled love between the man and the fountain. (*Paradiso* III 10–18)]

But then, following the moment of recognition (for Piccarda's is a beauty
now far in excess of that which Dante had formerly known and cherished in
Florence), comes the serpentine question, the question originally put to Eve in
the garden and conducive by way of her response – to the taking and eating of
the apple – to the agony of expulsion. 'Tell me', Dante says, 'would you not,
relegated as you are to the lowest of the celestial spheres, prefer to be a little
higher up, to see more, to understand more, and to be better connected?' ('Ma
dimmi: voi che siete qui felici, / disiderate voi più alto loco / per più vedere e per
più farvi amici?'; lines 64–6), at which point the truth of this issue, of what it
means for the creature to indwell, and in turn to be indwelt, by the Creator on
the plane of willing emerges in all its smiling substance; for not only is there no
real hierarchy in paradise, each of the elect knowing and enjoying God according
to his or her unique capacity for him, but to be in God is to be in him by way of
the most complete kind of 'inseatedness' (*circuminsessio*), of a species of mutual
inherence verifiable in the recesses of personality and reducible henceforth
neither to the purely creaturely nor to the purely creatorly.[9] This, then, or at any
rate something close to it, is Piccarda's meaning in the exquisite – and again
exquisitely smiling – passage beginning at line 67 and culminating in Dante's
most fulsome acknowledgement of Augustine, if not as an interlocutor in his
poem, then as a companion or fellow breaker of bread along the way (the 'in his
will is our peace' moment of line 84).[10] It is all a question, Dante has Piccarda
suggest, of 'inwilling' ('invogliare') as the ground and guarantee of man's being
and becoming as a creature called at last into the presence of God, of a mutual
in-abiding of the human and the divine on the plane of seeing, understanding
and choosing as the condition of his ultimate affirmation:

---

[9]    For the term(περιχώρησις), see Gregory Nazianzen, *Epistula* ci.6; xxii.4; Pseudo-
Cyril, *De sacro. trin.* xxiv; John of Damascus, *De fide ortho.* i.14, etc. See also Deneffe,
Stramara and Cross. In Dante, see the 'in te sidi' of *Paradiso* XXXIII 124–6: 'O luce etterna
che sola in te sidi, / sola t'intendi, e da te intelletta / e intendente te ami e arridi!' ('O light
eternal, who alone abidest in thyself, alone knowest thyself, and knowing, lovest and smilest
on thyself!').

[10]    Augustine, *Confessions* XIII ix 10: 'In bona voluntate pax nobis est.'

Con quelle altr' ombre pria sorrise un poco;
da indi mi rispuose tanto lieta,
ch'arder parea d'amor nel primo foco:
    'Frate, la nostra volontà qüeta
virtù di carità, che fa volerne
sol quel ch'avemo, e d'altro non ci asseta.
    Se disïassimo esser più superne,
foran discordi li nostri disiri
dal voler di colui che qui ne cerne;
    che vedrai non capere in questi giri,
s'essere in carità è qui *necesse*,
e se la sua natura ben rimiri.
    Anzi è formale ad esto beato *esse*
tenersi dentro a la divina voglia,
per ch'una fansi nostre voglie stesse;
    sì che, come noi sem di soglia in soglia
per questo regno, a tutto il regno piace
com' a lo re che 'n suo voler ne 'nvoglia.
    E 'n la sua volontade è nostra pace:
ell' è quel mare al qual tutto si move
ciò ch'ella crïa o che natura face.'
    Chiaro mi fu allor come ogne dove
in cielo è paradiso, etsi la grazia
del sommo ben d'un modo non vi piove.

[With those other shades she first smiled a little, then answered me so glad that she seemed to burn in the first fire of love: 'Brother, the power of love quiets our will, and makes us wish only for that which we have and gives us no other thirst. Did we desire to be more aloft, our longings would be discordant with his will who assigns us here, which you will see is not possible in these circles, if to exist in charity is here of necessity, and if you well consider what is love's nature. Nay, it is the essence of this blessed existence to keep itself within the divine will, whereby our wills themselves are made one; so that our being thus from threshold to threshold throughout this realm is a joy to all the realm as to the king who inwills us with his will; and his will is our peace. It is that sea to which all moves, both what it creates and what nature makes.' Then was it clear to me, how everywhere in heaven is paradise, even if the grace of the supreme good does not there rain down in one same measure. (*Paradiso* III 67–90)]

Now concerned as we are in this chapter with the image rather than with the idea as the means in Dante of pursuing the theological project, it is nonetheless worth pausing for a moment over this passage for what it tells us about precisely the kind of theological spirit he was. For if on the one hand Dante's too (but again how could it not be?) is a theology of the cross, it is, on the other, a theology of the cross in a special sense – in the sense, not only, nor perhaps even primarily, of the justification of self from beyond self, but of self as made equal by grace to the task in hand; hence the following lines from Canto VII of the *Paradiso* (the atonement canto *par excellence* of the *Commedia*), notable precisely for their commitment to the notion of man as by grace party to his own resurrection:

> Ma perché l'ovra tanto è più gradita
> da l'operante, quanto più appresenta
> de la bontà del core ond' ell' è uscita,
>   la divina bontà che 'l mondo imprenta,
> di proceder per tutte le sue vie,
> a rilevarvi suso, fu contenta.
>   Né tra l'ultima notte e 'l primo die
> sì alto o sì magnifico processo,
> o per l'una o per l'altra, fu o fie:
>   ché più largo fu Dio a dar sé stesso
> per far l'uom sufficiente a rilevarsi,
> che s'elli avesse sol da sé dimesso;
>   e tutti li altri modi erano scarsi
> a la giustizia, se 'l Figliuol di Dio
> non fosse umilïato ad incarnarsi.

[But because the deed is so much the more prized by the doer, the more it displays of the goodness of the heart whence it issued, the divine goodness which puts its imprint on the world, was pleased to proceed by all its ways to raise you up again; nor between the last night and the first day has there been or will there be so exalted and so magnificent a procedure, either by the one or the other; for God was more bounteous in giving himself to make man sufficient to uplift himself again, than if he solely of himself had remitted; and all other modes were scanty in respect to justice, if the son of God had not humbled himself to become incarnate. (*Paradiso* VII 106–20)]

Again, grace abounds, and abounds absolutely as the condition of everything coming next by way of man's coming home to his maker. But for all that, for all its moving within the context of a soteriology of impeccable credentials, the emphasis is unmistakably Dantean: man, for all the depths of his degradation, is not only lifted, but called upon in and through the Christ to lift himself to new life – a notion in turn informing Piccarda's account in Canto III of the *Paradiso* of the co-involvement of this or that individual man or woman in the working out of his or her historical and eschatological destiny. But for all the fresh nuancing of the idea (for it is the mark of Dante's genius as a theological poet that his, at every point, is a rethinking of the *idée reçue*, of the successive emphases to which he was heir), it is the image that matters here, for it is by way of what amounts to his reconstitution of personality in the round that the idea is at last confirmed in its power to new life, to the emergence of self in the fullness of self. Other than this, it subsists as a pure determination of the mind, as yet in waiting in respect of its power to resurrection.

With this, fundamental as it is to any account of Dante either as a poet or as a theologian (the two things coinciding within the economy of the text), we are even so in the foothills of an issue present to him, not merely intuitively, but as a matter of systematic concern; for, again as Contini used to say, his is a constant reflection on the act itself of composition, and this as but an aspect of its sacramentality, indeed of its sacredness as the way of self-actualization.[11] Anything approaching, therefore, an adequate account of this issue in Dante would have as of the essence to linger (a) over the range and refinement of Dante's rhetoric in the *Commedia*, of a rhetoric, however, throughout constrained by the 'dittar dentro' of the spirit as the ground of its legitimacy;[12] (b) over the continuing character of the poetic experiment in Dante, from the *Vita nova* to the *rime petrose* and from the allegorical *rime* of the 1290s to and beyond the great moral and erotic canzoni of his exile, each alike testimony to the same strain of technical-cum-existential anxiety in the text; and (c) over the mythopoeic component of Dante's mind and work, his tendency everywhere

---

[11]   'In realtà, la tecnica è in lui una cosa dell'ordine sacrale, è la via del suo esercizio ascetico, indistinguibile dall'ansia di perfezione' (Contini x). On the notion of 'a constant turning back on the act itself of composition', see Contini's still more radiant, and indeed now justly epigrammatic, remark (viii) to the effect that 'sarà chiaro come una costante della personalità dantesca sia questo perpetuo sopraggiungere della riflessione tecnica accanto alla poesia, quest'associazione di concreto poetare e d'intelligenza stilistica'.

[12]   *Purgatorio* XXIV 52–4: 'E io a lui: "I' mi son un che, quando / Amor mi spira, noto, e a quel modo / ch'e' ditta dentro vo significando"' ['And I to him: "I am one who, when Love inspires me, takes note, and goes setting it forth after the fashion which he dictates within me"'] – a passage decisive for the substance and psychology both of a precise moment in Dante's own development as a lyric poet and, in its moment-by-moment reconstruction by Dante himself, of the tradition in which he stands.

to fashion from the otherwise random data of his experience a universe of the spirit present to itself by way only of its consistency, of the transparency of each and every moment along the way to its deep rationale. For it is in these circumstances alone that the image as the co-efficient of every kind of psycho-ontological awareness in man stands properly to be appreciated for its well-nigh miraculous equality to the business in hand. Just for now, however, and dispensing for the moment with everything but the most minimal commentary, a final image, an image bearing this time on the nature and beauty of alongsidedness, as distinct from over-againstness, as the hallmark of specifically human being in the moment of its emergence. The basic question here is one which had long bothered the old theologians, Augustine to the fore among them; for how, precisely, is the individual attuned to the verticality of his or her ascent into God to make way for the horizontality of loving one's neighbour as oneself? How, in other words, is the ascensional to be reconciled with the social within the economy of the spiritual life? Augustine for his part had settled – in a famous to the point of notorious moment of the *De doctrina christiana* – for a distinction between *fruition* and *usage* as a means of settling this issue, the notion of usage, however, hardly reflecting either the substance or the seriousness of the gospel injunction.[13] For Dante, by contrast, the axes of concern thus understood stand in the moment of emergence to be liquidated in favour of something comprehending them both, in a species of consciousness delighting in otherness on the plane of the horizontal but undistracted by it. Something of the kind, at any rate, informs his nothing if not gracious account in *Paradiso* X of the bringing home of one spirit to another in all their radical diversity, in all the unique and, for this reason, infinitely precious character of their presence in the world. Thomas, hereabouts in paradise, is the master of ceremonies, his, however – in his acknowledgement of each in turn of his peers and predecessors either by name or by profession – being in one and the same moment a confirmation of difference and a taking up of that difference in something still greater than itself:

> Tu vuo' saper di quai piante s'infiora
> questa ghirlanda che 'ntorno vagheggia
> la bella donna ch'al ciel t'avvalora.

---

[13]    Augustine, *De doctrina christiana* I.xxii.20. Also on this issue, see Took, 'Arendt, Augustine, Dante and Loving One's Neighbour'. For Arendt's text, originating as a thesis completed under the supervision of Karl Jaspers, submitted for examination in Heidelberg in 1929 and entitled *Der Liebesbegriff bei Augustin. Versuch einer philosophischen Interpretation*, see Arendt. Also see Took 'Complementarity and Coalescence'.

Io fui de li agni de la santa greggia
che Domenico mena per cammino
u' ben s'impingua se non si vaneggia.

    Questi che m'è a destra più vicino,
frate e maestro fummi, ed esso Alberto
è di Cologna, e io Thomas d'Aquino.

    Se sì di tutti li altri esser vuo' certo,
di retro al mio parlar ten vien col viso
girando su per lo beato serto.

    Quell' altro fiammeggiare esce del riso
di Grazïan, che l'uno e l'altro foro
aiutò sì che piace in paradiso.

    L'altro ch'appresso addorna il nostro coro,
quel Pietro fu che con la poverella
offerse a Santa Chiesa suo tesoro.

    La quinta luce, ch'è tra noi più bella,
spira di tale amor, che tutto 'l mondo
là giù ne gola di saper novella:

    entro v'è l'alta mente u' sì profondo
saver fu messo, che, se 'l vero è vero,
a veder tanto non surse il secondo.

...

    Vedi oltre fiammeggiar l'ardente spiro
d'Isidoro, di Beda e di Riccardo,
che a considerar fu più che viro.

    Questi onde a me ritorna il tuo riguardo,
è 'l lume d'uno spirto che 'n pensieri
gravi a morir li parve venir tardo:

    essa è la luce etterna di Sigieri,
che, leggendo nel Vico de li Strami,
silogizzò invidïosi veri.

[You wish to know what plants these are that enflower this garland, which amorously circles around the fair lady who strengthens you for heaven. I was of the lambs of the holy flock which Dominic leads on the path where there is good fattening if they do not stray. He that is next beside me on the right was my brother and my master, and he is Albert of Cologne, and I Thomas of Aquino. If thus of all the rest you would be informed, come, following my speech with your sight, going round the blessed wreath. The next flaming comes from the smile of Gratian, who served the one and the other court so well that it pleases in paradise. The other who next adorns our choir was that Peter who, like the poor widow, offered his treasure to holy Church. The fifth light, which is the most beautiful among us, breathes with such love that all the world there below thirsts to know tidings of it. Within it is the lofty mind to which was given wisdom so deep that, if the truth be true, there never rose a second of such full wisdom ... See, flaming beyond, the glowing breath of Isidore, of Bede, and of Richard who in contemplation was more than man. This one from whom your look returns to me is the light of a spirit to whom, in his grave thoughts, it seemed that death came slow. It is the eternal light of Siger who, lecturing in Straw Street, demonstrated invidious truths. (*Paradiso* X 91–114 and 130–8)]

Here, then, is a collectivity, a chorality and, above all, a *caritas* testifying in its intensity to an order of being present to itself in its inclusiveness, in its countenancing the next man as a component and indeed as a co-efficient of historical selfhood. The other-than-self is known to self as but a condition of its emergence into the 'stature of the fullness' of its proper humanity. But of all this, in its exquisite abstraction, there is not a word in the text – simply depiction, the co-presencing of the elect as, somewhat after the manner of the Godhead itself, spiritually 'in-seated', saying all that needs to be said and, in truth, all that can be said.

**Works Cited**

Arendt, Hannah. *Love and Saint Augustine*. Ed. J.V. Scott and J.C. Clark. Chicago: University of Chicago Press, 1996.

Augustine of Hippo. *Confessionum libri XIII*. Ed. L. Verheijen, OSA in the *Corpus Christianorum Series Latina*, vol. 37. Turnholt: Brepols, 1990.

——— *De doctrina christiana*. Ed. J. Martin in the *Corpus Christianorum Series Latina*, vol. 32. Turnholt: Brepols, 1962.

Bernard of Clairvaux. *Opera genuina juxta editionem monachorum Sancti Benedicti*, vol. 2 (*VI opuscula et sermones de tempore et de sanctis*). Paris: apud Gauthier Fratrem et Soc., 1835.

*The Book of Common Prayer and Administration of the Sacraments and Other Rites and Ceremonies According to the Use of the Church of England* (successive editions).

Contini, Gianfranco. *Dante Alighieri. Rime*. Turin: Einaudi, 1965 (1946).

Cross, Richard. 'Perichoresis, Deification, and Christological Predication in John of Damascus'. *Medieval Studies* 62 (2000): 69–124.

Dante. *La Commedia secondo l'antica vulgata*, 4 vols. Ed. G. Petrocchi. Verona: Mondadori, 1966.

—— *The Divine Comedy*. Translated with a commentary by C.S. Singleton. Princeton, NJ: Princeton University Press, 1970.

Deneffe, August, SJ. '*Perichoresis, circumincessio, circuminsessio*: Eine Terminologische Untersuchung' *Zeitschrift für Katholische Theologie* 47 (1923): 497–532.

Stramara, D.F., Jr. 'Gregory of Nyssa's Terminology for Trinitarian Perichoresis'. *Vigiliae Christianae* 52.3 (1998): 257–63.

Tillich, Paul. *The Courage to Be*. Glasgow: Fontana, 1962 (1952).

Took, John. 'Arendt, Augustine, Dante and Loving One's Neighbour'. In *Essays in Honour of John Scott*, ed. J.J. Kinder and D. Glenn. Florence: Olschki, 2013, 105–19.

—— 'Complementarity and Coalescence: Dante and the Sociology of Authentic Being'. In *Conversations with Kenelm*. London: Ubiquity Press, 2013, 139–54.

# Chapter 6

# Law and Divine Mercy in Shakespeare's Religious Imagination: *Measure for Measure* and *The Merchant of Venice*

Paul S. Fiddes

*[handwritten margin notes: — p 125-6, concept, symbol]*

## Human and Divine Judgement

'Judge not, that ye be not judged.' These words of Jesus from the Gospel of Matthew 7:1 presented a problem to the rulers and lawyers of the Elizabethan age. Perhaps they still do for Christian believers called to the judicial bench, faced with the apparently stark command, 'Judge not'. How can judges *not* judge? This text is followed immediately by another, which elaborates it: 'For with what judgment ye judge, ye shall be judged, and with what measure ye mete, it shall be measured to you again' (Matt. 7:1–2; Geneva Bible translation). It is to this that Shakespeare refers in the title of his play, *Measure for Measure*. So, in its immediate context, the command warns that those who set out to judge others must expect to receive an equivalent condemnation for their own faults. The warning is echoed in the Epistle of Paul to the Romans, a book that had a weighty impact at the time of the English Reformation: 'in passing judgement on another you condemn yourself, because you, the judge, are doing the same things' (Rom. 2:1).

Elizabethan jurists coped with the direct command of Jesus not to judge by making a distinction between private and public spheres of life. Princes and other rulers were 'Gods by office' not 'Gods by nature';[1] as God's deputies, they were entrusted with the divine prerogatives of justice and mercy. Their authority to judge came from their public office, not their private opinions. Perhaps this is what is intended by Angelo in *Measure for Measure* when he says 'It is the law, not I, condemn your brother' (II, ii, 80), but we shall see that there is some deep

---

[1]    See Bishop Bilson in his coronation sermon before James I, sig. A6. See further Lever 14, on 'the demi-god, Authority' (1.2.112).

self-deception in this distancing of his personal life from his public function of judge, and so Shakespeare appears to be undermining this simple distinction. Certainly, the principle 'measure for measure' applies to making private judgements: those who judge others in ordinary social relationships must expect to receive the same kind of treatment in exact proportion to their own harshness and intolerance. But as Shakespeare explores the theme, the warning implied in the principle cannot be easily escaped in public judgements either.

Jesus' perplexing command not to judge cannot be resolved rationally. It makes an imaginative impact, opening up a space between the divine economy and the human economy of life, drawing attention to the gap between divine judgement and human judgements, which always stand under the warning of 'measure for measure'. Hearers enter the space created by the command, and engage with two questions about the interconnections between divine and earthly justice. First, how closely can the law of the land correspond to the justice of God, given that it can be only an imperfect image of the divine? Second, how closely can human law correspond to the mercy of God?

The second question may seem more surprising than the first, but the New Testament declares that God has pardoned all sinners through the sacrifice of the death of Christ. In the writings of St Paul the law of God now has a distinctly ambiguous status, despite this gift of God's grace. As one New Testament scholar observes, the notion of the 'justification' of the unjust, while employing a legal image, is 'contrary to all the rules of human justice' (Schrenk 45). While the righteousness and holiness of God remain unquestionable, it seems doubtful whether these are any longer to be best expressed in categories of law, except the new law of love. How then can this seemingly outrageous mercy of God be applied to the regulation of a human state and society? I want to hold these questions in mind as we engage with two of Shakespeare's plays in which law, justice and mercy play a leading part. I hope too that reflecting on these questions will enable us to explore the theme of poetry and the religious imagination.

## The Enigma of 'Lawful Mercy'

The plot of *Measure for Measure* hinges on the sudden revival, after a lapse of 19 years, of a law which imposes the death penalty on persons convicted of fornication, or those engaging in sexual relationships outside of marriage. In the city where the play is set, Vienna, this law has been on the statute book for many years, but has been allowed to lapse. The awakening of it to life, or rather death, is due to the decision of the Duke of Vienna, Vincentio, to take a break from government and to install in his place a lord named Angelo, who has a great reputation for both virtue and severity. The Duke intends to leave the city for an indefinite period, his whereabouts to be a mystery, while all his power of law is invested in Angelo, including the power of life and death. As he says to his chosen representative:

> Mortality and mercy in Vienna
> Live in thy tongue and heart: ...
> ... Your scope is as mine own,
> So to enforce or qualify the laws
> As to your soul seems good. (I, i, 44–5, 64–6)

We learn a little later that the Duke's 'holiday from reality' (Bloom 360) has been prompted by his uneasy realization that he has been too lenient in his rule, and has allowed many crimes to go unpunished. His plan to let someone else impose law more harshly might, we suspect, stem from a desire not to court unpopularity with the people. He puts a different spin on it by saying it would be unfair, or indeed tyrannous, to impose punishment for what he had himself allowed. Already, then, the ambiguities of human justice are being demonstrated.

Angelo takes up the task with zest, and chooses to begin by reviving the long dormant law against fornication. The first victim is a young man named Claudio who has made his fiancée, Julietta, pregnant, and Angelo intends to make his death an example of the law's strictness. This seems an especially repressive use of the law since Claudio and Julietta have entered into a marriage contract that both state and Church in Elizabethan England would have recognized as binding (Lever lxv); to be fully implemented, their union lacked only the transfer of a dowry, sacramental union and final public confirmation. 'Upon a true contract', protests Claudio, 'I got possession of Julietta's bed' (I, i, 134–5). They have delayed only because they need to win the consent of the relatives who keep the purse strings of the dowry. Claudio is technically guilty of a sexual offence according to the statute, but Shakespeare has been careful to mitigate the circumstances of the crime as far as possible; in one of the sources he apparently uses for the play, Claudio's counterpart has actually committed rape.[2]

For Shakespeare's audiences, the situation facing Claudio would not have seemed as absurd as it does to us. There was, it is true, no capital punishment in

---

[2]   Only in Shakespeare's play is the Claudio figure betrothed to the woman he sleeps with; compare Cinthio's novel *Hecatommithi* (1565) and George Whetstone's *Promos and Cassandra* (1578). Cinthio's Vico has forcibly seduced a virgin.

Elizabethan times for fornication, and only the most extreme members of the Puritan faction of the Anglican Church, such as Phillip Stubbes, were calling for the death penalty for both fornication and adultery.[3] The introduction of such a law was not totally unthinkable, and later, in 1650, the Puritan government of the Commonwealth actually put it on the statute books (Firth and Rait 387–9).[4] The phrase 'a change in the commonwealth' used by an alarmed Mistress Overdone (I, ii, 95), the well-worn prostitute, echoes the language of the Elizabethan Reform tracts which were calling for a new severity to be applied in London life. There is a general acceptance in the play, by both virtuous characters and rogues, that some control of the sexual appetite is not unreasonable, though expression of this varies. Claudio's sister, Isabella, reacts with moralistic fervour – it is 'a vice that most I do abhor, / And most desire should meet the blow of justice' (II, ii, 29–30) – while the pimp, Pompey, sees it as a kind of illegal poaching of game: 'groping for trouts, in a peculiar river' (I, ii, 83). There is enough here for us to suspend disbelief, and take the story seriously as a test case for the application of repressive laws, and ultimately as a test case for their correspondence to heavenly justice and mercy.

In the first conversation between Angelo and Isabella, most of the key issues emerge. Isabella, Claudio's sister, is a novice nun who desires to take her vows in a strict convent, wishing only that there were more restraints; undeniably virtuous, she also shows herself to be as sexually repressed as Angelo is, and with a hint of the self-righteous about her. She goes to Angelo to plead for her brother's life, but finds Angelo obdurate: 'Your brother is a forfeit of the law' (II, i, 71); 'The law, not I, condemn your brother' (II, ii, 81). Angelo, it seems, cannot be moved because he sees law as final and absolute in its own right; a kind of abstract process which is independent of the character of its administrator. Now, there are advantages in the independence of the law over the arbitrariness of the powerful. To be God's deputy, bearing the sword on God's behalf, meant that rulers themselves were to be accountable to the commands or law of God. Moreover, it was widely agreed that they should also respect and obey law made on earth, as an image (however inexact) of God's justice.[5] Nevertheless, Shakespeare stands with Erasmus, who declared in his *Education of a Christian Prince* that 'there can be no good prince who is not also a good man' (189). The connection between the administration of earthly justice and the person

---

[3]   This was lampooned in Nashe's *Anatomie of Absurditie*: see McKerrow 1:20.
[4]   The penalty was never applied.
[5]   See the dictum of Sir Henry Coke, in dispute with James I, that the King was 'not under man, but under God and the Law' (*non sub homine, sed sub deo et lege*): Holdsworth 430 and nn. 2–3.

of the judge – including the judge's own morality – is a theme that Shakespeare continually works at in dramatic form (Eure 410–11).[6]

Despite her own emotional inhibitions, Isabella thus urges the personal factor within the administration of justice: 'I do think that you might pardon him, / And neither heaven nor man grieve at the mercy' (II, ii, 49–50). The responsibility of standing imaginatively in the space between divine and human justice cannot be avoided. However harsh the law, the judge has some discretion to interpret and modify the law, fitting it to the particular situation. So she urges that his heart, like hers, might be 'touch'd with remorse'. We recall that the Duke had reminded Angelo precisely of this in handing over the power of 'mortality and mercy', balancing 'enforcing' the law with 'modifying' it, moderating 'terror' with 'love'. These contending forces were to be balanced, urged the Duke, 'as to your soul seems good', making clear the moral dimension of government (I, i, 19, 44, 64–6).

Angelo replies to Isabella in a way that recognizes the part his own will plays in the process – 'I *will* not do't' – but, when challenged, identifies his own will with the impersonal demand of the law: 'What I will not, that I *cannot* do' (my emphases). Isabella then advances a double argument: first, that mercy is the greatest attribute of human rulers, because it is most like God's own; and second, that every ruler should be aware of human weakness and frailty, including his own. These arguments are given an extra and theological dimension by appeal to the act of God in the atonement of human life. To Angelo's blunt statement, 'Your brother is a forfeit of the law', she responds:

> Alas, alas!
> Why, all the souls that were were forfeit once,
> And He that might the vantage best have took
> Found out the remedy. How would you be,
> If He, which is the top of judgement, should
> But judge you as you are? O, think on that,
> And mercy then will breathe within your lips,
> Like man new made. (II, ii, 73–8)

This speech is full of echoes from Paul's Letter to the Romans, with its promise of a new humanity ('man new made') as a result of God's act of atonement or

---

6    See, for example, the speeches of the Lord Chief Justice in *King Henry IV Part II*, V, ii, 35–44, 65–118.

'remedy' in Christ.[7] Romans also depicts the realistic psychology of a continuing struggle between the old man and the new man, a conflict between the old Adam and the man in Christ (Berman 141–50; Rom. 7:14–25). 'The evil that I would not, that I do', confesses St Paul, and it was a fundamental tenet of Reformation thought that the new man was 'at the same time justified and a sinner' (*simul justus et peccator*). Angelo, however, fails to recognize his own frailty and sinfulness, and stands under Paul's accusation that 'in passing judgement you condemn yourself'. Like Isabella, his fellow-ruler Escalus had asked him to consider whether he has been guilty in his own heart of the crimes for which he sentences others (II, i, 5–10; cf. II, ii, 137–42), and Angelo had proudly replied:

> Tis one thing to be tempted, Escalus,
> Another thing to fall
> ...
> rather tell me,
> When I that censure him do so offend,
> Let mine own judgement pattern out my death. (II, i, 17–18, 28–30)

These words turn out to be prophetic. Isabella is pleading for what she calls 'lawful mercy' (II, iv, 112). Angelo's version of this is the well-known doctrine of deterrence and public protection; when urged by Isabella, 'Yet show some pity', he claims: 'I show it most of all when I show justice; / For then I pity those I do not know, / Which a dismiss'd offence would after gall' (II, i, 101–103).

His argument is that mercy, or compassion, is owed more to possible future victims of crime, so that an example must be made of the offender. Isabella is then driven to her most impassioned outburst, along the lines that those who are allowed to represent divine justice on earth always resort to the most extreme means of punishing others. Merciful heaven knows when it is appropriate to split an obstinate oak with lightning and when it is right to spare the 'soft myrtle'. But for human rulers it is always 'nothing but thunder':

> Man, proud man,
> Dress'd in a little brief authority,
> Most ignorant of what he's most assur'd –
> His glassy essence – like an angry ape,
> Plays such fantastic tricks before high heaven
> As makes the angels weep. (II, ii, 118–23)

---

[7]    For example, Romans 3:21–6; 7:4–6; 8:1–4, 14–17; 12:1–2.

Angelo's mechanical application of law is absurd ('fantastic') because it punishes people harshly for having human weaknesses, and this play is more aware than most of the frailty of the human situation. Isabella would not express this in the manner of the rowdy crew of Lucio, Pompey and Mistress Overdone, who represent the dissolute man-about-town, the pimp and the brothel keeper; but they see essentially the same point. The comic scenes involving this amoral trio make clear that thorough enforcement of the law against fornication would soon depopulate the city of Vienna. Pompey enquires of Escalus:

> Pompey: Does your worship mean to geld and splay all the youth of the city?
> Escalus: No, Pompey.
> Pompey: Truly, sir, in my poor opinion, they will to't then ... If you head and
> hang all that offend that way but for ten year together, you'll be glad to give out a
> commission for more heads ... (II, i, 227–37)

Everyone except Angelo seems aware of the weakness of the human condition. Justice requires a reasonable relation between laws and elemental human nature, and the judge can assist in making this relation work. Escalus, Angelo's subordinate but wiser fellow-ruler, can 'qualify' or 'moderate' the law, as the Duke put it earlier; when the pimp and the bawd are arraigned before him, he dismisses them with a stern warning. But Angelo cannot take circumstances into account because he cannot recognize the failings in himself. He does not know himself. Towards the end of his first conversation with Isabella, an awakening of consciousness happens; she has done her work well (or perhaps the Apostle Paul has). Angelo begins to become aware of sinful desires within his own heart, and the result is not mercy for Claudio, but the resolve to possess Isabella sexually. In his second interview with her, he therefore proposes a bargain: he will pardon her brother if she consents to 'yield up the treasures of [her] body' to him. Aware now of his fallenness, he determines to fall with a vengeance. Isabella's reaction has a touch of hysteria in it, but must be understood in the context of her belief that to yield her body would mean eternal damnation of her soul. When Angelo puts the alternative, 'Then must your brother die', she retorts:

> And 'twere the cheaper way.
> Better it were a brother died at once,
> Than that a sister, by redeeming him,
> Should die for ever. (II, ii, 105–8)

She is, however, persuaded to pretend to yield to Angelo by Duke Vincentio, who has not after all journeyed far away, but – disguised as a friar – has been lurking around the city and the jail, keeping a watchful eye on everything. She also agrees to provide a substitute for herself when the night comes, one Mariana, whom Angelo had previously contracted to marry and then deserted since the dowry was not forthcoming. Pretending to be Isabella, Mariana spends the night with him and effectively consummates the marriage. When Angelo goes back on his word, despite thinking he has possessed Isabella, and sends a command for the instant execution of Claudio, the Duke intervenes and prevents it. However, still disguised as the friar, he lets Isabella think that her brother has been executed after all, and encourages her to tell her story to the Duke when he returns. The irony Shakespeare presents here is that Angelo has committed the same crime as Claudio, having sexual congress with his betrothed, while ordering that Claudio be executed for the deed. Shakespeare has, in fact, combined several sources to achieve this mirror-image. In the hectic final scene, the Duke requires the couple to marry on the instant and, when the couple return, announces Angelo's execution. He echoes Angelo's own view about the 'pity' of the law, which Angelo had interpreted in terms of deterrent punishment:

> The very mercy of the law cries out
> Most audible, even from his proper tongue:
> 'An Angelo for Claudio: death for death.
> Haste still pays haste, and leisure answers leisure;
> Like doth quit like, and Measure still for Measure. (V, i, 405–9)

Mariana, who wants to keep her new husband, pleads with Isabella to join with her in asking for mercy for Angelo. Isabella is notably silent, and has to be requested three times by Mariana. But finally, still thinking her brother to be dead, she does ask the Duke to have mercy on his killer. In quick succession Claudio is then produced, alive, and is pardoned to marry Julietta; Angelo is pardoned with the injunction to love his wife; and the Duke asks Isabella (who appears to have had the same aphrodisiac effect on him as on Angelo) to marry him. The three marriages are joined by a fourth as the Duke compels Lucio, who has slandered him badly, to marry the mother of his child – none other than Mistress Overdone, the keeper of the brothel. Though Lucio protests that marriage to a 'punk' (prostitute) is a worse punishment than 'pressing to death, whipping and hanging', we suspect he is glad to be alive. With some satisfaction the Duke announces that he has 'found an apt remission' in himself – mercy appropriate for the situation (V, i, 496). Many commentators have found the scene 'a perfectly mad coda' (Bloom 379), but Debora Shuger observes that the Duke seems to us to be exercising a 'strange justice' because it is his attempt, as a sacral ruler, 'to imagine what Christianity might look like as a political process', and so a venture in 'visionary theocracy' (131–3). We may add that any attempt to make divine justice manifest in human society is going to be an approximation and an experiment at best.

## A Space for Imagination

*Measure for Measure* is often referred to as a 'problem play', along with *Troilus and Cressida* and *All's Well that Ends Well*. One critic has defined a problem play thus: 'a perplexing and distressing complication in human life is presented ... [and] the theme is handled so as to ... probe the complicated interrelations of character and action in a situation admitting to different ethical interpretations' (Lawrence 4). So there is a clash of values, which is likely to 'evoke diverse, fluid reactions from audiences' (Shell 12). One instance of this clash is Isabella's reaction to the position in which she has been placed: 'Then, Isabel live chaste, and brother die! / More than our brother is our chastity!' (II, iv, 184–5). Claudio, not surprisingly, does not see it this way, and when he pleads with her to save him, she retorts that in his case 'mercy would prove itself a bawd'. Life or chastity? This is a conflict in which many have been placed, without the bizarre situation of Isabella. We are uncertain about whether to sympathize with her or not, remembering her belief that if she loses her virginity in this way she will be damned for ever (Muir 136–7). The stakes are high. But just when we veer towards her position, we are checked by two considerations. First, she seems totally unable to apply what she has herself claimed about the mercy of God to her own circumstances. 'She seems to imagine God as a kind of Angelo, a legalistic judge, who would sentence her entirely according to the letter of the law rather than its spirit' (Schanzer 100). It never occurs to her that it would be a travesty of justice for God to sentence her to eternal death for saving her brother's life, despite her moving appeal to forgiveness in the atonement. Second, she seems inconsistent in allowing Mariana to run the same risk of damnation. The Duke has assured her that it would be no sin, since Mariana is contracted in marriage to Angelo (IV, i, 72); but this is virtually parallel to the situation of Claudio and Julietta,[8] and this she continues to consider to be a 'vice'. The same legalistic view

---

8     There might be a slight difference, in that Claudio and Julietta are bound by betrothal, whereas Angelo and Mariana have contracted a 'conditional marriage'. See Lever liii–liv for this distinction.

of divine justice which made Isabella assume that she would be damned ought to have made her presume the same about Mariana (Schanzer 111).

The values held by Isabella make this a problem play. As Harold Bloom concludes, 'Shakespeare leaves us morally breathless' (359, 379–86). But the whole situation of applying law and justice in a fallen world is a problem of conflicting values that has no neat solution. What is this 'lawful mercy' which is appealed to several times? There is no easy resolution, but what resolution there is seems to lie in the character and wisdom of the judge, exercising the virtue of 'moderation'. This combines a number of elements – the classical virtues of Aristotle's 'reasonableness' (*epikeia*) and Seneca's clemency (*clementia*; see Elyot 2:80–1), together with the Reformer's ideal of Christian 'equity'. In this last idea there is an intersection between the Christian virtue of moderation and the legal principle of equity in basing judicial decisions on a reasonable appeal to natural justice, going beyond law as 'statute', but becoming part of common law.[9] For all his ambiguity and spin-doctoring, the Duke is presented as a 'gentleman of all temperance', mediating between extremes. There is thus no direct application to human law-making of the act of pardon shown by God in the cross of Christ, despite attempts by critics and theologians to make the play an allegory of atonement (Coghill, 'Comic Form in *Measure for Measure*' 14–27)[10] with the Duke as a symbol for God or Christ (Wilson Knight 82–96).[11] When Isabella finally asks for mercy for Angelo, after eloquent silence, she says nothing about the atonement. She resorts to a pragmatic and legal argument, that Claudio deserved his fate because he not only intended the sinful act with Julietta, but performed it, whilst Angelo's sinning with her remained only an intention (V, i, 448–52). But unless she is ignorant of the contractual relation between Claudio and Julietta, she is again inconsistent: Angelo has now performed a very similar act with Mariana. Once again, she is caught in a self-contradiction that arises from her legalistic approach, which remains even in the face of a plea for pardon.

---

[9]    William Perkins's *Hepieikeia: or, a Treatise of Christian Equitie and Moderation* is an extended meditation on Philippians 4:5, 'Let your moderation be known to all men. The Lord is at hand'. Perkins urges that the 'nearness' of divine justice demands a humble conduct in our justice; echoing Psalm 85:10 (often appealed to in Christian exposition of the atonement), justice must shake hands with her sister mercy in human judgement (O'Donovan 261).

[10]    Substitutions run throughout the play, bringing life to various characters (even Barnadine), but these are not related to atonement. Nuttall 262–76 finds an allegory of substitutionary atonement, but a 'gnostic' version in which the appeased Father (the Duke) is an evil creator.

[11]    Rather, language of divinity (V, i, 364–8) refers to the Duke's status as a sacral ruler (Shuger 54).

*Measure for Measure* thus plays around with issues that concerned jurists and theologians in Shakespeare's time: how can divine mercy and justice be applied in an imperfect world? Shakespeare does not offer a theory or a doctrine. The command of Jesus – 'Judge not' – opens up a space to be occupied, calling hearers to work out imaginatively what it might mean to stand in the gap between human and divine justice. Shakespeare, in bringing religious ideas of law and mercy together with dramatic poetry, opens up this space of imagination in which tensions can be explored, and in which we learn that there is no simple formula. There can be no immediate transfer of divine justice and mercy into the human realm (cf. O'Donovan 260). We can only stand in the space in a mood of equity. There are only human beings trying their best, doing what is reasonable in the spirit of the law, avoiding legalism, forgiving each other, motivated by God's act of pardon in Christ, and taking warning from the principle 'measure for measure'.

## Law and Grace, Calculation and Risk

In *The Merchant of Venice* Shakespeare had already, some years before, handled the themes of justice and mercy. The Jew, Shylock, embodies and anticipates the kind of legalistic approach to justice that we see in Angelo, and from which even the virtuous Isabella cannot shake herself free. This is not essentially a play about Jews and Christians, but about law and grace. The play is not in itself anti-semitic, but anti-legalist, and legalism (so we discover) can be found among Christians as much as among Jews.

Near the beginning of the play there is a revealing piece of exegesis from the Old Testament book of Genesis (Gen. 30:25–43), a passage usually omitted by directors as hopelessly obscure (I, iii, 66–85). Shylock recalls the story of Jacob working as a shepherd for his uncle Laban, and their agreement that Jacob should keep for his payment all the lambs that were born with striped or piebald-coloured fleeces. The wily Laban thought this was a good deal, but according to the story he had reckoned without Jacob's greater craftiness. When the rams were in the act of mating with the ewes, Jacob stuck up in front of them wooden poles that had been partly peeled of their bark, and the ewes apparently took the hint and conceived lambs with striped fleeces. Shylock tells this story as a defence of usury, or money-lending at interest. The way he reads the text is that Jacob was blessed in multiplying his assets. He made his possessions work for him, in breeding more wealth, and he received what he deserved for his hard work. So Shylock makes his money work for him, and concludes: 'This was a way to thrive, and he was blest: / And thrift is blessing, if men steal it not' (I, iii, 845). This is a legalistic hermeneutics; profit comes from skilful exploitation of assets, and work is always rewarded. However, Antonio immediately responds by offering a different exegesis of the story:

> This was a venture, sir, that Jacob serv'd for,
> A thing not in his power to bring to pass,
> But swayed and fashion'd by the hand of heaven.
> Was this inserted to make interest good?
> Or is your gold and silver ewes and rams? (I, iii, 86–90)

Antonio reads the story as an example of risk-taking, of 'venturing' or hazarding for which Jacob was dependent, not on his skills in breeding, but on the grace of heaven. Jacob could not guarantee the outcome of his act of sympathetic magic with the peeled rods.

Antonio was launched upon such a venture in his trading enterprises, hazarding all upon the toss of the ocean with a risk that no money-lender had to take. His friend Bassanio was about to venture forth on a hazardous quest of love to Belmont to win the Lady Portia, but Antonio was hazarding more for the sake of love and friendship in putting himself into the power of Shylock's bond, with a stake which was to be nothing less than his own life. For while Shylock offered to lend 3,000 ducats interest-free for three months, the penalty for failure to repay at the end of that time would be a pound of Antonio's flesh, to be cut off 'nearest the heart'. Antonio agrees to this bond, taking up the hazard of love to raise the money for Bassanio to make his journey of love.

This, then, is the fundamental contrast at the heart of the play, between the generous risks of love and the mathematics of commerce. Shakespeare's contemporaries would have perceived immediately that it is also a contrast between law and grace. Shylock symbolizes those who live by the law, or who live by the Old Covenant read only as a matter of law.[12] He is the 'Jew' of the Apostle Paul's arguments about condemnation by law and justification by grace;[13] it is not Shylock's race that the play condemns, but his theology. For when none of Antonio's ships come home safely to Venice at the end of three months and he cannot repay Shylock, his adversary insists on the demands of the law.

---

[12]  Coghill, in 'The Governing Idea', finds an allegory between the old law and the new law. But Shylock does not stand simply for the Old Covenant, but for a legalistic approach to the Old Covenant. Under the 'old law' he should also have shown mercy.

[13]  Romans 2:17–21; 2:29–3:2; 3:19–26; 4:1–3.

In the trial before the Duke, Antonio's supposed lawyer, who is really the Lady Portia in disguise, begs Shylock to exercise mercy:

> The quality of mercy is not strain'd,
> It droppeth as the gentle rain from heaven
> Upon the place beneath: it is twice blest,
> It blesseth him that gives, and him that takes. (IV, i, 180–4)

Like love, mercy and forgiveness take risks. As Jesus points out, in a gospel text, that the heaven sends rain equally upon the righteous and unrighteous (Matt. 5:45), so mercy does not take strict account of deserts. In this speech, Portia goes on to paraphrase St Paul on the nature of justification by grace and condemnation by the law, without explicitly mentioning the Christian story:

> ... therefore, Jew,
> Though justice be thy plea, consider this,
> That in the course of justice, none of us
> Should see salvation. We do pray for mercy,
> And that same prayer, doth teach us all to render
> The deeds of mercy. (IV, i, 193–8)

Shylock decides to stand by the law, and replies: 'My deeds upon my head! I crave the law, / The penalty and forfeit of my bond!' The first phrase echoes the words of the crowd before Pilate, 'His blood be on us and on our children' (Matt. 27:25), but the story of the cross of Jesus remains only implicit here in Portia's version of St Paul. This is apt, because both Christian and Jewish believers can be urged to read their Scriptures as witness, essentially, to a God of grace and not a God of strict legalism. As with Paul, it is a matter of reading for the spirit rather than the letter in the written text, for 'the letter killeth, but the Spirit bringeth life' (2 Cor. 3:6). Legalism insists upon a literal reading, and this is what Shylock does, not only with the Torah story of Jacob, but with his bond. He is constantly asking the audience whether what is asked of him is explicitly *in the text*. Portia asks, for example, that Antonio be permitted here and now to repay the money three times over, but the strict letter of the bond says three months. 'An oath, an oath,' cries Shylock, 'I have an oath in heaven / Shall I lay perjury upon my soul?' (IV, i, 224–5). Portia asks that Shylock allow a doctor to stand by to try and save Antonio's life when the flesh is cut, but Shylock refers again to the written text: 'Is it so nominated in the bond?' (IV, i, 255). Portia replies: 'It is not so express'd, but what of that? / 'Twere good you do so much for charity.' But Shylock is remorseless: 'I cannot find it, 'tis not in the bond' (IV, i, 258). As, however, Shylock vows to live by the law, so he is condemned by the law. Those who will not take the risks of love and forgiveness will find that the law brings death. Portia encourages him to take up his knife and cut, but then at the last moment points out the full implications of the letter of the law. The bond allows a pound of flesh, but there is no mention of taking any blood with it. The bond states one pound, so Shylock must not take one tiny scruple less or more than the weight stated. If Shylock fails to take the exact pound, or sheds any blood, then he must pay the penalty of having all his goods confiscated and must himself die. Such a task is impossible, and having made his decision, Shylock cannot now show mercy and retrieve the amount owed to him. The law of Venice further condemns him for having plotted against the life of a citizen, and may fine him up to the limit of one half of his estate; the other half is due to the defendant, Antonio, as compensation. Shylock is now dependent on the mercy of the Duke and Antonio, who offer him his life and the use of half his estate until his death, on the condition that he is baptized as a Christian.

Shakespeare has taken the plot in its entirety from an existing story, including the turning of the exact text of the bond against Shylock.[14] But he has permeated it with the Reformation theme of law and grace, with the contrast between the mathematics of gain and the absurdly generous multiplication of love. The same theme is worked out in the parallel plot-line of the play: during the three months that Antonio's agreement with Shylock is running, Bassanio journeys to Belmont and wins the beautiful, intelligent and (above all) fabulously rich Lady Portia. But, following the theme that Shakespeare has already established, Bassanio can only win Portia's hand in marriage by hazarding for it.

Portia has to live under a rule established by her rich father before he died, that anyone wishing to marry her has to choose one of three caskets – gold, silver and lead. The right casket contains her picture, and she has to marry the suitor who chooses it; those who enter the guessing game take a considerable risk, since they must vow on their honour never to marry anyone if they choose wrongly. The lead casket carries the threatening words, 'who chooseth me, must give and hazard all he hath', and Bassanio correctly chooses this casket, which invites the viewer to risk all. The unlikely outward form of the dull lead contains inside the portrait of the lady, and here Shakespeare employs another familiar theme in his plays – the difference between appearance and reality (Brown lii).[15]

---

[14]   See the first story of the fourth day in Ser Giovanni, *Il Pecorone* (Milan, 1558), text in Brown 140–53. For a similar rebounding of the wording of the bond against 'the Jew', see Declamation 95 of *The Orator* by Alexander Silvayn (1596), text in Brown 168–72.

[15]   The same lesson is finally rubbed in, with a good deal of hilarious sexual innuendo, by the women's trick with the rings (V, i, 280–5, 305–7).

The two themes – the law and appearances – are intertwined. Legalism is preoccupied with the outward appearance of things, the outer letter of the text rather than the spirit within the text. Love and forgiveness have to penetrate beyond the surface of mere law. Bassanio, as he considers his choice, precisely draws a parallel between the appearance of the caskets, law and legal religion:

> So may the outward shows be least themselves,
> The world is still deceiv'd with ornament –
> In law, what plea so tainted and corrupt,
> But, being season'd with a gracious voice,
> Obscures the show of evil? In religion,
> What damned error but some sober brow
> Will bless it, and approve it with a text,
> Hiding the grossness with fair ornament? (III, ii, 73–80)

Love, forgiveness and a regard for the inner spirit and open meaning of a text belong together, in an extravagant self-giving and 'surplus of the gift' (Gallagher 75) which can pierce beneath the surface of things. This is the theme that Shakespeare carries through into the climax of the judgement before the Duke of Venice, which is essentially a 'struggle for the act of reading' (Drakakis 104). Portia's successful quibble that the flesh must be taken without blood and to the exact weight comes from stories that Shakespeare probably used as a source, but Shakespeare brings to it the reflection on law and mercy explored above, and adds to it the need to travel beyond appearance to what is finally real. The monarch's sceptre, says Portia in her great speech on mercy:

> ... shows the force of temporal power,
> The attribute to awe and majesty,
> Wherein doth sit the dread and fear of kings:
> But mercy is above this sceptred sway,
> It is enthroned in the hearts of kings,
> It is an attribute to God himself. (IV, i, 186–8)

As in all Shakespeare's comedies, appearances are turned upside down by comic confusion in order to expose the truths lying beneath. Adopting the disguise of being a male lawyer, making appearance even more deceptive, gives Portia the opportunity to penetrate the surface of law and bring everyone, Jew and Christian, to face reality.

We must, however, try and catch something of Shakespeare's subtlety in his attack on legalism in the cause of grace and mercy. The play opens a space in which the complexity of the relation between human law and divine grace can be explored, in which there is no easy resolution. It is too simplistic to see the play as a Christian criticism of Judaism. In the scene of judgement, an ambiguity hovers around the interpretation of the flesh-bond. Who really is the legalist here, Shylock or Portia? It might be argued that Shylock's assumption that flesh implies blood, and that an approximate weight will do, is in fact reaching beyond the letter of the law to its spirit, and so ironically exemplifies the practice of 'equity'.[16] Perhaps too, as Terry Eagleton suggests (43–4), the very proposal of the flesh-bond by Shylock is not in its deepest sense a legal instrument at all, but a cry for Jewish flesh to be recognized as equal to Christian flesh; beneath the surface it may be a means of forcing us to recognize that Christians and Jews have a common body, exposed to the same life and death. Shylock stands within a long history of the abuse of Jewish flesh by Christians (I, iii, 101–26); revenge certainly motivates his claim on a pound of Christian flesh, but the very agreement gives Shylock a kind of gruesome intimacy with Antonio. Indeed, it is an Old Testament stress on the body. What stands between them, argues Eagleton, is not the mere currency of financial exchange, but flesh itself. Flesh is what they have in common, and when Antonio faces the payment of the forfeit, it is with a curious intensity that Shylock calls his flesh 'mine' (IV, i, 100). At the point of death, it is all too clear that we have a common humanity, a fact that Antonio himself denied in his behaviour towards Shylock. Shylock's great speech in defence of Jewish humanity affirms that what we all have in common is the body:

> I am a Jew. Hath not a Jew eyes? Hath not a Jew hands, organs, dimensions, senses, affections, passions? Fed with the same food, hurt with the same weapons, subject to the same diseases, healed by the same means, warmed and cooled by the same winter and summer as a Christian is? If you prick us do we not bleed? (III, i, 52–8)

Portia, on the other hand, overturns Shylock's claim by a piece of sheer legalism, a quibbling on the precise letter of the text: no mention of blood, and an exact pound. 'There is a ruthless precision about her sense of the text which exactly parallels Shylock's relentless insistence on having his bond' (Eagleton 37; cf. Charlton 159). There is also an uncanny resemblance here to Isabella's quibbling on the difference between 'intent' and 'action'. The point of Portia's argument is

---

[16]   A possible source, Silvayn's *Orator*, posits that the Jew claims to be working by equity or 'reasonable things' (Brown 170).

a theological one, that to live by law and neglect mercy is to die by the law.[17] The one who appeals to the law for his righteousness will end by being condemned by it. But she argues the point with legalistic methods that have no placc in Paul's rhetoric or elsewhere in the New Testament. This may simply be the strain of bringing together a folk tale with a theological reflection, but it does at least serve to raise questions about whether the Christians themselves in this play are innocent of legalism. That they are not innocent is shown by the terms of the so-called 'mercy' finally given to Shylock.

## Theology, Poetry and Imagination

These two plays tell us that when earthly rulers or lawyers judge, both their justice and their mercy are defective, but they may witness to the perfect union of the two in the character and acts of God. Through a convergence between theological concepts of law, mercy and grace on the one hand, and his use of metaphor and image on the other, Shakespeare opens up an imaginative space in which we can work at a human approximation to transcendent justice and mercy, to the grace that transforms law.

As we think about the relation between theology and poetry, we see that this space that is opened up for us is being created by a two-way movement that we might identify as imagination and revelation. Imaginative writing such as poetry and drama reaches out beyond itself to something of 'ultimate concern' to us. It would be mere fantasy if we did not sense that it was pointing to a final reality which can only be hinted at. The imagination transcends itself towards mystery, towards a reality which eludes empirical investigation and bursts open rational concepts. Some – though not all – poets will want to name this most real Reality as 'God'. But whilst a movement towards mystery is characteristic of poetry, quite the opposite might seem at first sight to be true of Christian theology. In poetry, images are used playfully and experimentally to hint at a kind of reality which the reason cannot properly comprehend. By contrast, theology asserts that the Final Mystery has actually disclosed itself to us, and human images and stories take their place in witnessing (however imperfectly) to this encounter with a self-revealing God. The initial movement with which theology is concerned is

---

[17]    See Galatians 3:10; Romans 2:12; Romans 7:9–11; 2 Corinthians 3:6–9. Coghill argues that Portia's argument is justified theologically ('The Governing Idea'), and Brown (116) that is it is justified dramatically.

not from the world to mystery, but from mystery to the world. As the theologian Karl Barth expressed it, 'revelation seizes the language' (1.1: 430).

Theology is bound to use symbol and metaphor, since no talk about God as the final and unique Mystery can do without these forms of discourse; literal talk about God is just not possible. But theology tends to use metaphor in an effort to fix meaning, to define and limit a range of possible understandings. On the other hand, poetic metaphor and narrative rejoice in ambiguity and the opening up of multiple meaning. Poetry emphasizes the playful freedom of imagination, while doctrine will always seek to reduce to concepts the images and stories upon which it draws. In short, literature tends to openness and theology to closure (Fiddes 8–26).

A Christian theologian will acknowledge that theology, poetry and imagination are, nevertheless, all responses to the self-disclosure of the Mystery we may name God. Theology witnesses deliberately, consciously and conceptually to the movement of the unveiling of God where poetry does not. Nevertheless, we may think that our very capacity for transcending ourselves which poetry exemplifies is being prompted in the first place by the self-opening of this Mystery to us. As the theologian Karl Rahner puts it, the human openness to Mystery can never be separated from God's own openness to us in gracious self-giving. To be a person, he writes, is actually to take part in 'the event of a ... self-communication of God' (127). The discipline of theology is thus essential for witnessing to the self-unveiling of the Mystery, but it will always need to be broken open through imagination for new exploration by the impact of poetry.

In her great speech on the 'quality of mercy', Portia quotes the Lord's Prayer and paraphrases St Paul on the nature of salvation by grace, without explicitly mentioning the Christian story at all. Isabella makes a more explicit reference to the 'remedy' that God found for humanity, but in support of an enigmatic idea of 'lawful mercy', which cannot be reduced to a formula. Shakespeare thus demonstrates his own form of religious imagination. Christian theological concepts are being brought into imaginative tension with a poetic and dramatic exploration of law and mercy in the plays, without commitment to any particular theological scheme, but as a call to explore a space that is being opened up so that we can experience something transcending it. *Measure for Measure* recommends the virtue of moderation as we stand in this space, while *The Merchant of Venice* calls us to a risky adventuring of love. They both summon us to a space in which we are to live, move and have our being.

## Works Cited

Barth, Karl. *Church Dogmatics*. Trans. and ed. G.W. Bromiley and T.F. Torrance. 14 vols. Edinburgh: Clark, 1936–77.

Battenhouse, Roy. '*Measure for Measure* and Christian Doctrine of the Atonement'. *PMLA* 61 (1946): 1029–59.

Berman, Ronald. 'Shakespeare and the Law'. *Shakespeare Quarterly* 18.2 (1967): 141–50.

Bilson, Thomas. *A Sermon preached at Westminster before the King and Queenes Maiesties at their coronations [...] by the Lord Bishop of Winchester*. London, 1603.

Bloom, Harold. *Shakespeare: The Invention of the Human*. London: Fourth Estate, 1999.

Brown, John Russell, ed. *The Merchant of Venice*. Arden Shakespeare Revised. London: Methuen, 1964.

Charlton, H.B. *Shakespearian Comedy*. London: Methuen, 1966.

Coghill, Neville. 'Comic Form in *Measure for Measure*'. *Shakespeare Survey* 8 (1955): 14–27.

—— 'The Governing Idea: Essays in Stage-Interpretation of Shakespeare'. *Shakespeare Quarterly* 1 (1948): 9–17.

Drakakis, John, ed. *The Merchant of Venice*. Arden Shakespeare. Third Series. London: Bloomsbury, 2010.

Eagleton, Terry. *William Shakespeare*. Oxford: Blackwell, 1986.

Elyot, Thomas. *The Boke Named the Gouernour*. Ed. Stephen Croft. 2 vols. London: Kegan Paul, 1883.

Erasmus, Desiderius. *The Education of a Christian Prince* (1540). Trans. L.K. Born. New York: Columbia University Press, 1936.

Eure, John D. 'Shakespeare and the Legal Process: Four Essays'. *Virginia Law Review* 61.2 (1975): 390–433.

Fiddes, Paul. *Freedom and Limit: A Dialogue between Literature and Christian Doctrine*. Basingstoke: Macmillan, 1991.

Firth, C.H. and R.S. Rait, eds. *Acts and Ordinances of the Interregnum, 1642–1660*. London: His Majesty's Stationery Office, 1911.

Gallagher, Lowell. 'Waiting for Gobbo'. In *Spiritual Shakespeares*, ed. Ewan Fernie. London: Routledge, 2005, 73–93.

Holdsworth, William S. *A History of English Law*. 4th edition. London: Methuen, 1927.

Lawrence, William. *Shakespeare's Problem Comedies*. New York: Ungar, 1960.

Lever, J.W., ed. *Measure for Measure*. Arden Shakespeare Revised. London: Methuen, 1965.

McKerrow, R.B. *The Works of Thomas Nashe*. 5 vols. London: Sidgewick and Jackson, 1910.

Muir, Kenneth. *Shakespeare's Comic Sequence*. Liverpool: Liverpool University Press, 1979.

Nuttall, A.D. *Shakespeare the Thinker*. New Haven, CT: Yale University Press, 2007.

O'Donovan, Oliver. *The Desire of the Nations: Rediscovering the Roots of Political Theology*. Cambridge: Cambridge University Press, 1996.

Perkins, William. *Hepieíkeia: or, a Treatise of Christian Equitie and Moderation*. Cambridge: John Legat, 1604.

Rahner, Karl. *Foundations of Christian Faith: An Introduction to the Idea of Christianity*. Trans. W.V. Dych. London: Darton, Longman and Todd, 1978.

Schanzer, Ernest. *The Problem Plays of Shakespeare*. London: Routledge, 1963.

Schrenk, Gottlob. 'Righteousness in the New Testament'. In *Righteousness*, ed. Gottfried Quell and Gottlob Schrenk, trans. J.R. Coates. London: Adam and Charles Black, 1951, 26–55.

Shell, Alison. *Shakespeare and Religion*. Arden Critical Companions. London: Methuen Drama, 2010.

Shuger, Debora Kuller. *Political Theologies in Shakespeare's England: The Sacred and the State in* Measure for Measure. Basingstoke: Palgrave, 2001.

Stubbes, Phillip. 'The horryble vice of whordome'. In *The Anatomie of Abuses*. London: Richard Jones, 1583.

Wilson Knight, G. *The Wheel of Fire: Interpretations of Shakespearian Tragedy*. Revised edition. London: Methuen, 1965.

## Chapter 7

# Wallace Stevens on God, Imagination and Reality

## John McDade

'Religion is poetry in which we *believe*, usually without knowing it to be poetry; hence it affects our behaviour ... the highest poetry is identical with religion' (Bates 49). This comment from Milton Bates, interpreting George Santayana's *Interpretations of Poetry and Religion* (1900), accurately presents Wallace Stevens's view of poetry and religion. For Santayana and Stevens, poetry and religion are human inventions that express and partly satisfy our 'longing for the ideal', springing from an impulse within us identified as the 'imagination' (Bates 49). The only difference between them comes from the consequences which flow from them: religion leads to new ways of behaving in the world (action and ethics), while poetry is an imaginative interpretation of the real. Our statements about God are invented, spun out of the poetic self as a spider produces the filaments that become its web. Stevens writes in a letter to Hi Simons, dated 28 August 1940:

> We no longer think that God was, but was imagined. The idea of pure poetry, essential imagination, as the highest objective of the poet, appears to be, at least potentially, as great as the idea of God, and, for that matter, greater, if the idea of God is only one of the things of the imagination. (*Letters* 369)

The three categories mentioned here – 'pure poetry', 'essential imagination' and 'the idea of God' – are said to be the highest aim of the poet, and given the relation that Stevens sees between poetry and religion, it is no surprise that the 'idea of God' is the supreme instance of the 'fiction' devised by the poetic imagination. God is central to the working of the human imagination and Stevens's dilemma concerns the status of this particular 'fiction': to say that the idea of God is one of the things of the imagination is to be faced with the question of whether there might be, in reality and actuality, something to which that fiction refers. His letter dated 21 December 1951 to Sister M. Bernetta Quinn is open to that possibility: 'I am not an atheist', he wrote, 'although I do not believe to-day in the same God in whom I believed when I was a boy' (*Letters* 735). In similar vein, he had written to Hi Simons on 9 January 1940 that he said he had come to realize that 'an anthropomorphic god is simply a projection of itself by a race of egotists, which it is natural for them to treat as sacred' (*Letters* 349). Humans cannot cope with a God whose being is beyond description: the vacuum is always replenished with material from the psychic and mythical storehouse. But this is where the problems lie. That humans make the divine in their own image and likeness has been known since Xenophanes (580–470 BC):

> But mortal men imagine that gods are begotten, and that they have human dress and speech and shape.

> If oxen or horses or lions had hands to draw with and to make works of art as men do, then horses would draw the form of gods like horses, oxen like oxen, and they could make their gods' bodies similar to the bodily shape that they themselves each had.

> The Ethiopians say that their gods are snub-nosed and black-skinned, the Thracians that they are blue-eyed and red-headed. (Fragments 4, 15, 16)

A reflective religious believer will recognize that anthropomorphic categories are projected on to divine figures out of impulses in our nature, and that if we are to engage with the divine in appropriate ways, these projections have to be deconstructed through a recognition that God cannot be imagined at all without distortion. But because he insistently joins 'imagination' and 'God' in ways that leave no opening for a God who is *beyond* imagination, was Stevens ever able to set out on that particular intellectual journey? Probably not. 'God' for him seems always to be imagined, never affirmed as 'the good beyond being' and beyond imagination, and so an insistence on linking 'God' and 'imagination' would seem to be wrong right from the start and to be the source of much of the confusion that one finds in Stevens and others. But his approach is valuable: he is concerned with the way in which we construct, picture, devise an imaginative account of God, with our versions of the divine. For Stevens, the imagining of God is of a piece with the imagining of other fictive gods and spirits – what naturalist philosophers call 'spooky realities' – and with the imagining of the world in poetry and art. Religion is an impulse that for Stevens and many modern atheists is continuous with poetic imagination generally and expresses the self and nothing beyond it.

Stevens judged that there are no versions of the divine other than imaginative ones available to us and so his focus is on how we construe and imagine God, gods and the real. He is primarily interested in religion as a work of the imagination, corresponding to what theologians call the cataphatic style, the use of positive categories to portray and imagine the divine in meaningful ways. In his writings on this matter, Stevens seems to have a confidence worthy of Feuerbach that all language about the divine is an unexamined imaginative projection of what we want to be there. But that is over: ours is 'an age of disbelief when the gods have come to an end, when we think of them as the aesthetic projections of a time that was passed' (Stevens, 'Two or Three Ideas' 844). With the demise of these projections, recognized finally as projections, 'men turn to a fundamental glory of their own and from that create a style of bearing in themselves in reality. They create a new style or a new bearing in a new reality' ('Two or Three Ideas' 844). In this godless age, the imagination can still create fictions, but they will be aesthetic fictions unclothed in religious images.

Because Stevens's view of religion is that it is the elaboration of fictive worlds, a work of semantic expansion and metaphoric colonization, his concern is with the poetry, with the fiction, with the 'style' gods have as creations of the imagination. The gods of the ancient world, on whom we look back now with interest but with disbelief, were, he says, 'clear giants of a vivid time, who in the style of their beings made the style of the gods and the gods themselves one' ('Two or Three Ideas' 841). In the address from which these remarks are taken, he speaks of the effect on us of this disbelief:

> To see the gods dispelled in mid-air and dissolve like clouds is one of the great human experiences. It is not as if they had gone over the horizon to disappear for a time; not as if they had been overcome by other gods of greater power and profounder knowledge. It is simply that they came to nothing. Since we have always shared all things with them and have always had a part of their strength and, certainly, all of their knowledge, we shared likewise this experience of annihilation. It was their annihilation, not ours, and yet it left us feeling that in a measure we, too, had been annihilated. It left us feeling dispossessed and alone in a solitude, like children without parents, in a home that seemed deserted, in which the amical rooms and halls had taken on a look of hardness and emptiness. What was most extraordinary is that they left no mementoes behind, no thrones, no mystic rings, no texts either of the soil or of the soul. It is as if they had never

inhabited the earth. There was no crying out for their return. They were not
forgotten because they had been a part of the glory of the earth. At the same time,
no man ever muttered a petition in his heart for the restoration of those unreal
shapes. ('Two or Three Ideas' 842)

This is a fine and subtle description: the gods are absent and we are
consequently 'annihilated', 'dispossessed' orphans. But a post-religious world
no longer peopled with these divine figures suits us very well, and Christian
believers need to understand the ease with which people today slide into post-
monotheist atheism, just as perhaps Mediterranean peoples slid into Hebraic
monotheism and felt no compelling desire to keep the classical gods (who were
a rotten lot anyway). Religion has been one of the aesthetic pleasures we create
for ourselves, a form of enchantment now left behind. No matter, Stevens says:
in an age of disbelief we can still create imaginative fictions through poetry and
art, by means of which the modern poet faces up to the 'monotony of reality'.
The poet now knows that reality can be deemed 'monotonous' only when it is
set against an imagined 'other reality' such as a spiritual world of unchanging
perfection that a Platonically infused Christian culture has devised. When,
through disbelief, there is nothing to which the world can be compared –
because there is neither God nor heaven nor hell – 'reality is returned, as if
a shadow had passed and drawn after it and taken away whatever coating had
concealed what lay beneath it' ('Two or Three Ideas' 847–8).[1] '[T]he great
poems of heaven and hell have been written', Stevens states, 'and the great
poem of the earth remains to be written. I suppose it is that poem that will
constitute the true prize of the spirit' ('Imagination as Value' 730). So religion
and poetry, although they overlap, can also be placed on a timeline: religion
was then, poetry is now; religious fiction was the product of earlier ages, and
when fictive religion ceases to be credible, the same quality of significance can
be attained through poetry and art:

> One of the visible movements of the modern imagination is the movement away
> from the idea of God. The poetry that created the idea of God will either adapt it
> to our different intelligence, or create a substitute for it, or make it unnecessary.
> These alternatives probably mean the same thing, but the intention is not to foster
> a cult. (Stevens, *Letters* 378)

---

[1]    Nietzsche seems to be the influence here. He located this impulse in a desire to escape
from the real world by constructing (imagining) a perfect world, in comparison with which
the reality of the world is found wanting.

Presumably because a 'cult' would be another form of religion and we can no longer return to naïve religious narratives, such is our depth of religious disenchantment. So what is imagination expected to do in a post-religious context and can it fulfil the same function as religion in an earlier age? In many ways, Stevens's poetry is an extended exploration of issues that are no less philosophical than aesthetic, bearing upon language and reality and the possible presence of God within both language and reality. Surely this is the distinctive quality of his poetic voice. In 'Imagination as Value', Stevens quotes Ernst Cassirer's *An Essay on Man* to the effect that imagination 'now has universal *metaphysical* value' and 'poetic imagination is the only clue to reality' ('Imagination as Value' 726; my emphasis). He distinguishes between, on the one hand, imagination 'as a power of the mind over external objects' – such as might be found in the sculptures of Michelangelo or the Jesuit church in Lucerne which fuses the 'real' and 'the visionary', presumably in High Baroque *trompe l'oeil* – and, on the other hand, 'the imagination as metaphysics' bearing upon how we construe reality and significance ('Imagination as Value' 726–7). It is a mistake to discuss only the question of imagination in relation to the arts and letters; more significant, he thinks, is the role that imagination plays in life itself, as he declares: 'Poetry is the imagination of life. A poem is a particular of life thought of for so long that one's thought has become an inseparable part of it or a particular of life so intensely felt that the feeling has entered into it' ('The Figure of the Youth as Virile Poet' 684).

'To regard the imagination as metaphysics', he says, 'is to think of it as part of life, and to think of it as part of life is to realize the extent of artifice. We live in the mind' ('Imagination as Value' 728). Here the word 'artifice' designates the interior image by which the world is taken into the thinking self. Poems are the 'artifice' through which we engage the real. In reading Stevens's work, the reader often has a sense of entering a world in which an engaged and introspective self draws the outside world into itself and recreates it fictively.[2] The great puzzle is that the mind that springs from the world has the capacity to turn back to the world in an act of intellectual interpretation. Reality becomes accessible to us heuristically, through acts of discovery and disclosure, and semantically, through the bestowal and creation of meaning. Interpretation is all and imaginative interpretation issuing in poetry and art is no less truth-seeking and truth-bearing than the other approaches open to us such as philosophy and science.

---

[2]     This is not far from Rilke: 'Nirgends, Geliebte, wird Welt sein, als innen' ('Nowhere, beloved, can world exist but within' [*Duino Elegies* 7]). In Margaret Miles's words, 'the primary task of living, for Rilke, is *imagining* the real: interior *representation* of Chartres, music, night, spring, earth and tree' (137).

Stevens thinks of poetry as 'at least the equal of philosophy' ('The Figure of the Youth as Virile Poet' 668).[3]

If this reading is correct, then the imagination in its fictive, poetic/religious productions intensifies what takes place all the time in our ordinary knowing. This is why Stevens can say that poetry is 'the imagination of life'. Poetry and the fictive work of imagination are not activities distinct from the other activities of the mind, but they are particular ways in which the meaning-creation and meaning-finding activities of the mind engage with 'the real' in ways that please our imaginative and intellectual taste. Truth is the object of both: a rational idea satisfies the mind; an imaginative idea satisfies the imagination. A rational idea may not satisfy the imagination, and an imaginative idea may not satisfy the mind, but the successful conjunction of the rational and the imaginative has consequences in providing us with the supreme fiction, the idea of God that establishes 'a divine beginning and end for us', telling us of our origin and goal, both rationally and imaginatively:

> From this analysis, we deduce that an idea that satisfies both the reason and the imagination, if it happened, for instance to be an idea of God, would establish a divine beginning and end for us which, at the moment the reason, singly, at best proposes, and on which, at the moment, the imagination, singly merely meditates.
> (Stevens, 'The Figure of the Youth as Virile Poet' 668)

The verbs here ('proposes' and 'meditates') are significant: the mind offers an idea for adjudication and rational acceptance, and the imagination 'meditates', presumably on the aesthetic quality of what is created; most of the time (all of the time?) they work separately, 'singly', not in concert. In Cassirer's words, the idea of God would offer a 'universal metaphysical value' as the fiction through which humans find 'what will suffice' to please and fulfil the mind (Stevens, 'Of Modern Poetry' 218). Of course there are fictive gods whom we imagine, whom we create out of our metaphors and projections, whom we know to be inventions. But they matter: such gods are how we express the meaning-creating dimension of ourselves and eventually we come to be pleased and satisfied by what we imaginatively devise. The God who is 'the supreme fiction' is most certainly created out of our imagining and is a product of the mind. But good theology, as taught by Maimonides and Aquinas in the Middle Ages and

---

3    In his letter to Sister Quinn dated 29 May 1952, Stevens wrote: 'My object is to write aesthetically valid poetry. I am not so much concerned with philosophic validity' (*Letters* 752).

strangely forgotten since then, knows that the condition of knowing 'the true God', of attaining genuine, non-delusory, monotheism, lies in removing God precisely from the web of such imaginings. This is the truth articulated in the biblical prohibition of images: authentic monotheism – an account of God that takes seriously that God cannot be captured in human categories without being betrayed – requires a cognitive and semantic separation between the referent 'God' and the meanings or 'senses' indirectly and metaphorically applied to that referent. One looks in vain for an awareness of this point in the way in which Stevens discusses God, the imagination and fiction. By contrast, classical theism, less tainted with romantic or philosophical idealism and keener to distinguish between 'the real' and 'the idea of the real', between the 'signified' and the 'mode of signification', does not think that the idea of God gives you access to God at all: *conceptio dei non est deus*, and the true God is attained only by relinquishing the *conceptio* in question. But for Stevens, there seems to be no God other than that reached through a fictive *conceptio*.

By definition, God is not an object of thought or imagination. But if God is construed in the imaginative categories of the mind, then echoing and paraphrasing St Augustine ('Si comprehendis non est Deus'), it is not God who is designated but a human, all too human, construal of the divine. It is significant that when, in 'Notes Toward a Supreme Fiction', Stevens evokes the story of Moses and the Burning Bush, he describes 'A lasting visage in a lasting bush / A face of stone ...' ('It Must Give Pleasure' 346). It is important for this poem, and for the rest of Stevens's poetic exploration of this theme, that God should be seen as having a 'face', because the idea of God is initially, and perhaps permanently, figurative, as he makes clear in a letter about the poem:

> The first thing one sees of any deity is the face, so that the elementary idea of God is a face: a lasting visage in a lasting bush. Adoration is a form of face to face. When the compulsion to adoration grows less, or merely changes, unless the change is complete, the face changes and, in the case of a face at which one has looked for a long time, changes that are slight may appear to the observer to be melodramatic. We struggle with the face, see it everywhere and try to express the changes. In the depths of concentration, the whole thing disappears. (*Letters* 438)

If the 'elementary idea of God is a face', then when we move, as we must, to a God who has no face, this can be either, on the one hand, a move into formal atheism and the denial that there is a God at all, or, on the other hand, a move into a form of theism that consciously forbids itself the consolations of imagery.

It is tempting to see Stevens's account of the issue as appropriately situated at the crossroad between atheism and non-figurative theism.

Stevens's proposal is that in the modern age the imaginative style of religion now gives way to the imaginative style of the poetic and the fictive. But why should the new poetic, the articulation of the supreme (non-religious) fiction that Stevens seeks be a better strategy than the God or gods of religion? He will try to answer this in his poetic charter, 'Notes Toward a Supreme Fiction', by insisting at the start that 'It Must Be Abstract' (329). The word 'abstract' is important here because it signals the denial of imagery and a return to a simplified perception of the world. Joan Richardson speaks of the influence on Stevens of Freud's case for the 'necessity of clearing away illusions of all kinds', among them 'the outworn remnants of religious attachments' (58). Stevens's strategy is to discover the 'essential poem at the centre of things', 'the central poem', 'the poem of the whole', 'the huge, high harmony that sounds', the 'Primitive Like an Orb' that is 'a nature to its natives all / Beneficence, a repose, utmost repose' (*Collected Poetry and Prose* 379). With good reason, Stevens is bewildered: 'I have no idea of the form that a supreme fiction would take', he admits and adds that 'the NOTES [the poem 'Notes Toward a Supreme Fiction'] start out with the idea that it would not take any form: that it would be abstract' (*Letters* 430).

What is interesting is that Stevens begins his exploration of the supreme fiction with the same strategy as theologians do when they want to prevent God from being colonized by an army of metaphors. His insistence that the Supreme Fiction 'Must Be Abstract' (the title of the first section of 'Notes Toward a Supreme Fiction') is meant to eliminate earlier, inherited fictions such as the idea of an 'inventing mind', such as God, and cleanse the mind of its old furniture, so that the sun can be seen again, 'cleansed' of the contaminations brought by a fictive heaven, and freed from the influence of the 'luminous master folded in his fire', probably Dante whose *Divine Comedy* charts the layered worlds of hell, purgatory and heaven with the consequence that 'The death of one god is the death of all' (Stevens, 'It Must Be Abstract' 329).

Yet the choice of this starting point ('the Abstract') does not remove his bewilderment about how to approach and characterize the 'supreme fiction' that is to stand in the place of the disappearing and dead gods. It is never easy to know where to start after the death of God. As Stevens expresses it in one of his letters, he simply does not know what he means:

> I ought to say that I have not defined a supreme fiction. A man as familiar with my
> things as you are will be justified in thinking that I mean poetry. I don't want to
> say that I don't mean poetry; I don't know what I mean. The next thing for me to

do will be to try to be a little more precise about the enigma. I hold off from even
attempting that because, as soon as I rationalize, I lose the poetry of the idea ... As
I see the subject, it could occupy a school of rabbis for the next few generations.
In trying to create something as valid as the idea of God has been, and for that
matter remains, the first necessity seems to be breadth. It is true that the thing
would never amount to much until there is no breadth, or, rather, until it has all
come to a point. (*Letters* 435)

Some lines earlier in the same letter, he writes of the 'abstract' quality of the
supreme fiction, by which I think he means its 'non-representational' or
apophatic quality:

The abstract does not exist, but is certainly as immanent: that is to say, the fictive
abstract is as immanent in the mind of the poet, as the idea of God is immanent
in the mind of the theologian. The poem is a struggle with the inaccessibility of
the abstract. (*Letters* 434)

It is a very revealing admission. 'I don't know what I mean', he can honestly say
and confess that, when he tries to be more precise, the poetry is impaired: he
is caught between too much clarity and too much connotation. When he tries
'to a little more precise about the enigma', he backs off from it for fear that
the too much rational attention will destroy 'the poetry of the idea'. He really
does not know what he is talking about. But that sense of not knowing how to
speak is good and right: the Dominican theologian Herbert McCabe used to
say that Thomas Aquinas thought that theologians simply do not know what
they are talking about and only by being aware of this could they do their job
properly. The classic hermeneutical formula from the Fourth Lateran Council
(AD 1215) dispels fogs of theological nonsense when it insists that there is
'no similarity between God and creature without an even greater dissimilarity'.
We might paraphrase this by saying that you must undermine your positive
statements about God by making even stronger negative statements about God:
if you say 'God is like this', you must immediately undercut it by affirming even
more strongly that God is even more unlike 'this'. In the terms we used earlier,
if we 'spin' religion out of the fiction-producing impulse of the mind, we must
not think that these schemes give us a mastery over the divine and it is only by
denying the affirmative statements that we set ourselves on a path towards the
God whose reality exceeds images.

　　By definition, theology is about *nothing* ('no thing'). Stevens's comments in
the above letter can be replicated in the experience of any theologian or any

'school of rabbis' trying to speak about God, as he seems to know. Why should it surprise us that Stevens encounters the same problems of knowing how to refer and how to predicate anything of a reality that by definition is indeterminate? God ('the abstract') is not accessible to language. Stevens's statement 'the abstract does not exist' corresponds exactly to the principle enunciated by the medieval scholastics, *Deus non est in genere*: God is not one thing in a category of things, so how can words of existence and attribution be predicated of either 'the abstract' or 'God'? As the theologian does not know how to proceed, neither does the poet Stevens: the web of words satisfies neither. If the poem is 'a struggle with the inaccessibility of the abstract', so is theology. How can we get it right if we do not know what it is? And 'where' is it? Not a silly question at all, I think. Joseph Riddel, reviewing the publication of Stevens's letters in 1967, interprets Stevens's 'Notes Toward a Supreme Fiction' in this way:

> ... its occasion is the process of the mind contemplating what it can conceive of but not possess – an ultimate reality – except that it possesses the supreme in its very grasp of the possibilities of the supreme. The mind, that is to say, possesses its moment of the supreme in the act of meditating the idea of the supreme; for the idea is its own creation. If the imagination exists only in relation to otherness, it *realizes* itself only in the phenomena of its own creation – what we call the poetic image, the fiction ... this impulse [towards the supreme fiction] is nothing less than the primal impulse of the imagination seeking the 'centre of reality', seeking repose or order, a place to realize itself. For the 'centre of reality' lay assuredly within the self, even as reality lay without. (527)

A little further on, he continues:

> For the supreme fiction, Stevens seems to discover, exists not beyond nor out of this world, but in the center of the self, and in the imagination's new beginnings. It is the image of the human need to discover its humanness, and the pleasure it affords is the pleasure of bringing into reality, or image, what otherwise is only the formlessness of desire. (530)

This is helpful in making clear that the supreme fiction is our internal version of what is real. Reality comes to expression in us through the idea that we devise of it; the idea conveys the real in a significant way. Riddel can say that the imagination expresses itself 'in the phenomena of its own creation' and in these phenomena – the images and linguistic webs of imagined versions of the real – it expresses the 'human need to discover its humanness'. The supreme fiction then is how we construe the real in ways that please us and that enable us to be at ease with our identities by constructing a 'house of imaginative meaning' drawn from, but ultimately tangentially related to, the world outside.

Stevens entertained, he tells us, 'the idea that, in the various predicaments of belief, it might be possible to yield, or to try to yield, ourselves to a *declared fiction* ... the same thing as saying that it might be possible for us to believe in something that we know to be untrue' (*Letters* 443; my emphasis). You can believe in something if you think it is real and true: that was the strength of religion in an age not conscious of its fictions – and still is, I hope – unless we succumb to a non-realist version of God-talk. But can you really be said to 'believe' in a declared fiction, as distinct from 'entertaining' such a fiction? If you know that what you might believe in is fictive, the product of the imagination, how can you credit it? Belief in God is surely inseparable from a fundamental trust in the world and our place in it. Can you put your trust in a lie that you know to be a lie, even a lie that gives you pleasure, as if it were true? Stevens records a conversation with a student one evening as they walked home together:

> I said that I thought we had reached a point at which we could no longer really believe in anything unless we recognized that it was a fiction. The student said that that was an impossibility, that there was no such thing as believing in something that one knew was not true. It is obvious, however, that we are doing that all the time. There are things with respect to which we willingly suspend disbelief; if there is instinctive in us a will to believe, whether or not it is instinctive, it seems to me that we can suspend disbelief with reference to a fiction as easily as we can suspend it with reference to anything else. There are fictions that are extensions of reality. There are plenty of people who believe in Heaven as definitely as your New England ancestors and my Dutch ancestors believed in it. But Heaven is an extension of reality. (*Letters* 430)

Stevens's opening sentence claims that we are now able to believe only in what we construct through imagination, what he calls 'fiction'. His assumption, of course, is that our reflective grasp of all our instruments of understanding, including religion and art, recognizes that everything to which we give our trust, our faith, our credence, is devised by us. We are now sophisticated enough, he suggests, not to be frightened by our critical 'coming of age' and can now believe while knowing that what we believe depends on our creativity: truth, even when it is discovered, is framed by the categories which the mind brings to the world. Presumably the argument is that the only meaning there is the one that flows from our impulse to interpret mute reality because we are the 'semantic point' at which the world develops semiotic categories and imaginative vision. We see the world imaginatively, metaphorically, in *a priori* categories embedded in us – surely echoes of Kant here. Our sign-bearing systems shape how we engage with the world, and they come back to us as interpretations of 'the real'.

And so, to create a metaphor or fiction is not to engage in mendacity. We use them and other semantic devices meaningfully, aware that metaphor and semantic expansion is part of our activity of seeing and giving meaning. Metaphor and imaginative description are not fraudulent: we trust them and use them in reasonable ways, in ways that promote understanding. The meanings we produce, the connections we create through seeing one thing as another in metaphorical predication, must be regarded as versions grounded in 'the real' – an important designation for Stevens.[4] 'Fictive', then, is not a word to be feared, but to be accepted as natural and inevitable. The issue is central to the work of Hans Vaihinger (1852–1933) whose work *The Philosophy of 'As If'* is discussed by Freud in his *The Future of an Illusion*, which Stevens read carefully in 1928 and 1929. Freud, quoting from Vaihinger, wrote as follows:

> 'We include in the group of fictions not only indifferent theoretical operations but also conceptions created by the noblest minds, to which the heart of the nobler part of mankind clings and which mankind will not allow to be taken away. And this we certainly do not wish to do. We will allow all that to remain as *practical fiction*, but it perishes as *theoretical truth*'. (Freud 92)

(Kant's removal of God from 'speculative reason', and his retention of God within 'practical reason', lies behind this statement.) Chief among these noble conceptions that are to be allowed to 'remain', of course, is the idea of God, and clearly the status of the 'supreme fiction' that would possibly replace God bothered Stevens, and with good reason. Freud's comment on Vaihinger's proposal of belief in something 'as if' it were true must have struck Stevens and fed into his thinking:

> This argument claims that in our mental activity there are a great number of assumptions whose baselessness and even absurdity we fully realize. These are called fictions, but given various practical reasons, it is claimed that we must act

---

4    An instance among many: Stevens's poem 'Earthy Anecdote' describes deer frightened and harassed by a prairie fire that is seen as 'a firecat that bristles in the way'. He comments: 'There's no symbolism in the "Earthy Anecdote". There's a good deal of theory about it, however; but explanations spoil things' (*Letters* 204), and adds: 'I intended something quite concrete: actual animals, not original chaos' (209).

'as if' we believed in them. This is said to be the case with religious doctrines because of their incomparable importance for maintaining human society ... This reminds me of one of my children, who was characterized at a young age by his high regard for accordance with reality. When the children were being told a story and were listening with fixed attention, he would come up and ask: 'Is that a true story?' On hearing that it was not, he would leave with an expression of disdain. It is only to be expected that people will soon treat the tales of religion in a similar way, despite any support for 'as if'. (Freud 91–2)[5]

Yet Stevens is not as convinced as Freud that a fiction that we know to be devised by us should be simply discounted as unworthy of belief. He describes himself as obsessed with this idea of the 'supreme fiction':

When I get up at 6 o'clock in the morning ... the thing crawls all over me; it is in my hair when I shave and I think of it in the bathtub. Then I come down here to the office and, except for an occasional letter like this, have to put it to one side. After all, I like Rhine wine, blue grapes, good cheese, endive and lots of books, etc., etc., etc., as much as I like the supreme fiction. (*Letters* 431)

Stevens's closing remark is meant to be light-hearted of course, but there is a serious issue here, as I suspect Stevens knew: does the supreme fiction that brings intellectual and aesthetic pleasure do anything more for us than these other things such as wine, grapes and cheese, except that it does it in a way that pleases and satisfies the mind and not the taste buds? Is the supreme fiction a vehicle of an intellectual hedonism sated by what is on offer, perhaps much as an Oxford don in the 1960s might have savoured a clever remark by Isaiah Berlin. Does the supreme fiction do more for us than a conversation with Isaiah Berlin (or his brother, the even greater Irving, who gave us 'White Christmas' and 'God Bless America')?

Surely it achieves more than that. The supreme fiction would be how our humanity is delivered to us through the imaginative web we create in relation to the external world: we play enchanting variations, asides on an oboe, intellectually and sensually as a way of accessing the real. This may be what Stevens's 'supreme fiction' is about. Stevens will speak of 'the poem of the mind' composed by the mind in order to *satisfy* the mind. This will deliver truth experienced aesthetically. Of course the key poem here is 'Of Modern Poetry',

---

[5]    Cf. Richardson 58–62. Stevens comments on Freud in 'The Noble Rider and the Sounds of Words' (651).

with its desire to find words that 'repeat, / Exactly that which it wants to hear ... wholly / Containing the mind' (218–19).

What do the words of the poem bring about? Not an understanding of the reality outside the poet or the listener: the poem is not a dispatch from a far country or the conveying of one person's experience to another. Although the poet's words spoken on a new stage are accountable to 'the men and women of the time', the focus of attention quickly passes to what takes place internally, within the listener's mind. The 'poem of the mind' enables the listener to be deeply in touch with herself. The poet has to find words that enable the listener to hear him- or herself in the words of the poem, words which enable the 'finding of a satisfaction'.

What does the listener come to understand? Nothing directly about the world itself, I would suggest, but only about how the world is conveyed imaginatively in the fiction offered in poetry. There is an imaginative transformation through art that gives us access to the real, via a detour which is the poem itself. The function of the poet in relation to the people, Stevens says, is to 'make his imagination theirs and that he fulfils himself only as he sees his imagination become the light in the minds of others. His role, in short, is to help people live their lives' ('The Noble Rider' 660–1). How strange it is, and yet how significant, that the final lines of 'Of Modern Poetry' evoke scenes from Dutch seventeenth-century genre painting: 'a man skating, a woman dancing, a woman / combing'. These are the realized images of artistic transformation that give us access again to 'a man', 'a woman', the emblematic signs of ordinariness. Modern poetry is to return us, *pleased*, to the real, the un-dramatic and the ordinary.

If this works, it will be, I suspect, an intensely solipsistic experience. The poem will cast a spell on the mind and bring it to a pitch of perception and awareness. The listener, through the words of the 'modern poetry' that is to stand in place of God, is to hear the words and thereby hear him- or herself intimately, as in an emotional exchange in which 'two people' experience themselves becoming 'one' (surely a sexual reference here). The 'metaphysician in the dark' (the poet) produces sounds (words) which wholly contain the mind raised to a heightened understanding. Stevens wants us to think that the real is transformed by imagination in such a way that we grasp the real pleasurably in its poetical reordering. Against the accusation that art is an escape from the real, a preference for the imagined over the real (Plato), Stevens insists that a poetry that deals with reality does not remove us from it, but returns us there:

> There is, in fact, a world of poetry indistinguishable from the world in which we
> live, or, I ought to say, no doubt, from the world in which we shall come to live,

> since what makes the poet the potent figure that he is, or was, or ought to be, is that he creates the world to which we turn incessantly and without knowing it and that he gives to life the supreme fictions without which we are unable to conceive of it. ('The Noble Rider' 662)

Stevens's quest for the supreme fiction intends it to have a determinative power over us so that what we create imaginatively governs us by enchanting us with its version of the real. He continues in ways which surely evoke the experience described in 'Of Modern Poetry' of the insight and understanding which comes to us when the poem works:

> The deepening need for words to express our thoughts and feelings which, we are sure, are all the truth that we shall ever experience, having no illusions, makes us listen to words when we hear them, loving them and feeling them, makes us search the sound of them, for a finality, a perfection, an unalterable vibration, which is only within the power of the acutest poet to give them. ('The Noble Rider' 662–3)

We should not ignore the phrase 'all the truth that we shall ever experience, having no illusions', because it signals the only transcendence available to us in the imaginative spell of the 'supreme fiction', the transformation of the real through the act of imagination. We have a 'deepening need' for words that convey to us a 'finality' and 'perfection'. Just as earlier ages, Stevens suggests, devised images, dramas and styles of deity and gave us fictions in which we could believe because we assumed them to be real, so now we live within poetic, imaginative fictions that we know to be both true and fictive.

In Stevens's perspective, there is nothing outside the fictive against which the fictive can be judged in terms of accuracy or veracity, because the fictive is how the real comes to delight and please us. The real is available to us, presumably, only in the categories of the imagination. So on what basis can 'the real' have any distinct status apart from its mediation in 'the poetic' or 'the imaginative' or 'the fictive'? It is this very frustration, I think, and the ambiguities it contains, which prompts Stevens's repeated circling of the question of language, the imagination, fiction and 'the real'. And it is this frustration that haunts all his discussion of God, imagination and fiction. If the real is accessed – and its meanings created – by the activity of the imagination, is the real no more than what surfaces in our schemes of imagining, without a true engagement with *what is*? It is a poetic transcription of Kant's distinction between the *phenomena* with which we engage and the *noumena* that elude the mind. Is the world constituted by the real that is God, as Aquinas held? Or is the world constituted by the imagination's re-working of it? That is surely the central question and I think that Stevens never really settles it. There are echoes of this in his poem 'A Child Asleep in Its Own Life' with its evocation of 'one, unnamed, that broods / On all the rest, in heavy thought' (468).

Who is the 'one, unnamed' who broods on the old men 'in heavy thought'? Old men who have no reality except in the 'universe of that single mind', who is 'sole emperor' in relation to them, transcendent ('distant') yet immanent ('close') in ways that create music in the child's dreams ('the chords')? God, I suggest, is evoked all through this poem, but is not named, and this is deliberate. Stevens gives us the evocation of the divine creative presence, but with God formally occluded.

At this point, for contrast, it may be helpful to point to some ideas drawn from classical theism evoked by this poem. Aquinas's formula for God is simply *ipsum esse* (*Summa theologiae* 1, 4a, 2), 'actuality itself'. God is the real, and the true puzzle for Christian theology is not that God exists, but that everything else that is not God exists. All our meanings are ultimately grounded in the reality of God's making an order of being, a creaturely, freely constituted world that the mind, emerging from properties within that world, comes to explore and express. In this realist theological perspective, the world has an objective status which can be interpreted artistically, and if art enchants us, it is because the world, antecedently, is suffused with the beauty of the divine action. The enchantment of beauty then is not the consequence of aesthetically pleasing imaginings, as it seems to be in Stevens's aesthetic, but what happens when we come into contact with a world sustained by 'actuality', *ipsum esse*. The world as it comes from God is an extension of the expressiveness proper to the divine being itself, suffused with the qualities of goodness, truth and beauty that then provide the measure for artistic expression.

From this classical theistic perspective, the truth and beauty of the world are features of things as they come from God. The work of the poet or artist connects with the real as a finite 'making' (in words, objects and sounds) that corresponds to, evokes and in some measure participates in God's creation, his act of 'making the world be'. The divine intellect 'thinks' the world and, by thinking it, makes it, and the artist analogously 'thinks' a version of the world and makes it in his or her chosen medium. What goes on in Bach's mind might be the best analogy for what goes on in God's mind.

Stevens's poem 'A Child Asleep in Its Own Life', with its resonances of classical theism, is not intelligible outside this theological context. One of the strengths of this theistic account is that it views the world as constituted objectively in an order of truth and goodness, and this differs considerably from the presuppositions which guide Stevens's treatment. Stevens, I suggest, fails to do justice to God because he is intent on viewing God as an object of the imagination, rather than as the reality who cannot be imagined without betrayal and idolatry and whose reality secures the possibility of truth and actuality. Because he cannot find a way to secure the distinct status of the real, he is led to equate God, fiction and the imagination in ways that in the end undermine the possibility of the imaginative mind engaging truly with the real. By making God a product of human imaginings, his aesthetic, although it deals with what he insistently calls 'the real', is, in the end, not an engagement with 'what is', but with the mind's grasping of 'the real'. His aesthetic is rather an intellectually pleasurable, sometimes solipsistic enchantment of the mind through what it imagines as it re-works, re-configures, re-views the world via its imaginings. The role of the world, we might say, is to end up in the poet's mind as a source of satisfaction. It is this which brings Stevens closer to Rilke than to Aquinas.

The Christian doctrine of creation, by contrast, sees 'the real' not as finally reached after the poet has internalized it and re-worked it imaginatively, but as springing from God's thinking that thereby makes it. Stevens seems to expect the poet to do what classical theism thinks that God does: by thinking, to make real. He is expecting the poet to 'think the world', just as God is said to think and thereby create the real by speaking it ('And God said, "Let there be light," and there was light' [Gen. 1:3]). For Aquinas, the condition of there being a world at all lies in the originating movement of expressiveness proper to God (Word), accompanied by a no less originating movement of bewitching fascination (Love), as a consequence of which the world comes to be. The world is strangely an autonomous extension *ad extra* of the otherness, the generativity within God that achieves 'hypostatic' status. Aquinas treats the movement of knowledge and love within God as the origin, principle and exemplar of the procession of created things from God in their diversity; there is thus a crucial connection between God being triune (Father, Son and Spirit) and God being creator: 'The going out of the persons [of the Trinity] in the unity of essence is the cause of the going out of creatures in the diversity of essence' (*Commentary on the Sentences* 1, d.2, *divisio textus*). 'The eternal processions [of the persons in God] are the cause and reason [*causa et ratio*] of the production of creatures' (*Commentary on the Sentences* 1, d.14, q.1, a.1).[6]

---

6    The Cathedral in Palermo in Sicily was built by Arab workmen, and they were permitted to place an Arabic inscription from the Qur'an above one of the doors that read 'When God made the world, he did not make everything': there is, in other words, still the scope for human 'making' as a participation in the creation of a 'true, beautiful, good' world.

This enables Aquinas to secure creation as the object of divine goodness flowing directly, by extension almost, from the dynamic life of God. His argument is that if there is a *Word* in God, an exuberant expressiveness proper to the divine nature, and if there is also *Love*, the impulse of charity, goodness and self-gift, then within the generativity of the real (*ipsum esse*) arises the fictive making that produces the world. God's self-imaging Word – for Aquinas and Bonaventure, the Word is the image and model not only of God but also of the creatures that will come from God – is the condition of the world's existence. For Aquinas, then, the Word within God is the originating 'supreme fiction' that creates the world; the Word that 'wholly contains' the divine mind, 'below which it cannot descend, / Beyond which it has no will to rise' ('Of Modern Poetry' 219); no less truly, the Love within God is 'the finding of a satisfaction', God's articulation of his reality in a way that, when it is extended *ad extra*, makes the world to be pre-eminently an object of love. So, because there is a divine Word that, carried outwards, gives rise to things, our (lesser) words are ways in which we internalize and explore the things that bear the mark of divine goodness. When we create visual, verbal and auditory art, we enact and evoke, in ways proper to our nature, the divine act of imagining. Through art and poetry, we echo and extend the inventing that makes the world be in the first place. So for Aquinas and the classical Christian theism that follows him, the whole of the 'real' is the product of a 'supreme fictiveness' in God and that is why it is good, the locus of delight and pleasure. Stevens's exploration of the status of the fiction at the heart of reality is more theological than he may have realized.

## Works Cited

Bates, Milton J. 'Stevens and the Supreme Fiction'. In *The Cambridge Companion to Wallace Stevens*, ed. John N. Serio. Cambridge: Cambridge University.

Freud, Sigmund. *The Future of an Illusion*. Ed. Todd Dufresne. London: Broadview Editions, 2012.

Miles, Margaret R. *Reading for Life: Beauty, Pluralism and Responsibility*. New York: Continuum, 1997.

Richardson, Joan. *Wallace Stevens: The Later Years 1923–1955*. New York: Beech Tree Books, 1988.

Riddel, Joseph H. 'Wallace Stevens – "It Must Be Human"'. *The English Journal* 56 (April 1967): 525–34.

Rilke, R.M. 'Duino Elegy 7'. In *Selected Poems*. Oxford: World Classics, 2011, 159–65.

Serio, John N., ed. *The Cambridge Companion to Wallace Stevens*. Cambridge: Cambridge University Press, 2007.

Stevens, Wallace. 'A Child Asleep in Its Own Life'. In *Collected Poetry and Prose*, ed. Frank Kermode and Joan Richardson. New York: Library of America, 1997, 468.

—— *Collected Poetry and Prose*. Ed. Kermode and Richardson. New York: Library of America, 1997.

—— 'The Figure of the Youth as Virile Poet'. In *Collected Poetry and Prose*, ed. Kermode and Richardson, 666–85.

—— 'Imagination as Value'. In *Collected Poetry and Prose*, ed. Kermode and Richardson, 724–39.

—— 'It Must Be Abstract'. 'Notes Toward a Supreme Fiction'. In *Collected Poetry and Prose*, ed. Kermode and Richardson, 329–44.

—— 'It Must Give Pleasure'. 'Notes Toward a Supreme Fiction'. In *Collected Poetry and Prose*, ed. Kermode and Richardson, 344–52.

—— *Letters of Wallace Stevens*. Ed. Holly Stevens. London: Faber and Faber, 1967.

—— 'The Noble Rider and the Sounds of Words'. In *Collected Poetry and Prose*, ed. Kermode and Richardson, 643–65.

—— 'Of Modern Poetry'. In *Collected Poetry and Prose*, ed. Kermode and Richardson, 218–19.

—— 'Two or Three Ideas'. In *Collected Poetry and Prose*, ed. Kermode and Richardson, 839–50.

# PART III
## Inspiration: Poetry and Poetry Reading

# Chapter 8

# Poetry as Scripture, Poetry as Inspiration

Jay Parini

## The Idea of Scripture

Poetry is largely a secular enterprise, although the line of religious verse might be considered an obvious exception, a place wherein poems acquire a devotional aspect. We see this especially in poetry that falls into the meditative tradition, as in John Donne's *Holy Sonnets* or the sacramental poems of Gerard Manley Hopkins, where poetry becomes an exercise in natural incarnation, celebrating what he called 'the rise, the roll, the carol, the creation' in a way that the details of the universe inexorably speak to a Creator-God (Hopkins, *Poems* 70). In some cases, such as T.S. Eliot's 'Ash-Wednesday' or *Four Quartets*, the poetry itself echoes or gestures in the direction of liturgy, as the poems trace the evolution of a sacred vision in rhythms that assume a distinctly liturgical cadence. On the other hand, scripture – 'holy writ' – is simply poetry that has been deemed worthy of liturgical significance or useful in a spiritual way and was therefore canonized. It is worth thinking about the idea of poetry as scripture itself before thinking about secular poetry in this context.

Of course Jews and Christians often consider the Bible as the Word of God – a message beamed from above, embodied in a sequence of texts. In certain quarters, this belief is quite literal, with these scriptures regarded as emerging from God's mouth directly – an improbable notion that seems to obsess the evangelical wing of the Protestant church, especially in the United States. The origins of this belief lie in certain Old Testament passages, as in Deuteronomy 11:13–15, where it seems obvious that God is talking and one should, even must, listen and conform:

> So if you faithfully obey the commands I am giving you today – to love the Lord your God and to serve him with all your heart and with all your soul – then I will send rain on your land in its season, both autumn and spring rains, so that you may gather in your grain, new wine and olive oil. I will provide grass in the fields for your cattle, and you will eat and be satisfied. (New International Version)

It should be said that Jews – except in the most orthodox circles – have rarely been obsessed with a literal belief in the Hebrew scriptures, and the existence of a vast Rabbinic tradition of commentary has dampened the thirst for literal readings: too many conflicting readings exist for anyone to want to pin anything down. The belief in biblical inerrancy – a fairly recent phenomenon that takes literal readings to a level of absurdity – is not just a Protestant fundamentalist quirk, as we sometimes imagine. Pope Paul VI, rather famously, promulgated the dogmatic constitution *Dei Verbum* in 1965, affirming the Roman Catholic belief in Holy Scripture as the Word of God.

In chapter 3 of that document, entitled 'Sacred Scripture, Its Divine Inspiration and Interpretation', one gets a good summary of the notion:

> Those divinely revealed realities which are contained and presented in Sacred Scripture have been committed to writing under the inspiration of the Holy Spirit. For holy mother Church, relying on the belief of the Apostles (see John 20:31; 2 Tim. 3:16; 2 Peter 1:19–20, 3:15–16), holds that the books of both the Old and New Testaments in their entirety, with all their parts, are sacred and canonical because written under the inspiration of the Holy Spirit, they have God as their author and have been handed on as such to the Church herself. (Flannery, Ch. 3:11)

Such thinking ignores the historical origins of these texts – the books of the Old and New Testaments represent the work of many hands. The Gospels, for example, can hardly be said to belong to writers with the names attached to them: Matthew, Mark, Luke or John. These names stand in for a variety of authors, a quilt of narratives, parables and aphorisms that gathered in the decades after the death of Jesus. In the early centuries of Christianity, these particular Gospels acquired prominence in the religious practice of those who followed the teachings of Jesus, and many others were rejected; eventually, various councils confirmed the sequence and number of Gospels and established the canonical books that make up the New Testament itself. The Council of Trent of 1546 might be regarded as a vote of confidence for what was, until that moment, a beloved miscellany of writings. The letters of Paul, quite obviously, were simply that: letters. They were situational, written to a specific community and addressing particular problems. There is no sense within the writing that Paul for a moment imagined that anybody in the future would take his correspondence as God's literal word.

Looking back at the Old Testament, it seems useful in this context to think about the Book of Psalms. This is simply an anthology of Hebrew lyrics from a certain era, an early version of some *Oxford Book of Hebrew Poems*. One finds here 150 poems that seem fairly consistent in manner, subscribing to a particular form, the so-called praise poem, which employs similar types of repetition and parallelism. They were lyrics, probably sung musical accompaniment. A number of them celebrate important occasions, such as weddings or coronations. Others are lamentations of one sort or another – a vein of poetry that continues to thrive, as poets seem perpetually out of sorts with their world. A number of the Hebrew psalms are clearly instructional, making legal points. They were collected over a lengthy period and represent the work of many hands, although tradition has it that David wrote them. But this David is no more real than Matthew, Mark, Luke or John.

*Dei Verbum* turns heavily on the notion of inspiration, and it is worth pondering what this actually means. The term 'inspiration' itself has clear root meanings: to inspire is to breathe in, to take in the air around you, to absorb it, to give it back. *Spiritus* in Latin means breath or wind, but it also means soul or spirit, depending on the degree of literalness you seek. When Christians talk about scripture as the inspired Word of God, they mean that God breathed life into certain words, thus separating them from the rest of our words.

I myself have no wish to privilege biblical poems, as in the Psalms of David, over secular poems. And this is not to diminish the weight of sacred scriptures. I happen to spend quite a lot of time with the Christian Bible, and find the practice of reading bits and pieces in the liturgy of the Church both useful and, at times, dislocating, as the nature of the liturgy is such that one de-contextualizes passages. This often works quite well, as certain passages are remarkably self-contained, though it is always good to keep reminding oneself that in any liturgical setting we are hearing fragments of poetry – sometimes narrative poetry – ripped out of context.

Those of us who dwell in the English language should feel blessed by the 47 translators of the King James Bible, who (400 years ago) had a peculiar gift for phrasing – although they drew on earlier inspired translators, such as William Tyndale, an English contemporary of Martin Luther, who undertook his own translation of the Bible with astonishing verve. The cadences of the King James version ring in our heads, as they have rung in the heads of poets down the centuries, shaping their syntax and diction, their way of using metaphors. It is hard to imagine poetry in English without the language of the King James, which forms a kind of root-work from which later verses could grow.

This is as true for American poets as for British. For example, consider a tiny poem by Walt Whitman, 'As Adam Early in the Morning':

> As Adam early in the morning,
>
> Walking forth from the bower refresh'd with sleep;
>
> Behold me where I pass – hear my voice – approach,
>
> Touch me – touch the palm of your hand to my Body as I pass:
>
> Be not afraid of my Body.

One hears the biblical cadences in the balanced syntax of those lines and in the diction, as in 'walking forth' or 'bower', or in the poet's commanding of the reader to 'Behold' or 'Touch'. Those cadences also inhabit the odd final injunction: 'Be not afraid of my body.' Even in the mid-nineteenth century, one surely would have said 'Do not be afraid', rather than 'Be not afraid'. Whitman, everywhere in *Leaves of Grass*, his huge compendium of verse, assumes a prophet's tone: prophetic in the sense of one who speaks on behalf of God, who calls attention to things that are out of sorts, who interprets the will of God for the people. The notion of a prophet as one who foretells the future is a later wrinkle, and not an essential one. A prophet is like Adam in the garden, naming the world in all its bright particulars. As Emerson noted in his essay, 'The Poet', the poet names something because he sees it, or comes 'one step nearer to things' than any other (297). Towards the end of the essay, he concludes: 'The condition of true naming, on the poet's part, is his resigning himself to the divine aura which breathes through forms, and accompanying that' (298).

## The Sacrament of Poetry

I suspect that poetry, as a sacramental art, has a great deal to do with an Emersonian appreciation of the spirit (call it divine, perhaps) breathing through the visible forms of the universe. That appreciation underlies such famous lines as the opening of Psalm 121: 'I will lift up mine eyes unto the hills, from whence cometh my help.' In fact, there is not a great deal of natural detail in Hebrew scripture; nor is there much in Homer. It is with Shakespeare, with German and English poetry of the eighteenth century, or with the great Romantic poets, that one begins to see nature clarified, coming alive with bright particulars, properly embodied.

In his prefaces to Shakespeare, Alexander Pope certainly regarded Shakespeare as an almost divine font of wisdom: 'The poetry of Shakespeare was inspiration indeed; he is not so much an Imitator, as an instrument of Nature; and 'tis not so just to say he speaks from her, as that she speaks through him' (184). Yet if Shakespeare certainly counts among the most particularizing – and therefore inspired – of poets, one returns to the ancient Greeks and Romans for poets who regarded themselves as inspired. Classical poets often imagined that the poem was delivered from above, from a source beyond the natural reach of the poet's grasp. The poet became a vehicle or transmitter of a message. He or she wrote in a state of rapture. In the end, the poet looked at the work and did not know where it came from or how it journeyed through his or her mouth. Socrates, for instance, told Ion that poets write because they are 'inspired and possessed' (Plato, *Ion* 533c–534b).

In the German lyric, especially after Goethe, God himself became the animating quality of the universe in idealistic philosophy. Even Kant, of course, presupposed a divine source. Yet the Romantics, in England and America, tended to strip all notions of higher power from the equation, although they maintained their reverence for nature, and the idea of poetry as inspiration dominated their thinking about how poems come into being. For Wordsworth, poetry is almost certainly a form of secular scripture.

Nature, for Wordsworth, is a holy presence, the manifestation of spirit. And *The Prelude* is essentially a poem of incarnation. The world of the child is unmediated, closer to God, and closer to nature. And nature teaches the child, as well as the man, about life, thus humanizing him. As Geoffrey Hartman puts it:

> If nature fails, the child's development is either arrested, and he becomes an idiot whose 'life is with God,' or a premature adult, doomed to cynicism or alienation. If nature succeeds, the child is organically ready to be humanized, and humanization is the second developmental step covered by *The Prelude*. The two steps are, of course, interrelated: and the road from 'love of nature' to 'love of man,' even though built, in Wordsworth's case, on a strong and sensuous foundation, is so precarious that its charting occupies the greater part of his secular poem. (16)

I would quarrel with the notion of *The Prelude* as a secular poem, however, in that Wordsworth's nature is anything but disconnected from the spirit. It flows from, and returns to, a divine source, and there is that avowedly sacramental quality to the writing, its invitation to take a place in the reader's life once occupied exclusively by scripture.

I often re-read *The Prelude*, especially in its 1805 iteration, and when I do I think of it as a kind of Holy Writ, something that could be canonized by a future council of some kind. Although Wordsworth's great poem reveals a deeply ingrained humanism, there is never much doubt about the presence of God, as toward the end of Book XIII (1805 version), where the poet praises his friend Coleridge for assisting him in naturalizing his 'supernaturalism':

> And so the deep enthusiastic joy,
> The rapture of the Halleluja sent
> From all that breathes and is, was chasten'd, stemm'd,
> And balanced by a Reason which indeed
> Is reason, duty and pathetic truth:
> And God and Man divided, as they ought,
> Between them the great system of the world
> Where Man is sphered, and which God animates. (236)

At least in this earlier version, Wordsworth regards the world as thoroughly animated by God, and all human activity reached into the divine realm, involving the 'great system of the world'. In his poetry, world and word meet, assuming a transformation that, at its base, is nearly liturgical.

## Poetry and the Production of Scripture

In dealing with poetry as scripture – as an extension of Holy Writ, in other words – one brushes against a commonplace of literary and historical thinking, as represented in *Natural Supernaturalism* by M.H. Abrams, where he writes: 'It is a historical commonplace that the course of Western thought since the Renaissance has been one of progressive secularization' (13). This may hold true if one is thinking within certain frameworks, which are largely political. But when dealing with poetic language, there is, to me, no sense in which this statement yields much in the way of meaning. Poetry is language put under pressure, language drawn to the world in such a way that the representation of the world in language is revelatory. Indeed, that most secular of poets, Wallace Stevens, once wrote that 'Description is revelation' (339). In saying that, he put his finger on the core of what I am talking about here, the idea of poetry as a kind of scripture, whatever its theological frame.

Taking Gerard Manley Hopkins as an example, one goes to the centre of language as incarnation. His *Journal* is full of moments of description that give way to revelation, and which prepare us for reading his poems. It was in May 1870 that he wrote his well-known passage on bluebells: 'I do not think I have ever seen anything more beautiful than the bluebell I have been looking at. I know the beauty of our Lord by it' (*Journals and Papers* 199). He goes on, attempting to get at the specific aspects of a particular bluebell and its inherent glory:

Its inscape is mixed of strength and grace, like an ash tree. The head is strongly drawn over backwards and arched down like a cutwater drawing itself back from the line of the keel. The lines of the bells strike and overlie this, rayed but not symmetrically, some lie parallel. They look steely against the paper, the shades lying in the bells and behind the cockled petal-ends and nursing up the precision of their distinctness, the petal-ends themselves being delicately lit. (199)

In the precision of his descriptive language, its attentiveness to unique forms in nature (embodied in that eccentric coinage of his, 'inscape'), Hopkins achieves a concreteness that ushers us to the heart of his poetry. That concreteness illumines poems such as 'The Starlight Night', which opens:

> Look at the stars! Look, look up at the skies!
>> O look at all the fire-folk sitting in the air!
>> The bright boroughs, the circle-citadels there! (Hopkins, *Poems* 26)

Here, as so often in Hopkins, the poet asks us to 'bid' for the something desired, to purchase the glory of a landscape. The word 'bid' connects by etymology to *bidden*, the Middle English word for prayer, in the sense of begging or 'putting in a bid' for mercy or access to God. In a sense, each of his poems constitutes a bid of this kind. We can read Hopkins as scripture without making many adjustments. 'God's Grandeur', for instance, aspires to the condition of Davidic psalm:

> The world is charged with the grandeur of God.
>> It will flame out, like shining from shook foil;
>> It gathers to a greatness, like the ooze of oil
> Crushed. Why do men then now not reck his rod?
> Generations have trod, have trod, have trod;
>> And all is seared with trade; bleared, smeared with
>> toil;
> And wears man's smudge and shares man's smell:
>> the soil
> Is bare now, nor can foot feel, being shod.
> And for all this, nature is never spent;
>> There lives the dearest freshness deep down things;
> And though the last lights off the black West went
>> Oh, morning, at the brown brink eastward, springs——
> Because the Holy Ghost over the bent
>> World broods with warm breast and with ah! bright wings. (*Poems* 26)

The poem is a praise poem, of course, and yet it builds to the astounding image of the Holy Ghost like a great bird, brooding over this fallen world that nevertheless rises each day with dawn. God's 'grandeur' flashes through the world, making itself evident, even though men refuse to 'reck his rod', or pay attention to his strictures, his heed. The poem seems on every level to have a design on the reader that seems apposite to what psalmists of ancient Israel had in mind: poems that were meant to kindle the affections, to draw the reader closer to God.

### Reading Poetry as *lectio divina*

Now Hopkins is writing in a self-consciously religious vein, whereas most poets do not – especially not in the past century. Of course poetry often reaches into areas that could be called 'spiritual' – one of those nebulous and overused words that seems almost beyond concise definition. What interests us here is not so much the specific spiritual content of poetry but our way of reading poems as sacred, aspiring to a kind of numinous affect. And what this entails is our sense of reading as *lectio divina* or 'holy reading', which goes back many centuries, with its origins in Benedictine practice. This practice involves reading with, as St Paul said in Romans, one's 'mouth or heart'. It is a matter of saying the words reverently, slowly and perhaps aloud: thus allowing the meaning to drift forward. Undoubtedly, this is the best way to read any poetry.

The practice of *lectio divina* interested Guigo II, a Carthusian monk of the twelfth century, and he isolated various stages in the process, including *lectio*, *meditatio*, *oratio* and *contemplatio*. One begins quite simply by reading, preferably aloud. The sound of the words is important, as meaning will inhere in those sounds, and they will have a uniqueness reflected by the quality of expression, diction, syntax and so forth. After one has read the poem aloud, lingering over each phrase, one begins the process of meditation, which involves thinking about the meaning of the language, its nuances and after-effects. It would be rare for anyone reading a secular poem to move into *oratio* or prayer; but if one thinks of prayer as merely intense listening, that does not seem a stretch of the imagination.

Poetry gestures in the direction of silence. In some ways, it is an organized version of that silence. As Eliot writes in the fifth section of 'Burnt Norton': 'Words, after speech, reach / Into the silence'. It is the pattern of the words, the way they lie on the page or assemble in the mouth, that creates the possibility of stillness. In the practice of *lectio divina*, the fourth stage in the process opens into contemplation, which is ultimately a form of connection to God or, perhaps, the deepest layers of human consciousness, where the mind of an individual reader connects with the collective mind. At the very least, this fourth stage (*contemplatio*) involves a sense of quiet absorption in layered meanings.

I will end with a poem by Mary Oliver, a contemporary American poet who has written with inspired simplicity and grace about the natural world. I would like to look at this poem not so much as secular verse but as a text that can be read deeply and, perhaps, usefully as well in the tradition of *lectio divina*. The poem is 'White Flowers' and it begins: 'Last night / in the fields / I lay down in the darkness / to think about death'. The poet instead falls asleep, 'as if in a vast and sloping room' that fills with flowers opening all summer. When she finally wakes, the morning light is 'just slipping' in front of the stars and the speaker finds herself 'covered / with blossoms'. She wonders if she has slipped down into some 'sleep-sharpened affinity' with the depths or whether that 'green energy' has risen from the earth 'like a wave / and curled over' the poet. She concludes by saying that never before in her life had she felt 'so near / that porous line' where her own body was 'done with / and the root and the stems and the flowers / began' (58).

This beautiful poem works to locate the connections between nature and spirit, between the human body and the body of the earth. It is a poem in the long tradition of *ars moriendi*: the art of dying. In this tradition, the subject tries to learn how to die well, with death not as something to fear but as something inviting, a movement, that is, from one state of being into another.

I have read this poem aloud to myself many times, allowing the alliterative moments to suck at the words, as in the movement from 'warm fields' to the next line, 'When I woke ...' Oliver has something of Theodore Roethke's density in describing the natural world when she writes about 'diving down / under the sugary vines'. I also think of Roethke when she talks about feeling 'plush' or 'slippery' as well as 'empty' in the arms of the earth. The 'green energy' that she describes is difficult to assess, or describe; it refers, I believe, to the natural wave of life, the spiritual radiance that shines through everything that is seen in a proper light, which is to say the light of eternity.

One can move with this poem, and so many good contemporary poems, as if through a prayer. That prayer is a bid for mercy. It is a bid for peace, for stillness, for the ability to look without fear or expectation, accurately and clearly, into the heart of light. The stage of contemplation comes in the after-reading, in the glow of focused attention, as one listens beyond the words themselves, or through them, into the silence.

After all, a word is a gesture, a finger pointing at the moon. And it is important not to keep one's eye too fixed on the finger alone. Sometimes one asks for the moon itself.

## Works Cited

Abrams, M.H. *Natural Supernaturalism*. New York: Norton, 1971.

Eliot, T.S. *Collected Poems, 1909–1962*. Centenary edition. New York: Harcourt Brace, 1991.

Emerson, Ralph Waldo. 'The Poet'. In *The Essential Writings of Ralph Waldo Emerson*, with an introduction by Mary Oliver, ed. Brooks Atkinson. New York: Random House, 2000, 287–306.

Flannery, Austin, OP, ed. *Vatican Council II: Constitutions, Decrees, Declarations*. Northport: Costello, 1996.

Hartman, Geoffrey H. *The Unremarkable Wordsworth*. Minneapolis: University of Minnesota Press, 1987.

Hopkins, G.M. *The Journals and Papers of Gerard Manley Hopkins*. Ed. H. House and G. Storey. Oxford: Oxford University Press, 1950.

—— *Poems of Gerard Manley Hopkins*. Ed. Robert Bridges. London: Humphrey Milford, 1918.

Oliver, Mary. *New and Selected Poems*. Boston: Beacon, 1992.

Plato. *Ion*. Trans. Benjamin Jowett. New York: Scribner's Sons, 1871.

Pope, Alexander. 'Preface to Shakespeare'. In *The Major Works*, ed. Pat Rogers. New York: Oxford University Press, 2006, 184.

Stevens, Wallace. 'Description without Place'. In *Collected Poems*. New York: Knopf, 1954, 339.

Whitman, Walt. 'As Adam Early in the Morning'. In *Leaves of Grass*: *The Walt Whitman Archive*. Accessed 3 March 2011. <http://whitmanarchive.org/published/LG/>.

Wordsworth, William. *The Prelude or Growth of a Poet's Mind* (1805). A new edition by Stephen Gill. Oxford: Oxford University Press, 1970.

# Chapter 9

# The Poet as 'Worldmaker': T.S. Eliot and the Religious Imagination

## Dominic Griffiths

> All creatures want to utter God in all their works; they all come as close as they can in uttering him, and yet they cannot utter him. Whether they wish it or not, whether they like it or not, they all want to utter God, and yet he remains unuttered. (Meister Eckhart 204)

T.S. Eliot's later poetry is, to quote Meister Eckhart, an attempt to 'utter God'. His works are religious, not only in that they draw symbols extensively from the great religious traditions, but also in a broader sense; this, as I will argue, is the sense in which all art is religious, in as much as it unfolds worlds, opens possibilities and enacts the will to hope. To argue this position I will engage with the work of Martin Heidegger and Paul Ricoeur. From Heidegger I will discuss the meaning of 'worldmaking' and from Ricoeur develop an understanding of the poetic and religious imagination. Both these thinkers offer us rich ontological and phenomenological insights into the nature of art and worldmaking.

Heidegger defines the world as 'the ever non-objective to which we are subject as long as the paths of birth and death ... keep us transported into Being'. He writes that the world is 'not the mere collection of the countable or uncountable, familiar and unfamiliar things that are at hand ... The *world worlds*' (*Basic Writings* 170). What Heidegger offers in these brief comments is a way of conceiving of the world which, to use his term, 'destructs' the history of modern philosophy and its rigid Cartesian dualism between the subject and object. Heidegger wants to draw our attention to a more 'authentic' experience of the world – one which is not characterized as a separation from Being, but rather a *being* with Being, which in English translation is captured in the hyphenated phrase, being-in-the-world. Thus the genuine 'world' that Heidegger conceives of is the 'ever non-objective' that encompasses us and our existence, and so transcends the 'mere collection' of things.

Properly understood, the world does not offer itself to us as a material collection of objects of contemplation and explanation; rather, it keeps us 'transported' and bound into the shaping of human existence itself. When we alter the world we are not manipulating a separate object, but changing our experience of reality. The expression 'the *world worlds*' conveys this by drawing attention to the use of the word 'world' as both noun and verb. For Heidegger, this kind of neologism emphasizes a particular quality of a word which may be concealed in ordinary usage. We think of the 'world' as a collection of things, of geography, of peoples, and this gives the ordinary impression of the world as a material thing made up of objects. What Heidegger's tautology draws out is the more authentic experience of the world as something that is happening, that is unfolding and projecting itself, through human becoming, into a future. This future is the 'ever non-objective' because its existence is a potential that always remains undisclosed and yet is always constantly unfolding. As we project ourselves into it, it recedes always away – and thus we remain ever subject to the 'paths of birth and death' that the world offers.

A significant part of Heidegger's philosophy is concerned with re-engaging our existence with and attuning it to a more conscious recognition of this mysterious, yet fundamental, fact about reality, which he calls the 'mystery' of Being (*Discourse on Thinking* 56). Heidegger's later work proposes that a central way in which we can reinvigorate this attunement in ourselves is through the open encounter with the artwork. The artwork offers a genuine encounter with the true nature of a thing by revealing it within its broader horizon of meaning. This horizon reveals that this thing, this object, is, in fact, no mere thing, but a fragment of Being itself. Placed within the space that the artwork grants, the thing is illuminated, and this illumination reveals a *world*.

Central to this experience that we encounter in the artwork of revelation, of *worlding*, is the role of imagination, and to explore this role I will draw on the work of Ricoeur. In his 'Lectures on Imagination', he argues that it is through 'productive imagination' that individuals can gain access to a world transformed from their own.[1] The productive imagination can transform existing categories, drawing from current reality while at the same time producing something without an original; 'something from nowhere' (Taylor 98). This split between ordinary and imaginative reality Ricoeur calls an 'epoché'; essentially a suspension of ordinary experience to allow a space or openness for imaginative possibilities to become manifest ('The Metaphorical Process' 154; *The Rule of Metaphor* 248). Part of the aim of this chapter is to explore this moment of epoché by focusing on examples which demonstrate it. Ricoeur ascribes four categories to productive imagination. First is the domain of social and cultural imagination which he

---

[1]    Ricoeur's 'Lectures on Imagination', presented in 1975, are unpublished. However, Taylor provides an overview of the lectures which I refer to extensively.

relates specifically to the idea of utopia. The second domain is epistemological imagination, and pertains to theoretical models available to science. The last two are of particular interest to this argument as they concern poetic imagination and religious symbols (Taylor 94–7). The first part of the chapter will explore the nature of poetic imagination and the second part religious symbols.

Ricoeur writes that poetic imagination 'unfolds new dimensions of reality' (Taylor 97). This unfolding potential is made possible through language itself, particularly metaphor, which can alter reality in new and unexpected ways. Though his theories offer us a 'logic of discovery' which allows for the analysis of how metaphor works, he maintains that there remains a 'kernel of opacity', a measure of impenetrability which defies full explanation (Taylor 98). This elusive quality of language continually beckons us, yet, in the words of Eliot, leaves 'one still with the intolerable wrestle / With words and meaning' (*Complete Poems and Plays* 179, 'East Coker' II.20–1).[2] Because of this measure of impenetrability, metaphoric truth is thus not a question of conformity or 'adequation' in terms of how successfully one thing conforms to or confirms itself in comparison with another. Rather, for Ricoeur, truth is 'manifestation', as Heidegger also believes; it is a revealing or unconcealing of being which offers a new disclosure of reality, effacing itself 'for the sake of what is said about reality' (Taylor 98).

Poetic language is no less concerned with reality than other forms of language – scientific language, for example – that seem to be more directly referential. Rather, its 'complex strategy' involves a 'suspension and seemingly an abolition of ordinary reference attached to descriptive language' (Ricoeur, 'The Metaphorical Process' 153). This is the effacement of poetic language, the sacrifice of its own meaning, in order to grant the epochal space for imaginative possibilities to emerge. Yet, through this suspension of direct reference to everyday things, poetry makes a 'primordial reference' to 'the deep structures of reality to which we are related as mortals who are born into this world and who dwell in it for a while' (Ricoeur, 'The Metaphorical Process' 153). For Ricoeur, this 'split-reference' is essentially the distinction in which 'ordinary' language, in poetic form, opens a new dimension in imagination which offers the 'projection of new possibilities of re-describing the world' ('The Metaphorical Process' 154).

To explain how poetic imagination works more fully, I will offer some examples. The first comes from Heidegger himself in the 1935 essay 'The Origin of the Work of Art', in which he discusses the 1886 painting by Van Gogh of

---

[2]     All quotations from *Four Quartets* come from the *Complete Poems and Plays*, and are referenced by page number, followed by quartet name, movement number in roman numerals and line number/s in arabic numerals. Attentive readers of this chapter should have a copy of the poem open.

a pair of shoes, which Heidegger is said to have seen at a 1930 exhibition in Amsterdam.[3] We can stare at this painting as a depiction of things, objects, equipment. There is nothing to it. It is just a painting of some shoes, the shoes, for Heidegger, of a peasant woman, or perhaps, for other interpreters, Van Gogh's own shoes. If we just stare at them indifferently, as cast-off objects that we might see next to a dustbin, then they are not even equipment, merely discarded things of no value; junk. But the painting beckons; it calls us to go beyond the mere thingness of the object. This is the *work* of art, work in the verb sense. The painting, by its very existence, discloses this 'particular being in its Being' (*Basic Writings* 164). In the artwork, to use Heidegger's language, the truth of beings has set itself to work; art, he says, is truth 'setting itself to work' (*Basic Writings* 164).

As with all great artwork, it is difficult to fully articulate this truth because of the 'kernel of opacity', which compels us to both experience and interpret the work, and yet transcends our attempts to offer any final, definitive meaning. Nonetheless Heidegger ventures to describe what this painting reveals to him about the world it contains. He writes that from

> the dark opening of the worn insides of the shoes the toilsome tread of the worker stares forth. In the stiffly rugged heaviness of the shoes there is the accumulated tenacity of her slow trudge through the far-reaching and ever uniform furrows of the field swept by a raw wind. On the leather lies the dampness and richness of the soil. Under the sole stretches the loneliness of the field-path as evening falls. In the shoes vibrates the silent call of the earth, its quiet gift of the ripening grain and its unexplained self-refusal in the fallow desolation of the wintry fields. (*Basic Writings* 159)

In this famous description, Heidegger tries to evoke a truth that the painting expresses for him. To do this evidently requires an imaginative engagement with the artwork. In this phenomenological 'nearness' to the work, we find ourselves 'suddenly somewhere else than we usually tend to be' (*Basic Writings* 161). The experience is one of 'transport' and 'enchantment' (*Contributions to Philosophy* 48–9), where the world shows up 'as a holy place' and the things in it as 'radiant, charismatic, sacred beings' (Young 52). To explain this more technically, we can refer back to Ricoeur's notion of the 'epoché', the split between ordinary and imaginative reality which the encounter with the artwork can bring about.

---

[3]   There remains a question here as to whether he actually did see the painting. See Thompson 107–9 for an overview of this issue.

Evidently Heidegger's own description of what the painting depicts is made possible through his imaginative engagement with it, allowing an original hermeneutic self-disclosure to emerge.

This enigmatic, original perceiving of the potential meaning of the painting transports us, via Heidegger's interpretation, into the imagined life of the peasant woman. This is a life structured according to the needs of those who dwell closely with the rhythms of the earth, attentive to its change in season and the needs of the soil in order to allow it to produce its 'quiet gift' (*Basic Writings* 159). A vital requirement of this life is sturdy, stout shoes. For the peasant woman, the shoes are an everyday object, taken for granted. Probably, as with most equipment that surrounds us, the shoes only become conspicuous to her as things when their nature as equipment, as use-objects, fails – when the sole of one is worn through or the lace snaps. The artwork transforms the shoes into objects brimming with a startling mystery, a hiddenness which offers its discovery to anyone willing to be in 'nearness' to the artwork. When this happens, the painting speaks (*Basic Writings* 161) and its speaking reveals a world. This world is not contained in the exhibition room; it is not, as both Heidegger and Eliot claim, even part of the artist's intention.[4] Rather it is a dialogic moment that exists between the viewer and the artwork. Heidegger's verbal account of his encounter with the painting attempts to express this moment, to illustrate how the unfolding of truth happens in the artwork.

For this discussion, following these insights from Heidegger and Ricoeur, I will focus on some of Eliot's later poetry to show how he too is a 'worldmaker', and how an encounter with his poetry can reveal the truth of a particular world. In the opening lines of 'East Coker', the second of his *Four Quartets*, Eliot draws our attention to a thing, a house (*Complete Poems* 177): 'In my beginning is my end. In succession / Houses rise and fall, crumble, are extended, / Are removed, destroyed, restored' (I.1–3). Houses, in a normal lifetime, seem to be mostly solid objects, lasting equipment. They do not wear out like a pair of shoes, but rather they are built to have the quality of endurance, to outlast their builders, possibly to shelter and provide dwelling for many generations of human beings. A house is an everyday object, like a shoe; it is just there, where we saw it the day before. But Eliot, like Van Gogh, uses the artwork to transform the thing, and to reveal a depth to it that is mostly hidden in everyday existence. 'Houses live and die', the passage continues, 'there is a time for building / And a time for living and for generation', but also a time for decay, when the wind will 'break the loosened pane' and 'shake the tattered arras woven with a silent motto'

---

[4]    See Heidegger, *Discourse on Thinking* 44, and Eliot, *Selected Prose* 43–4.

(I.9–13). The passage links the object 'house' metaphorically – more precisely, metonymically – to the generations of a family line. The double meaning creates a complex symbol which interweaves the life of a house with those who dwell there. To see this is to recognize, like Van Gogh's shoes, that a house expresses a world.

The passage captures an intersection of two temporal cycles. One is the linear cycle of a single life, which is finite and marked by its natality and death: 'In my beginning is my end' ('East Coker' I.1, 14). This sentiment is echoed in Heidegger's essay, where he writes that the 'beginning already contains the end latent within itself' (*Basic Writings* 201). This linear cycle falls within the broader temporal cycle of human dwelling, 'a time for living and for generation' ('East Coker' I.10). While the individual is born and dies, the cycle of regeneration extends from before the past and beyond the future of one person. We live in a constant 'succession' ('East Coker' I.1), a renewing genealogy. The things we create, even those things that will outlive an individual life, are also part of this cycle and it is this interweaving of beings, marked by time, which is both captivating and evocative in the passage.

These lines, like the painting, hold a mystery which they beckon us to discover. Through 'a nearness' with the words, we are invited and compelled to move beyond them. We experience, in Eliot's language, 'the sudden illumination' (*Complete Poems* 186, 'Dry Salvages' II.44). We find ourselves, as Heidegger writes, 'suddenly somewhere else'. Ricoeur's epochal distinction between ordinary and imaginative reality explains how phenomenologically the poetic language and the productive imagination move us beyond the words themselves, connecting us to those 'deep structures' which shape human dwelling ('The Metaphorical Process' 153). Perhaps this brief suspension finds readers contemplating the unimagined, unknowable ancestors who begot them, trying, as Eliot says later in the poem, to search 'past and future' (*Complete Poems* 189, 'Dry Salvages' V.16) for a deeper clue as to who they are. Or readers imagine the endless cycle of building and destruction that marks human existence, a constant, ever-renewing and necessary violence that we perpetuate to make the earth habitable. Houses, like humans, live and die, and the passage communicates this to us while at the same time offering us the opportunity to contemplate it for ourselves.

Thus imagination gives us the ability to 'produce new kinds of assimilation and to produce them not above the differences ... but in spite of and through the differences' (Taylor 99). Eliot, interweaving the meanings of the 'house' in terms of both thing and genealogy, produces a new, original assimilation. The two senses stand side by side for us, the import of each enriched by the presence of the other. As Ricoeur says, this creates 'imaginative interrelation across difference' which produces 'new metaphoric resemblance' (Taylor 99). These resemblances are not contained in each thing separate from the other, but together are 'transformative of existing reality' (Taylor 98).

Arguably present in Eliot's mind when he wrote this passage in 1939 was the foreboding anxiety of imminent war and a despair that Western civilization was, for the second time in his life, inexorably drawing towards its destruction. These opening lines of 'East Coker' are somewhat eerily prescient of what was to follow in the year that the quartet was published; on 7 September 1940 began the sustained bombing of English cities by the Luftwaffe. Yet, in spite of this bleak time, critics regard 'East Coker' as the most optimistic of the *Quartets*, a poem that made an 'extraordinary impact' at the 'darkest moment of the war' (Gordon 353). The reason for this is arguably because the most important message in *Four Quartets*, and particularly 'East Coker', is the sense of hope that, even in the face of adversity, pervades the human condition; a realistic hope tempered by the wisdom gained from the disappointment and anguish of living a finite life.

In the second part of this essay, I will reflect on the significance of the 'religious imagination' in Eliot's poetry. The working of this imagination, though evident in his pre-conversion poetry, becomes explicit after his conversion to Anglo-Catholicism in 1927. In defining 'religious imagination', I again take guidance from Ricoeur, who discusses how the productive imagination contains a religious dimension. Once this definition is developed, I shall consider it in light of some passages from *Four Quartets*.

Ontologically central for Ricoeur's philosophical anthropology is human capability, which is essentially the open possibility that humans have to act in the world. This openness exists primarily because of language, which makes all other human capabilities meaningful (Ricoeur, 'Ethics' 280). As in Heidegger's thought, our ability to act in and upon the unfolding world makes temporality a central feature of Ricoeur's philosophical anthropology. Human existence, as the site of possibility, is futural in its orientation and 'constantly projecting itself in front of itself towards a possible way of being' (Vanhoozer 7). Imagination is pivotal in how this projection can come to be, because it allows us phenomenological access to an idea of ourselves which has not yet been manifest in ordinary reality. This means that a human being is not 'limited to the here and now, that is, to present actuality' (Vanhoozer 7). Rather, we exist as beings in the midst of our finitude, carrying the past with us as we shape the future. As Eliot puts it in the compelling opening of 'East Coker', 'In my beginning is my end' (*Complete Poems* 177, I.1).

For Ricoeur, human capability, the ability to act meaningfully in the world, aside from having a temporal character, is also shaped by our innate 'originary goodness' ('Ethics' 284). Here Ricoeur is explicit about the structure of human ontology, which he understands in the biblical sense as 'creation, createdness' ('Ethics' 284). Our orientation to the good is rooted in our being, as an originary motivation. To act for the good is to strive to realize human capability in its fullest potential. Life, from natality, has already been given the potential for fullness; it is already possessed of a 'surplus of being' which is 'nothing other than *possibility*' and the reason humanity can hope (Vanhoozer 7). To quote Kevin Vanhoozer in this context: 'We are not as we shall be' (7). Thus hope is part of the human condition and shapes human capability, which is motivated by a will to transform existence.

Central to how this 'surplus of being' is expressed, for Ricoeur, is through poetic language, which provides the most complex and sophisticated way of responding to this plenitude by offering its own 'surplus of meaning', particularly through the techniques of narrative and metaphor (Vanhoozer 8). This is clearly evident in the above passage from 'East Coker' which, though relatively short, offers an abundance of rich complex interpretation and reflection. For Ricoeur these techniques allow us to express the possible, and it is in this realm of possibility where hope can be made manifest. This draws us back to the theme of the productive imagination, but especially to the last of the four types of productive imagination, namely, religious symbolism. It is particularly here, in this imaginary space, where Ricoeur locates the will to hope. He argues that it is primarily in this sphere where goodness is fully expressed, writing that 'all religions are different attempts in different language games to recover the ground of goodness, to liberate, so to say, the enslaved freedom, the enslaved capability' ('Ethics' 284).

Thus religious discourse offers us a language of hope and freedom; the metaphors and narratives of religious events are the symbolic and imaginative 'schematization of liberation' which allows us to recognize and to act on the ontological, originary goodness rooted in us. For Ricoeur, a powerful exemplar of this is the 'Christian symbol of the perfect man ready to give his life for the sake of his friends' ('Ethics' 285). This belief offers Christians 'freedom in the light of hope', essentially an understanding and acceptance of existence lived in sure knowledge of the Resurrection, an event of promise and hope (Ricoeur, *Essays* 105). Thus hope, the 'passion for the possible', is allied with imagination, for it is the power of imagination which offers the possibility of renewal, by granting new possibilities of meaning and action (Ricoeur, *Essays* 106).

For Ricoeur, imagination has a metaphysical role that goes beyond the 'simple projection of vital, unconscious, or repressed desires' (*History* 126–7). Instead it offers a 'prospective and explorative function' for envisioning what is humanly possible. He goes so far as to argue for the 'redemption through imagination' where 'hope works to the fullest human capacity' (*History* 127). Though these images of reconciliation are 'myths', they offer a vision of a shared human destiny, and are the starting points for decisive change in the world. He writes that 'every *real* conversion is first a revolution at the level of our directive images. By changing his imagination, man alters his existence' (*History* 127).

As mentioned earlier, pivotal for Ricoeur's philosophical anthropology is the centrality of temporality and possibility in shaping human existence. Here he stands in the shadow of Heidegger's *Being and Time*, taking up Heidegger's project of describing temporality but also, as we have already seen, transforming it by offering an ontology grounded in goodness (Vanhoozer 25). This transformation becomes even more apparent when we consider the concept of hope, for which, Ricoeur complains, Heidegger's account leaves little room (Vanhoozer 25). It is worth reflecting on what Heidegger thinks of hope because it stands in marked contrast to Ricoeur's conception. Though both share some fundamental assumptions about human existence, their orientation of that existence differs profoundly. For the early Heidegger, the fact that we are temporal, futural beings does not imply that we should be hopeful. In fact, in *Being and Time*, hope is framed as an inauthentic mood which creates expectations about reality which, if not patently false, at least distract us from the call to authentically face our finitude. Heidegger writes that he who 'hopes takes himself *with* him into his hope ... and brings himself up against what he hopes for. But this presupposes that he has somehow *arrived at himself*' (*Being and Time* 396; my emphases). Hope may bring 'alleviation', but this means that it is still related to 'our burdens' (*Being and Time* 396). The mood of hopefulness, instead of creating a space which opens up genuine possibilities for existence, in fact closes them, because these hopeful possibilities are, in some deep way, already shaped by an individual's past burdens and expectations. For Heidegger, we are futural beings, ahead of ourselves, and our existence can never be given at any moment. Thus we should never expect to fully 'arrive' at ourselves. To imagine this arrival as possible implies assuming an inauthentic orientation to our existence. Essentially, hope produces an illusion of the self which occludes facing up to one's own finitude and, to use Heidegger's term, one's 'thrownness' (*Geworfenheit*).

Ricoeur's existential outlook for human existence is far more positive than Heidegger's because it is framed and guided by a radically different conception of freedom. For the Heidegger of *Being and Time*, authentic *Dasein* stands in its being-towards-death resolute before the nothing of Being, before the 'possibility of the absolute impossibility' of its being (294). This is all there is and to hope for more is to be trapped in a beguiled fearfulness, a foolish unrealistic hope that attempts to shelter the individual *Dasein* from facing its authentic, finite self. Heideggerian freedom lies in grasping this authentic self, an experience which he suggests is similar in mood to Nietzsche's bleak vision of human destiny:

> In some remote corner of the universe, poured out and glittering in innumerable solar systems, there once was a star on which clever animals invented knowledge. That was the haughtiest and most mendacious minute of 'world history' – yet only a minute. After nature had drawn a few breaths the star grew cold, and the clever animals had to die. (Nietzsche 42)

In contrast, for Ricoeur, freedom exists in the 'light of hope'. The idea of 'Christian freedom' specifically, a notion he takes from Luther, belongs 'existentially to the order of the Resurrection' (*Essays* 107). This conception of freedom is paradoxical because the hope that it inspires exists between 'what is heading toward death and what denies death'. The 'hope of resurrection' is a living contradiction of actual reality, because it 'proceeds from what is placed under the sign of the Cross and death' (*Essays* 107). Ricoeur writes that 'freedom in the light of hope is not only freedom for the possible but, more fundamentally still, freedom for the denial of death, freedom to decipher the signs of the Resurrection under the contrary appearance of death' (*Essays* 107). Thus the logic of hope is one of 'superabundance', an 'absurd' logic whose meaning is opposed to the abundance of 'senselessness, of failure, and of destruction' (Ricoeur, *Figuring the Sacred* 206). This law of superabundance provides a rich and complex existential meaning to our existence which is 'irreducible to a mere wisdom of the eternal present' (*Figuring the Sacred* 206). Ricoeur, following Kierkegaard, perceives in hope the freedom for a 'passion for the possible' which offers a different orientation to 'all Nietzschean love of destiny ... to all *amor fati*' (*Figuring the Sacred* 206).

How is the religious imagination, then, depicted in the poetry of T.S. Eliot? As mentioned earlier, Eliot converted to Anglo-Catholicism in 1927 and this had a marked effect on the content of his poetry. This is illustrated starkly by comparing his 1925 poem 'The Hollow Men' with his next poem 'Ash-Wednesday', published in 1930. While this is a clear and somewhat convenient division, one should not overlook the moments throughout Eliot's poetic corpus which are attentive to communications and illuminations of a divine sort. However, I shall limit my discussion to his last great poem and return again to 'East Coker', to the passage from the fourth movement of this quartet depicting the 'wounded surgeon' (*Complete Poems* 181–2, IV.1). In these almost garish lines both the poetic and religious dimensions of the productive imagination are evident. In addition, we can clearly discern the impulse of hope which Ricoeur holds so central to the religious imagination in the symbols depicted in the passage.

In their evocation of a renunciation that is life-giving, the lines are clearly located within the tradition of Christian asceticism, but Eliot, through metaphor, presents Christ in a way which beckons the reader to engage and reflect on the meaning of this portrayal of him. Christ is our surgeon assisted by his nurse, the Church, yet paradoxically, in order for our health to be restored, 'our sickness must grow worse' (IV.10). This speaks directly to the superabundance of hope which is so central to the Christian message and to Ricoeur's conception of the religious imagination. The 'enigma' and mystery of our 'disease', 'Adam's curse' (IV.5, 6, 9), holds within it the means of our salvation. Though we are both sinful and mortal, we must obey the 'sharp compassion' (IV.4) of our healer and his Church, accepting faithfully that it is only through consuming the 'dripping blood' and 'bloody flesh' that we can be healed (IV.21–2). It is worth noting the regular and strongly traditional poetic form and metre of the lines, which reflect the 'intellectual and emotional structure' of 'East Coker' as a whole and link Christ's 'redemptive task' both in content and the deliberate precise form to that of a surgeon (Kramer 94).

Eliot is very deliberate in creating images which seem immediately counter-intuitive to our ordinary conception of disease and its treatment. There is no sense of our recovery being a gentle, restorative affair, convalescing quietly in a soothing hospital environment. Rather there is an urgency and directness to our treatment; we must surrender to our physician and ingest his medicine. Though the medicine itself is suggestive of cannibalism, this is again deliberately counter-intuitive, for this act of consumption, seemingly savage and repulsive, holds the mystery of transubstantiation, and thus our salvation, in its midst. Thus Eliot reminds us why 'we call this Friday good' ('East Coker' IV.25); it is because of the suffering Christ and his crucifixion that we live, in Ricoeur's words, in the 'hope of resurrection'. In Eliot's lines we perceive the 'living contradiction' of actual reality, for the fullness of our lives is held in the freedom our disease grants us, 'freedom for the denial of death' in spite of the certainty of our physical death.

The above passage from *Four Quartets* is explicitly Christian in image and content, and so I shall briefly consider another which is not. I do this to substantiate, but also to complicate, Ricoeur's claim that 'all religions are different attempts ... to recover the ground of goodness', and to support the claim made earlier that religious discourse offers us a language of hope and freedom ('Ethics' 284). In the passage below, Eliot again interweaves the poetic and religious imagination, reminding us of the capacity of language, as Ricoeur says, to open up new worlds (Kearney 44). This passage comes from the second movement of the third quartet, 'The Dry Salvages', where the poet moves to consider a god from a different tradition, the Hindu tradition of the *Bhagavad Gita* (*Complete Poems* 187–8). The passage opens by alluding to Krishna's admonishment of Arjuna before a battle of the Kurukshetra War.[5] The *Gita* is a conversation between them. Krishna appears as a charioteer and comes to aid Arjuna, who is engaged in the battle to recover land which is rightfully his. Arjuna tells Krishna that if victory requires killing relatives, then he would rather forego the battle, because it will lead to the death of family members, disrupt Hindu society and create caste confusion (Kramer 120). Krishna admonishes Arjuna for his worrying about the future and urges him to 'fare forward' ('Dry Salvages' III.14, 26, 39, 45); because Arjuna is of the Kshatriya caste, the warrior caste of Hindu society, it is his duty to fight, and thus he cannot shirk his own nature. The line the 'future is a faded song' (III.3) signifies that Arjuna must remain true to the action that his caste status requires of him, regardless of its future consequences, for once the future has unfolded, it too becomes the past. Also, Krishna, because he is divine, perceives time in a way that Arjuna cannot. Krishna understands the nature of the true Self, *Atman*, which is unborn and undying and therefore knows that, regardless of the outcome of the battle, Arjuna was born and will die and then reincarnate into another life. Thus, from Krishna's perspective, we must 'not think of the fruit of action' (III.38) and be paralysed by the fear of inaction, but remain mindful that 'the time of death is every moment' (III.36).

In this movement of 'The Dry Salvages', Eliot, via Krishna, calls for life lived which accords to duty and self-sacrifice, reminding us, via Arjuna, that the certainty of death diminishes our need to worry over the consequences of the future; rather, the action called for in the event itself, namely, for Arjuna upon the battlefield, must be most befitting of what Arjuna represents, in terms of his caste and position. Arjuna tells his doubts to Krishna and is guided according to the precepts of the complexity of Hindu belief. Much like Christ in the Garden of Gethsemane, who understands that his sacrifice will be for the freedom of humankind but is afraid of the torturous death that awaits him, Arjuna is conflicted by the demands of duty in the realization that it demands killing. Yet both Christ and Arjuna accept their respective destinies, in spite of their realization of the possible consequences.

---

[5]     See Balakrishnan and Sri for accessible overviews of Eliot's allusions to Upanishadic themes in his poetry and plays.

While it is apparent that Christ and Arjuna represent radically different religious traditions, Eliot traces a common wisdom in these traditions, which, as he writes in one of his essays, he believes 'is the same for all people everywhere' and which the language of poetry is 'most capable' of communicating (*On Poetry* 226). Keeping in mind the Heraclitean fragment 'the way up and the way down are the same' (*Complete Poems* 171), which underpins *Four Quartets*, we must search for those deeper patterns of meaning which draw human experience together. What the above passage gives us is a 'schematization of liberation', to use the words of Ricoeur. Krishna reminds us that the certainty of death gives us the unfolding present moment; that, if we are too focused on the future, then what is lost and denied is the sacramentality of the present. Genuine freedom is not found in the image from *Four Quartets* of 'time counted by anxious worried women / Lying awake, calculating the future' (*Complete Poems* 185, 'Dry Salvages' I.41–2), but rather in recognizing that, though we will all experience suffering and death, our 'real destination' (*Complete Poems* 188, 'Dry Salvages' III.42), we cannot hide from our own life because of this knowledge. We cannot bid 'fare well' to living, but must 'fare forward' (III.44–5) into the unknown and uncertain sea of life, mindful of the duty which both binds us to life and to living it fully, and which will ultimately separate us from it. Thus the 'right action is freedom / From past and future also' (*Complete Poems* 190, 'Dry Salvages' V.41–2).

As all the examples illustrate, our engagement with the artwork brings to the fore the imaginative epoché, the space which allows worldmaking to manifest. Through an open encounter with the artwork, particularly through the language of poetry, we can encounter the world in a way which transforms existing categories of meaning, producing wholly new ones. Yet these categories re-affirm the 'deep structures' of reality to which we all, as mortals, belong, while allowing us new possibilities of re-describing the world (Ricoeur, 'The Metaphorical Process' 153–4). Central to this is Ricoeur's claim that it is here where we can locate the will to hope and recognize the capability we all have to 'recover the ground of goodness' in us ('Ethics' 284). Particularly in the last two examples, though from different religious traditions, we can discern a language of hope and freedom which allows us to find our own language to 'utter God'.

In conclusion I will leave the reader with the passage which ends *Four Quartets*, one that is richly compelling and hopeful (*Complete Poems* 197–8, 'Little Gidding' V.26–46). The lines speak of arriving at 'the end of all our exploring' and finding it to be 'where we started' (V.27–8). In the image of the 'unknown, remembered gate' (V.30), Eliot suggests that hope is always already inside us, and that the journey of life is compelled onward by that same hope.

Those who know the poem will recognize that this passage gathers together themes and symbols from the earlier quartets – 'the children in the apple-tree', the sea, the rose (V.35, 38, 46) – all imagery integral to the deeply personal work that Eliot does in his poem, examining the choices, places and histories that formed him, and searching for a sense of peace. Apart from the 'tongues of flame ... in-folded / Into the crowned knot of fire' (V.44–5), which alludes to the heavenly fire that seemed to come down on the apostles on Pentecost, and the quotation from the English mystic Julian of Norwich (the lines 'all shall be well', V.42–3), the passage is not explicitly or exclusively Christian. What is deeply religious, in Ricoeur's understanding, is the sense of fullness and maturity in the lines, ripeness that is at once a homecoming and a ceaseless, hopeful openness to the future. What the reader shares with Eliot is not so much an experience of his world, but of ourselves as worldmakers, able to cross the invisible boundary between the everyday world and that same world revealed as a mysterious potential that 'worlds'.

## Works Cited

Balakrishnan, Purasu. 'An Indian View of T.S. Eliot's *Four Quartets*'. *American Scholar* 60.1 (1991): 73–89.

Eliot, T.S. *The Complete Poems and Plays of T.S. Eliot*. London: Faber and Faber, 1969.

——— *On Poetry and Poets*. London: Faber and Faber, 1957.

——— *Selected Prose of T.S. Eliot*. Ed. Frank Kermode. San Diego: Harcourt, 1975.

Gordon, Lyndall. *T.S. Eliot: An Imperfect Life*. New York: Norton, 2000.

Heidegger, Martin. *Basic Writings*. Ed. David F. Krell. San Francisco: HarperCollins, 1993.

——— *Being and Time*. Trans. John Macquarrie and Edward Robinson. Malden: Blackwell, 2006.

——— *Contributions to Philosophy (From Enowning)*. Trans. Parvis Emad and Kenneth Maly. Bloomington, IN: Indiana University Press, 1999.

——— *Discourse on Thinking*. Trans. John Anderson. New York: Harper and Row, 1969.

Kearney, Richard. *Dialogues with Contemporary Continental Thinkers: The Phenomenological Heritage*. New York: Manchester University Press, 1989.

Kramer, Kenneth. *Redeeming Time: T.S. Eliot's Four Quartets*. Lanham: Cowley, 2007.

Meister Eckhart. *The Essential Sermons, Commentaries, Treatises, and Defense.* Trans. Edmund Colledge and Bernard McGinn. New York: Paulist Press, 1981.

Nietzsche, Friedrich. *The Portable Nietzsche.* Ed. Walter Kaufmann. New York: Penguin, 1988.

Ricoeur, Paul. *Essays on Biblical Interpretation.* Trans. Robert Sweeney. Philadelphia: Fortress, 1980.

—— 'Ethics and Human Capability'. In *Paul Ricoeur and Contemporary Moral Thought*, ed. John Wall, William Schweiker and David Hall. New York: Routledge, 2002, 279–90.

—— *Figuring the Sacred: Religion, Narrative, and Imagination.* Trans. David Pellauer. Minneapolis, MN: Fortress, 1995.

—— *History and Truth.* Trans. Charles Kelbley. Evanston, IL: Northwestern University Press, 1965.

—— 'The Metaphorical Process as Cognition, Imagination, and Feeling'. *Critical Inquiry* 5.1 (1978): 143–59.

—— *The Rule of Metaphor: The Creation of Meaning in Language.* Trans. Robert Czerny. London: Routledge, 2007.

Sri, P.S. 'Upanishadic Perceptions in T.S. Eliot's Poetry and Drama'. *Rocky Mountain Review* 62.2 (2008): 34–49.

Taylor, George. 'Ricoeur's Philosophy of Imagination'. *Journal of French Philosophy* 16.1 and 16.2 (2006): 93–104.

Thompson, Iain. *Heidegger, Art, and Postmodernity.* Cambridge: Cambridge University Press, 2011.

Vanhoozer, Kevin. *Biblical Narrative in the Philosophy of Paul Ricoeur: A Study in Hermeneutics and Theology.* Cambridge: Cambridge University Press, 1990.

Young, Julian. *Heidegger's Later Philosophy.* Cambridge: Cambridge University Press, 2002.

# Chapter 10

# *Non tantum lecturi sed facturi*: Reading Poetry as Spiritual Transformation

Antonio Spadaro SJ

In his book entitled *Prayer and Poetry*, first published in French in 1926, Henri Bremond wrote that the spiritual and poetic experiences shared 'the intensity of the activities of the deeper soul' (155). These included, he specified, recollection, simplification, a rhythm of activity and passivity, and receptiveness. Bremond, however, reversed the traditional practice of explaining the mystical experience from the vantage point of poetic experience. In his view, it was the mystical experience that clarified the mystery of the poetic and creative experience rather than contrariwise.

Bremond's thinking about the relationship between mysticism and poetry starts from the following assumption: 'It is not the poet who illuminates the mystery of the mystics; on the contrary, it is the mystic, and the mystic in his most sublime states, who helps us to penetrate the mystery of the poet' (187).[1] In other words, the psychological mechanism used by grace to raise us to prayer was, he thought, the same as that set in motion in poetic experience. Bremond's interpretation requires us to rethink not only the nature of poetry but, more importantly, how we read poetry. If the poetic experience is – in Bremond's words – 'explained' by the mystic experience, the reading of poetry is presumably somehow related to the disposition to pray. Writers of many different traditions worldwide have made this point. Proust, for example, dedicated several pages to describing the 'salutary role' of reading, alluding to the opening up of some hidden space within the psyche (24–8).[2] The similarity to prayer here does not need to be stressed. Bremond defines this kind of reading as intensively creative, or, as he puts it, a 'poetic reading' (168) or 'a lower poetical stage' (155).

---

[1]    Also, in Bremond's words: 'It is from the mystic that we can learn to understand the poet' (85).

[2]    The well-known text referred to here appeared for the first time in *La Renaissance latine* in 1905, and was published the following year as a preface to the translation of *Sesame and Lilies* by John Ruskin. See Spadaro, 'Marcel Proust e la sapiente bellezza della lettura'.

Let us explore Bremond's insight. There is no such thing as a generic 'spiritual experience', so we need first to choose which tradition of spirituality we might use for the purpose of understanding what it means to read poems poetically. Of the several different traditions I shall choose the one that I am most familiar with, Ignatius Loyola's *Spiritual Exercises*.

## The Exercise of Reading

The text of the *Spiritual Exercises* was not written to be read sequentially. It contains a series of guidelines that the person giving the exercises should use to help the exercitant to pray. It delicately indicates ways of meditating and praying, leading the exercitant to contemplate a chosen mystery through the power of the imagination and the spiritual senses.

The dynamic of the exercises is very complex and works at various levels. The French semiologist Roland Barthes explained it very well (41–4). Even if unable to capture the essence of a spiritual experience, Barthes correctly suggested that, in the case of the exercises, 'we are not reading *one* text, but rather *four* texts, disposed in the shape of the small book in our hands' (41). The first text is the one Ignatius addresses to the person who gives the exercises, to the director of the retreat. The director then adapts this text to the personality of the exercitant, thus producing another text of his/her own. This is what he calls the second 'text'. In their turn, the exercitants turn to God in their prayer, which constitutes the third text, and here God is the receiver. Ignatius compares this last level of communication between the exercitant and God with the way two friends talk or a servant speaks to his master (*Spiritual Exercises* §54). Finally, the fourth text is much more difficult to identify, being the response that the exercitant receives from God, who moves and attracts him (*Spiritual Exercises* §175).

On closer reading, however, the *Spiritual Exercises* offer more levels of communication than the four described by Barthes. The text implies, for example, the relationship between the retreatant and the director, as well as the relationship between the director and God. The latter relationship is nuanced, only hinted at by Ignatius as a sort of 'laissez-faire', rather than giving instructions about what the director should be 'doing'. Noteworthy, and also documented in the Directories, is the network of relationships among those who give the exercises and who must themselves have received and practised the spiritual exercises. Finally, a further text should be kept in mind. This is what God intended for Ignatius, who describes its nature briefly in his *Autobiography*: 'At that period God dealt with him as a teacher instructing a pupil' (53).

Most importantly the *Spiritual Exercises* do not illustrate an experience. They encourage the exercitant to undergo an experience. They invite him or her to become involved in this experience in at least three ways. First, the exercitant is asked to imagine being physically present at a scene. Second, they are called to identify with the characters in the scene and with their feelings. Finally, they are called to live again step by step the events of the chosen mystery. Each spiritual experience is thus associated with a constituent element of the grammar of narration, namely, setting, character and plot (Ryan 119).

In describing the scene of the mystery (to be contemplated) Ignatius avoids ornate images and sophisticated language. He summarizes the mystery in a few sentences – or more precisely three 'points' – which allude to an impenetrable mystery while allowing the spirit to open up to its own vision. The person giving the exercises suggests these points to the exercitant, and the exercitant's task is – as Italo Calvino rightly perceived – 'to paint frescoes crowded with figures on the walls of his mind, starting out from the stimuli that his visual imagination succeeds in extracting from a theological proposition or a laconic verse from the gospels' (86). Ignatius's style is sharp, precise, but also dry and concise, able to evoke rather than define or exhaust the powers of imagination. The *Exercises* do not focus on giving further detailed knowledge of Jesus' life. Their purpose is to involve the exercitant fully in the life of Christ. Consequently, much is left to the exercitant's free reconstruction.

## The Text as Door

Marguerite Yourcenar understood the importance of the reader's free reconstruction. In the notebook written for her masterpiece, *Memoirs of Hadrian*, set in the second century CE, she commented: 'The rules of the game: learn everything, read everything, inquire into everything, while at the same time adapting to one's ends the Spiritual Exercises of Ignatius Loyola' (330). This method is summarized in the expression: *como si presente me hallase* ('as if I were present in the place') (*Spiritual Exercises* §114). Yourcenar added: 'pursue each incident to the very moment that it occurred; endeavour to restore the mobility and suppleness of life to those visages ... set aside, if possible, all beliefs and sentiments which have accumulated in successive stratas between those persons and us' (331). The language of narrative is, in this sense, the language of experience.

The second prelude to the contemplation of the Nativity is as a paradigmatic example of the 'engaging' dynamic proposed by Ignatius Loyola:

Here this will be to see with the eyes of the imagination the road from Nazareth to Bethlehem, considering the length and breadth of it, whether it is a flat road or goes through valleys or over hills; and similarly to observe the place or grotto of the nativity, to see how big or small it is, how high, and what is in it ... to see the persons namely Our Lady, and Joseph, and the servant girl, and after his birth, the child Jesus. Making myself into a poor and unworthy little servant, I watch them, and contemplate them, as if I were present, serve them in their needs with all possible respect and reverence; then I will reflect within myself to draw some profit. (*Spiritual Exercises* §112; §114)

The spiritual exercise implies a full, even emotional, involvement on the part of the exercitant. They feel 'various movements [*mociones*] produced in the soul' and are called 'to perceive and understand to some extent' (*Spiritual Exercises* §313). The two verbs 'to perceive' and 'to understand' form an inseparable pair. They designate a particular form of knowledge for which definite 'rules' are needed (*Spiritual Exercises* §§313–36).[3]

What can we gather from all this? The most conspicuous conclusion is that making the exercises is not equivalent to reading them. The exercitants should rather follow and perform what Ignatius's book suggests: they should watch, feel and do, 'feel with the sense of touch'[4] and discern between inner motions. In this way the exercitant is called to enter a truly virtual space, the so-called *composición viendo el lugar*, the visual composition of the place (*Spiritual Exercises* §47).[5]

The text is thus an entrance to a story. A superabundance of details would drain the reader's imagination. It would limit its space. Personal involvement is the precondition by which reading becomes an experience, allowing the reader's imaginative and perceptive powers to come into play, 'making the exercitant adjust and differentiate his or her focus' (Iser 26). Ignatius wrote, in short, a text which requires that we exercise ourselves if we wish to read it. This is the reason why the author explains the meaning of the title by referring to physical

---

[3]    In fact, Ignatius presupposes that there are 'three kinds of thought processes in me, one sort which are properly mine and arise simply from liberty and will, and two other sorts which come from outside, one from the good spirit and the other from the bad' (*Spiritual Exercises* §32), and therefore the retreatant must 'discern' between the 'spirits' and their effects, namely, thoughts and inner motions (feelings such as peace, turmoil, confusion or joy). In this way, in fact, it is possible to recognize the action of God in one's own life, as well as the forces leading the retreatant away from Him.

[4]    For example: 'To touch with the sense of touch, for example embracing and kissing the places where these persons tread and sit' (Ignatius, *Spiritual Exercises* §125).

[5]    Here the term 'virtual' does not mean 'fictitious' or 'illusory' or the opposite of 'real'. It should be read as meaning 'potential' (Levy 23).

exercises. He clarifies: 'For just as strolling, walking and running are exercises for the body, so "spiritual exercises" is the name given to every way of preparing and making ourselves ready' (*Spiritual Exercises* §1). Each reading can therefore turn into a performance. Ignatius does not describe the experience of the *Exercises*. He rather suggests an experience, guides it and inspires it. And, importantly, he recommends the conditions for it.

## The Unliterariness of the *Spiritual Exercises*

The preface to the first edition of the vulgate of the *Spiritual Exercises* of 1548 reads: '*non ... tantum lecturi sunt exercitia, sed ... facturi*' (Polanco 80).[6] The *Exercises* aim, that is, at influencing our lives and actions through the spiritual exercise ('Directorium anonymum' 883). Reading the text of the *Exercises* is like looking up a train timetable: it is unquestionably useful for travellers who travel, but boring and useless for those who stay behind. We could well say that the text is 'somewhere else' or that it refers to 'some other place' different from the printed text. By text we usually mean simply 'what is communicated' by the author to reader. This limited meaning does not work when applied to Ignatius's text.

In the case of the *Exercises*, the literary quality of the written text is disregarded. The 'truth' of the exercitant's spiritual experience lies in the vivid effect that the written page has on them, not in the written page. In this sense the exercitant becomes the real 'author' of the exercises. They are totally absorbed in the situation that they are experiencing. How can this lack of unity – in a literary sense – of the *Spiritual Exercises* help us read poetry? We can draw, I believe, three conclusions.

## Reading as Performing a Virtual Work

The first conclusion is that, from an Ignatian point of view, reading is not an event which comes to the text extrinsically or incidentally. In order to exist, a text must indeed be read. To read a book, again from an Ignatian point of view, can only mean to 'read' yourself in it, namely, in how you experience that book.

---

6    The translation in the *Textus italicus* reads: 'questa spesa de fatiga et opra non solo è per quelli li quali haveranno da legere solamente questi tali esercitii, ma chi li eserciterà, overo più tosto l'insegnarà ad altri. Conciosia che a recepere frutto grande sia poca cosa haverli letto, se alcuno in quelli non se sia diligentemente esercitato et non habbia trovato maestro dotto in cose spirituale' (Calveras and de Dalmases 652).

In the words of the philosopher Luigi Pareyson, reading is synonymous with 'to perform'. In this case the expression 'to perform' has the same meaning as in music. The reality of a piece of music lies not in 'the inert and mute pages of the score', but rather 'in its living and sonorous performance' (Pareyson, *Truth and Interpretation* 59). To give a performance of a work does not mean 'surrendering to the effect the work has on you and passively remaining under its influence'. To give a performance is rather 'an act by which we master the work itself rendering it alive and present, i.e. enabling it to operate its effect' (Pareyson, *Estetica* 222; my translation). A performance is not secondary or optional. On the contrary, it is co-original with the work. A performance binds together the unchangeable identity of the work and the changing personality of the interpreter giving the performance. A work cannot be separated from its performance. Again according to Pareyson, reading takes place only if the reader *himself* intends to 'perform the work in itself [*l'opera in se*], so that the reader's performance is the work itself, brought by him to its present life, and at the same time it is the reader's interpretation of that work'(*Estetica* 229; my translation).

A work lives of and through its performances, although its meaning transcends those same performances. From this point of view the personality of the interpreter concentrated on expressing himself does not hinder the performance. In fact it is the one necessary precondition for the performance to take place. Unsurprisingly then, Pareyson recommends being faithful to the work as follows:

> make of yourself, of your entire personality and spirituality, of your way of thinking, living and feeling, a means of understanding, a condition of accessing and an instrument of revealing, a work of art; remember that you are not expected either to have to renounce yourself or to want to express yourself ... remember instead that you personally must interpret the work. It is exactly that work that you must interpret, and at the same time it is exactly you who must interpret it. (*Estetica* 231; my translation)

A literary work can only be dealt with in a manner both obedient and free: obedient to the uneliminable objectivity of the written page of the text, and free in the approach and interpretation of it. From this virtuality springs the dynamics enabling the literary work to operate as well as the reader. Ignatius himself teaches us that fidelity to the story goes together with 'pious' meditation which reconstructs freely and creatively through the imagination (Spadaro, 'Gli "occhi dell'immaginazione"'). In fact the former is the necessary prerequisite of the latter.

Texts are not printed in the reader's mind automatically and naturally. Whatever is given must be received, and the way in which it is received depends on the reader as much as on the text. Because it is not a one-way process, reading does not consist in an act of internalization pure and simple. The reading process is better described as a dynamic interaction between text and reader, where the meaning remains only potential until the reader brings it to completion.

## Meaning as Dynamic Event

The second conclusion, proceeding immediately from the first, is, then, that the meaning of the text is a dynamic event. Reading is not an act. It is a process, something happening in time, the meanings being activated piecemeal. The text does not disclose itself completely in its wholeness, nor does the reader perceive its entirety simultaneously. The relationship between the text and the reader is consequently quite different from the relationship between an object and the observer of that object. It would perhaps be more appropriate to speak of a mobile point of view 'moving' within that same meaning which we seek to catch.

The reader is therefore akin to a traveller. He or she travels through the 'poietic' text from his itinerant point of view, uniting all he sees in his memory, mixing memories from his own life, as well as images and recollections from the reading of earlier pages of the text. In so doing, he creates a consistent pattern of reading (Iser 16). At no time, however, is he able to see the entire picture of his journey (Iser 16). Likewise for Ignatius, the exercitant who sets imaginatively on a journey along the road from Nazareth to Bethlehem can say what it is like only if he journeys in the company of Mary and Joseph. On the journey the exercitant remains involved with his memory, his desires, his tensions, his curiosity and his difficulties in a process of, we may say, 'conversion'. Just as in the exercises, reading, in the strong sense of the term, is always able to activate a dynamics of conversion.

In the *Exercises*, 'to convert' does not mean refusing to acknowledge the past for a radically new future. Memory is not an unchangeable transcription of what has happened. The past influences the present as long as, in its turn, the past is recaptured and reshaped by the present. A profound conversion is possible only when the past retains, with a change in sense, a significance for present actions. 'To convert', therefore, signifies reviewing the past as a basis for the future. If we regard reading as a gradual 'exercise', then it becomes clear how reading has a bearing on our memory, enriching or changing its meaning. In the light of the

*Exercises*, becoming involved in reading a text means entering a situation with all our heart (memory, intellect, will, Ignatius would say, and therefore with our expectations, recollections and understanding of what is real) and succeeding in reading ourselves through the text and in the text. The text leads us to experience a process of conversion.

### Reading as Spiritual Experience

The third conclusion regards the importance in our journey of faith, of expressing our experiences poetically. Anyone who has been educated in the spirituality of the *Exercises* knows that the involvement in the mystery that he or she is called to contemplate is never aseptic, never detached. The exercitant cannot be divorced from the story. In the *Exercises*, God is not contemplated in himself or by leaving behind history, the world and images transmitted through the senses. On the contrary, God is sought and found exactly in history, in the world and through sensible images (Perniola 117). The primary object of Ignatian contemplation is not God. It is rather the historical world and the saving events that happened in history where he has revealed himself. Whoever is acquainted with this spiritual path will be familiar with stories told and rendered poetically. He or she will be able to read them and pay attention, as explained all along, to the experience of feeling and recognizing the motions happening in the soul. The good and bad spirits which Ignatius mentions also operate in us when we read a poem or watch a film. Being a source of spiritual consolation or desolation, some images or expressions often have a profound impact on us. They are often 'felt' but not 'recognized'. In order to be able to 'recognize' them, the hermeneutic method of spiritual discernment must be applied.[7]

Michael Paul Gallagher offers two insights deriving from applying the Ignatian 'rules' (Gallagher, 'Teologia').[8] The first is that 'consolation may look like a true consolation, when in fact it might be otherwise' (Gallagher, 'Teologia' 47; my translation). A poem, he writes, 'may give a kind of fulfilment and inner comfort, but this is not a good reason for saying that we are in the presence of a true consolation' ('Teologia' 47). Ignatius's second contribution, he continues, 'lies in his constant attention to the whole process of spiritual motions in a person'

---

[7]    As a help for the first two weeks of the exercises, Ignatius offers the 'rules for discernment' (*Spiritual Exercises* §§313–27 and §§328–36).

[8]    The translation of quotations from this essay is mine. The author's comments regard cinema in particular, but they can also be applied to literature. See also Gallagher, *Fede e cultura*, 155–72.

('Teologia' 47). He considers not only 'the consoling effects shown in the person's mood, but also general direction of the mood as well' ('Teologia' 47). This means 'testing how long the feelings that have been aroused last' by the reading of the poem and then 'wondering where they are leading the person' ('Teologia' 48).

Let us take an example. A poem, for instance, suggests that human life is absurd. Obviously it states something not Christian. However, exactly by radically presenting the problem and questioning all that concerns human life, that poem may help a reader rouse from a dull life with which he is only superficially content. It may 'wake up' others who do not search, who do not listen and who cannot be silent because they are already satisfied, that is to say, men who are shut up within themselves, unable to hear the call of grace (Rahner 502). The literature and cinema of the absurd can work spiritually on blinkered mentalities of this kind. It can trigger a sense of anxiety and disquiet which, in the long run, may turn out to be a means of salvation, waking them up from false certainties, making them drop the masks of appearances. This is the precise application of the first Ignatian rule of spiritual discernment reserved for those who 'go from one deadly sin to another'. In people of such disposition the good spirit 'causes pricks of conscience and feelings of remorse by means of the natural power of rational moral judgement' (*Spiritual Exercises* §314).[9]

The readers educated in the spirituality of the *Exercises* will be used to questioning themselves or discussing with a spiritual guide the motions they have experienced reading a poem or novel or watching a film. They will be familiar with noticing – as Ignatius often asks in the *Exercises* – the 'points' or the 'most relevant parts', where they have experienced 'some insight, consolation or desolation' or 'greater motions and spiritual relish' (*Spiritual Exercises* §62; §118; §227). Ignatius of Loyola the reader was the first to make this kind of experience during his convalescence after being wounded during the taking of Pamplona by the French in 1521. It was a reading of this kind that aroused his experience of spiritual discernment. A reading of this kind can in turn become a pattern for reading a poetical text.

## Works Cited

Barthes, Roland. *Sade, Fourier, Loyola*. Trans. Richard Miller. New York: Hill and Wang, 1976.

---

9    According to St Thomas, 'synderesis' is a special natural habit which 'goads us toward what is good and to murmur about what is bad' (*Summa theologiae*, 1, 79, 12).

Bremond, Henri. *Prayer and Poetry*. Trans. Algar Thorold. London: Burns Oates, 1927.

Calveras, Jose and Candido de Dalmases, eds. *Sancti Ignatii de Loyola Exercitia spiritualia* (Monumenta Historica Societatis Iesu 100; Monumenta Ignatiana ser. II: Exercitia spiritualia S. Ignatii de Loyola et eorum directoria, t. I). Rome: Institutum Historicum Societatis Iesu, 1969.

Calvino, Italo. *Six Memos for Next Millennium*. Cambridge: Harvard University Press, 1988.

'Directorium anonymum'. *Exercitia spiritualia S. Ignatii de Loyola et eorum directoria*, vol. II. Madrid: MHSI-Monumenta Ignatiana, 1919.

Gallagher, Michael Paul. 'Teologia, arte, discernimento'. *Civiltà Cattolica* II (1995): 388–98.

—— *Fede e cultura. Un rapporto cruciale conflittuale*. Cinisello Balsamo: San Paolo, 1999.

Ignatius of Loyola. *The Autobiography of St Ignatius Loyola*. Ed. J.F.X. O'Connor. New York: Benziger, 1900.

—— *Spiritual Exercises*. Text and commentary in *Understanding the Spiritual Exercises* by Michael Ivens. Leominster: Gracewing, 1998.

Iser, Wolfgang. *The Act of Reading*. London: Routledge and Kegan Paul, 1976.

Levy, Pierre. *Becoming Virtual: Reality in the Digital Age*. Trans. Robert Bononno. London: Plenum Trade, 1998.

Pareyson, Luigi. *Estetica. Teoria della formatività*. Milan: Bompiani, 1996.

—— *Truth and Interpretation*. Trans. Robert T. Valgenti, ed. Silvia Benso, with a foreword by Gianni Vattimo. New York: Suny, 2013.

Perniola, Mario. *Del sentire cattolico. La forma culturale di una religione universale*. Bologna: Il Mulino, 2001.

Polanco, Juan de. 'Praefatincula editioni primae vulgatae versionis exercitiorum praemissa (1548)'. In *Sancti Ignatii de Loyola Exercitia*, ed. Calveras and de Dalmases, 79–81.

Proust, Marcel. *On Reading*. Ed. Damion Searls. London: Hesperus, 2011.

Rahner, Karl. 'La missione del letterato e l'esistenza cristiana'. In *Nuovi Saggi II*. Rome: Paoline, 1968, 487–507.

Ryan, Marie-Laure. *Narrative as Virtual Reality: Immersion and Interactivity in Literature and Electronic Media*. Baltimore, MD: Johns Hopkins University Press, 2001.

Spadaro, Antonio. 'Gli "occhi dell'immaginazione" negli Esercizi di Ignazio di Loyola'. *Rassegna di Teologia* 35 (1994): 687–712.

—— 'Marcel Proust e la sapiente bellezza della lettura'. *La Civiltà Cattolica* II (1998): 480–5.

Yourcenar, Marguerite. *Memoirs of Hadrian*. Trans. Grace Frick, in collaboration with the author. London: Secker and Warburg, 1974.

## Chapter 11

# Reading as Active Contemplation

### Jennifer Reek

## Introduction(s)

In his influential 1989 book *Breaking the Fall: Religious Readings of Contemporary Fiction*, the late Robert Detweiler, Professor of Comparative Literature at Emory University and a leader in the interdisciplinary field of literature and religion, proposed that we engage in a practice of 'religious reading' that is imaginative, playful and communal. He reminds us that:

> as critics such as Gaston Bachelard and Roland Barthes have shown us, one can learn a variety of reactions to a text, of which interpretation is only one. Sometimes texts need to be absorbed, taken in and then offered up not to a relentlessly analytical readership but rather to a contemplative fellowship. One can learn to relax with texts, play with them, take them less than seriously and thereby employ them as a means of escaping our privacies on occasion and of indulging the *conversation* that we claim to value but seldom make time for. (34)

Detweiler suggests that such reading is religious 'in its very openness to others; its willingness to accommodate and adapt; its readiness to entertain the new, the invention, while honouring the old, the convention; its celebration of the text's possibilities rather than a delimiting of them' (35). This imaginative way of both reading and being religious is contrary to most interpretive traditions and religious institutions, which 'tend to be closed, restrictive, defensive and prescriptive' (35).

I wish to take this sense of religious reading as both point of departure and guide to what I image as a reading pilgrimage with three unlikely 'word-fellows': Ignatius of Loyola, the sixteenth-century Basque saint and founder of the Society of Jesus, the French poet Yves Bonnefoy and the French thinker Hélène Cixous. Inspired by Detweiler's 'religious reading', I seek, with their assistance, to illuminate and enact a poetic spirit of reading and writing as a type of active contemplation. I do this by elucidating similarities among dissimilarities and by tracing movements from immobility to motion, from death to new life, in the texts of these subjects, each of whom were led through their reading/writing practices on transformative interior journeys. Necessarily, this marking of poetic and spiritual movements requires an appropriate way of proceeding, one that is non-linear and sometimes wandering as I attempt to listen to the poets and follow their lead, to enter into conversation with them and the reader.

Before setting out, allow me to introduce this unusual gathering. Long considered France's most important post-war poet, Yves Bonnefoy has written at least seven major collections of poetry, as well as memoirs, art criticism, translations and prose poems. For Bonnefoy, 'poetry is what tries to make music of what occurs in life' ('Interview' 169). His work reveals an explicit concern for the sacred; his poems have a spare, stripped-down, sacramental quality, with space and silence surrounding words that express the concrete elements of life – simple, elemental words: rock, water, bread, fire – yet reveal what Bonnefoy refers to as 'presence', 'a sacred order ... at the very heart of daily things' ('Interview' 163). Hélène Cixous is not a poet by common measure. Yet she has called herself one, using a definition worth taking as our own as we go forth, as it aligns with our metaphor of pilgrimage and the practice of 'religious reading'. She writes: 'I call "poet" any writing being who sets out on this path, in quest of what I call the second innocence, the one that comes after knowing, the one that no longer knows, the one that knows how not to know' ('The Last Painting' 114). Cixous thinks and writes poetically, regardless of the area in which she is working. She has written more than 40 books and over a hundred articles: drama, experimental fiction, memoir, philosophy, literary theory and criticism, yet such a list is misleading because of the genres and disciplines she has breached. Her style is the opposite of Bonnefoy's in its excessive plenitude, yet, like him, she seeks to spiral down into deeper truths that have transformative potential. She is Jewish, not practising, not religious in a conventional sense, yet, as Heather Walton notes, she aspires to a 'religious writing' that is 'not to be found in any particular text or type of creative work but is to be understood as an energy source' (149). Ignatius is the most outwardly religious of the three and least likely to be considered a poet. Yet arguably he thought, prayed and, to borrow from Hölderlin,[1] dwelt poetically. He created the text of his *Spiritual Exercises* to be lived, prayed and performed imaginatively, poetically.

---

[1]    In a late poem perhaps best known from Martin Heidegger's study of Hölderlin, the poet writes: 'poetically, man dwells on this earth'. See 'In Lovely Blueness ...' in *Poems and Fragments* 601.

It may also be helpful here to provide beginning definitions of the terms 'poetics', 'poet' and 'poetry'. For now, perhaps it is enough to say that what I mean by 'poetics' is well expressed by Richard Kearney in his book *Poetics of Imagining*: 'in the broad sense of the term – an exploration of the human powers to make (*poiesis*) a world in which we may poetically dwell' (8). This definition resonates with Heidegger, who stresses in his essay '"... Poetically Man Dwells ..."', titled after Hölderlin's phrase, that when he is speaking of poetry, he is not speaking of 'the literature industry', for which he expresses some disdain for its tendency to make poetry into an object to be studied 'in educational and scientific terms' (214). Poetic dwelling, for Heidegger, shifts the relations between human and poetry, fostering a recognition that, though we act as if we are masters and shapers of language, in truth, 'language remains the master of man' (215). A poet, Heidegger says, is a maker, but a maker who seeks not to master language but to listen to its call in the imagination (216). 'What they make is merely imagined. The things of the imagination are merely made. Making is, in Greek, *poiesis*' (214). Poetry, in Heidegger's thinking, 'is the instituting of a world, the uncovering of the matrix of meaning in which an historical age lives and dwells' (Caputo 235). What the poets make is poetry, but the making itself is poetics. We can distinguish poetry in a basic way by its unique relationship to language, by what it does in both form and content, for 'the language of a poem is constitutive of its ideas' (Eagleton 2). Reading the work that is made, the poetry, is what reveals the poet's orientation, her poetics. Poetics defined in this way is what allows me to call all three of my word-fellows 'poets'. Hence I read these writers not because they compose religious verse, but rather because their work makes new worlds in the imagination that open up transformative possibilities for being religious in ways that allow for poetic dwelling.

## Letting the Path Work

At seminars in 1985–86 on 'poetry, passion, and history', Cixous spoke of reading as both interior journey and communal activity, moving from first to second person to bring her listeners into her way of reading. She said:

> I want to plant some paths, some slowness, some trees, some thought and silence. The texts that accompany me on this journey work on this inside of an outside, on an inside-outside ... These texts make us travel so that from an apparently immobile contemplation we are led to infinite discoveries. ('Poetry' 112)

Cixous often writes of these infinite discoveries and of the great transformations she has undergone through reading the texts of the writers she loves most. These texts, she states in the same seminars, 'all speak with insistence of a going toward, or of an active orientation. It is this movement toward something or somebody that opens what I would call "being in the direction of chance"' (112). The response to this movement toward life is a much different way of being, of reading, than we are often accustomed to. It is a form of humility, Cixous implies, 'a playing to find while losing. A thousand poets promise that if we lose ourselves – and we must – there always remains the path. That's what Heidegger told us in his *Holzwege*, his paths that lead nowhere. We have to let the path work' (112).

We may be fortunate in our wanderings to travel at least a trace of Heidegger's poetic paths to nowhere. For both Heidegger and Cixous, poetry, at least poetry at a certain level, is essential for authentic human living, even salvific. What level of poetry are they engaging? One that arises from the depths, with an imperative placed upon us to read it. As Heidegger urges, referring to Hölderlin and Rilke: 'We others must learn to listen to what these poets say' ('What Are Poets For?' 94). Alice Jardine wonderfully phrases the problem of our difficulty in learning to listen when she writes of the ideology of Cixous's *écriture féminine*[2] and its seeds in the thought of Heidegger:

> For Heidegger, the human subject in the modern world has come to be not-himself because he has simply forgotten how to let Being be in language. 'Modern Man' must slow down. He is no longer astonished by the quiddity of things: the redness of red, the wordness of a word. (108)

Yet Heidegger and Cixous also recognize that poetry matters little if at all to an increasingly utilitarian, technological world. Heidegger asks, in an essay of the same title, 'what are poets for?' after a phrase in Hölderlin's poem 'Bread and Wine': 'What are poets for in a destitute time?' (91)

---

2    This practice resonates with our concerns of alternative ways of knowing and communal reading. It is frequently misunderstood and difficult to define, as it has much fuller meaning than a literal translation of 'feminine writing'. One of the clearest definitions I have found is by Verena Andermatt Conley: 'a working term referring less to a writing practiced mainly by women than, in a broader logical category, to textual ways of spending. It suggests a writing, based on an encounter with another – be it a body, a piece of writing, a social dilemma, a moment of passion – that leads to an undoing of hierarchies and oppositions that determine the limits of most conscious life' (vii).

Heidegger answers after Hölderlin in his poem: in these most destitute times the poet is able to 'discern the danger that is assailing man', she is the one 'capable of seeing the threat of the unhealable, the unholy' and by that discernment, unveiling tracings of the gods and the god who have fled (117). The destitution is made more so by human ignorance of its severity, and because of this lack of awareness, 'there fails to appear for the world the ground that grounds it' and the world hangs in the abyss. There is hope, however, if the world turns away from the abyss, which is only possible through the poet, who reaches into the abyss unlike any other human and restores awareness of the poetic in our being (92).

Cixous puts the problem poetically, echoing a passage of Heidegger's essay:[3]

> [I]n these feeble and forgetful times, when we are far away from things, so far from each other, very far from ourselves, in these sad and forgetful times, of feeble looks, too short, falling aside from things, far from living things, where we don't know how to read, to let senses radiate, and we are cold, a glacial air is blowing around our souls, around the words, around the moments, our ears are frozen, the years have four winters and our ears hibernate, we have need of translation. (*Vivre l'orange* 46–8)

We have need of translation. Who will translate for us? Who will open our ears, remind us how to read, discern the dangers, thaw our souls, reach into the abyss? Heidegger urges us to learn how to listen to true poets who know their vocation in this destitute time, ours the same as Hölderlin's, traced from the time of the gods' departure. And therein is the crux of this chapter: if poets are defined as those who best serve as such translators, then my word-fellows may indeed all be called poets, for they not only perform such translations, but they do so because they themselves were the beneficiaries of translations by others that they experienced as transformative. Their creative and spiritual lives come to life as they allow poetical texts to deeply affect them, which Heidegger tells us 'does not consist in a clutching or any other kind of grasping, but rather in a letting come of what has been dealt out' ('"... Poetically Man Dwells ..."' 225).

In this understanding, poetry matters because it knocks us off those straight and narrow paths of mediocrity and utilitarianism into something out of the

---

3    I am thinking particularly of this passage from Heidegger's 'What Are Poets For?': 'The essence of technology comes to the light of day only slowly. This day is the world's night, rearranged into merely technological day. This day is the shortest day. It threatens a single endless winter. Not only does protection now withhold itself from man, but the integralness of the whole of what is remains now in darkness. The wholesome and sound withdraws. The world becomes without healing, unholy' (117).

ordinary. Both Bonnefoy and Cixous know this very well. Sandra Gilbert has described Cixous's *The Newly Born Woman* in words that can easily be extended to Bonnefoy and Ignatius: reading Cixous, she writes, 'is like going to sleep in one world and waking up in another' (x). Ignatius, Bonnefoy and Cixous go to sleep in one world and wake up in another by reading. In our reading of them, we are offered the same opportunity if we are willing to let their work take our own spiritual measure.

Cixous and Heidegger place paths that encourage fruitful exploration of the texts of our poets: the idea of turning, or metanoia; the transgression of the boundary between inner and outer; movement within immobility; and *Gelassenheit*, a term used by Meister Eckhart and developed by Heidegger, that is, in the words of Detweiler, 'a condition of acceptance that is neither nihilistic nor fatalistic but the ability – and it may be a gift – to move gracefully through life's fortunes and accidents, or to wait out its calamities' (35). These paths are hermeneutical and spiritual, and thus my main concern is to suggest that, in reading and creating as poets, this odd trio may show us as readers what could be considered a 'religious imaginary', transforming our 'insides' so that we might transform our 'outsides' by poetically finding 'God' in all things. To bring out the features that might be inherent in such an imaginary, I will attend to those moments in the poets' lives and texts where the two intermingle most intensely. In this poetic realm, texts are taken into bodies and bodies enter texts, making for a transgressive and unstable environment ripe for transformation.[4]

### 'From an Apparently Immobile Contemplation ...'

Here is a commonality that mobilizes a joint attack on binaries of spirit/body, inner/outer, remaindered from the past. The three poets each undergo a transformation by chance, or grace, depending on your beliefs, while in what I will call spaces of immobility. They are transformed in these spaces by reading books given to them or stumbled upon, accidental readings, wonderful accidents, gifts that must be grace (and there I show my hand). The immobility of Ignatius is physical and forced upon him. Cixous is stilled by loneliness and desperation;

---

[4]    I am grateful to David Jasper for conversations on the destabilizing nature of the mingling of texts and bodies. In his book *The Sacred Body*, Jasper delves beneath the surface of things, making transgressive moves from body to text and back again. 'Texts into bodies and bodies into texts', he writes, eventually daring us to join him in what is both a deeply theological and hermeneutical journey by asking the question 'For what is it to dive into the depths, to risk the impossible vertical?' (182).

Bonnefoy, by ennui and mediocrity. Living and reading become so close in this consideration that it is sometimes difficult to see where one lets off and the other begins. For Cixous, writing is the energy of life/the energy of life is writing. For Ignatius, the text is something he inhabits. For Bonnefoy, the poem is a dwelling created out of words and empty spaces that surround them.

## The Pilgrim Poet

Let us begin our little textual pilgrimage with Ignatius, the one who calls himself 'the pilgrim' in his autobiography, which he narrated to another Jesuit (*A Pilgrim's Journey* 13). His experience of immobility and the transformation that it generated is the most obvious and easily delineated of the three poets. This immobilization is crucial for the foundational event of the saint's spiritual life: his conversion experience. In 1521, Ignatius, then a soldier, spent nine months recuperating from a horrible injury suffered when a cannonball shattered his leg in the battle of Pamplona (*A Pilgrim's Journey* 39).[5] After a few months he was well enough to want to read his favourite fare, chivalrous romances, but his sister-in-law Magdalena, matron of the Loyola castle, gave him the only books she possessed: Jacobus de Voragine's *The Golden Legend* and Ludolph of Saxony's *The Life of Jesus Christ* (*A Pilgrim's Journey* 43–4). What did Ignatius do in this immobility of the body? He was compelled by outside circumstance to turn inside, the outer immobility allowing for an inner dynamism.[6] He read, and read poetically; a letting go into the text that became part of him as he reacted to his reading. He entered the narratives of the saints, especially perhaps of Francis and Dominic, as they are mentioned specifically in the autobiography:

> While reading the life of our Lord and those of the saints, he used to pause and meditate, reasoning with himself: 'What if I were to do what Saint Francis did, or what Saint Dominic did?' Thus in his thoughts he dwelt on many good deeds, always suggesting to himself great and difficult ones, but as soon as he considered doing them, they all appeared easy of performance. Throughout these thoughts he used to say to himself: 'Saint Dominic did this, so I have to do it too. Saint Francis did this, so I have to do it too.' (*A Pilgrim's Journey* 47)

The tough soldier begins to note his affective responses to his reading, an embodied reading, for the emotions are experienced bodily (recall Cixous,

---

5    Ignatius was wounded in May 1521 and left for Jerusalem in February 1522.
6    I am grateful to David Jasper for this wording.

'These texts make us travel so that from an apparently immobile contemplation we are led to infinite discoveries'). Ignatius begins his interior pilgrimage as he starts to perceive a difference in his responses to the religious and adventurous texts. From this initial distinction will arise the practices of the discernment of the spirits, the core of the *Exercises*,[7] and the prayer of the senses. Michael Ivens describes the latter as 'the exercise which culminates the contemplative day ... characterized by a concentrated sense-presence with a minimum of discursive thinking. The sensing is bodily/imaginative and its immediate object is the physical realities of persons and things' (97).

From the autobiography:

> There was this difference, however. When he thought of worldly matters, he found much delight; but after growing weary and dismissing them, he found that he was dry and unhappy. But when he thought of going barefoot to Jerusalem and eating nothing but herbs and imitating the saints in all the austerities they practiced, he not only found consolation in these thoughts, but even after they had left him he remained happy and joyful. He did not consider nor did he stop to examine this difference until one day his eyes were partially opened, and he began to wonder at this difference and to reflect upon it. From experience he knew that some thoughts left him sad while others made him happy, and little by little he came to perceive the different spirits that were moving him; one coming from the devil, the other coming from God. (*A Pilgrim's Journey* 48)

I suggest that Ignatius has gone so far inside himself in his reading that he begins to incorporate the texts into his body. His reading spurs him to an eventual incredibly intricate and delicate awareness of his bodily responses, which he transmutes in an equally intricate and delicate way into the workings of his *Exercises*. Yet, within the rigid structure of the *Exercises* are a flexibility and playfulness, and a recognition of the importance of the senses, the freedom of the human person, and the delicate movements of the soul. He has read to an excess in his immobility, not only desiring to imitate but to be what he in fact was already becoming.

I think of Ignatius most often as pilgrim and poet. Therefore, it was with delight that I re-encountered a forgotten text by Roland Barthes (the eponymous *Sade, Fourier, Loyola*, an even odder threesome than my own), the only one I know of who has insisted on calling Ignatius a writer and his *Exercises* writing. Not only writer, but inventor of a new language, one that

---

7    See, for example, Dulles xv.

the exercitant must learn so as to be able to converse with God. Barthes reads the *Exercises* as writing, releasing the text from its bond of religion (9), he claims, and by doing so is able to discover multiple texts and an alternative economy, one, like Cixous's, of gift, which perhaps we might think of as a religious imaginary, recalling Detweiler's distinctions between his religious reading and institutional religion. Barthes notes that first there is the literal text, which Ignatius gives to the director of the retreat. The director interprets that text and offers it to the retreatant, in the process creating a new text. The retreatant performs it, imperfectly, as the gift offered to God, who receives it and offers God's own text back to the exercitant. Each giver and receiver is also a writer, writing a new text, creating a new language (41–4). Though Barthes does not use this wording, these languages are truly incarnational. 'The body in Ignatius is never conceptual; it is always *this* body: if I transport myself to a vale of tears, I must imagine, see *this* flesh, *these* members among the bodies of the creatures' (62). As Barthes notes, Ignatius founds 'meaning on matter and not on concept' (62). In Barthes's reading, resonances can be felt with Cixous's idea of writing the body. Like Cixous, Barthes reads with great pleasure. He perceives the text's life-giving nature and refuses to reduce it to an object:

> Nothing is more depressing than to imagine the Text as an intellectual object (for reflection, analysis, comparison, mirroring, etc.). The text is an object of pleasure ... at times the pleasure of the Text is achieved more deeply (and then is when we can truly say there is a Text): whenever the 'literary' Text (the Book) transmigrates into our life, whenever another writing (the Other's writing) succeeds in writing fragments of our own daily lives, in short, whenever a coexistence occurs. (7)[8]

Barthes in his reading pays attention to his own affective responses, as Ignatius would urge. In the process, he brings the saint to life, into greater intimacy with himself. Though some miss the wild joy of Ignatius, preferring a static domesticated version of the saint, piously bedecked in luxurious robes in Rome, Barthes, through his visceral reading, knows it: 'What I get from Loyola's life',

---

[8]    Text/text here is clearly not meant in the traditional sense of words that make up a work and give it a stable meaning that can be uncovered, but rather in the structuralist and post-structuralist sense of an unstable space where 'meaning is generated by the intertextual relations between one text and another and by the activation of those relations by a reader' (Allen 227).

Barthes writes, 'are not the saint's pilgrimages, visions, mortifications, and constitutions, but only "his beautiful eyes, always a little filled with tears"' (8).[9]

## *The Poet-Thinker*[10]

Cixous describes herself as 'only a poet' in her essay 'The Last Painting or the Portrait of God'. 'But not without God; being only a poet, I am really obligated to count on God, or on you, or on someone' (106). Perhaps that is reason enough for a linking with Ignatius. Still, they are an odd couple. So distant and yet somehow so close. I imagine they would have been great correspondents. As disciple of Jacques Derrida and author of the playful book *Portrait of Jacques Derrida as a Young Jewish Saint*,[11] Cixous reminds me of Ignatius in her mimetic excess. What do I mean by that phrase? There are at least two aspects. I turn to the philosopher Edith Wyschogrod, who brings the texts and lives of saints and postmodern writers into conversation in her book *Saints and Postmodernism: Revisioning Moral Philosophy*. First, she notes that the imperative of the hagiography is 'listen'; the successful response is not one of replication, but an identification with the 'spiritual rebirth and transformation' of the saint whose story is being told that inspires 'a new

---

9    Barthes assists my project in naming Ignatius a writer. He notes that many Jesuits deny their founder this privilege and sees in this something more telling: 'Here we find once more the old modern myth according to which language is merely the docile and *insignificant* instrument for the serious things that occur in the spirit, the heart or the soul. This myth is not innocent; discrediting the form serves to exalt the importance of the content: to say: *I write badly* means *I think well*' (39).

10    I borrow this appellation from Jacques Derrida who applied it to Cixous, whom he considered an intellectual and spiritual companion. The feeling was mutual: see, for example, Cixous and Calle-Gruber, *Rootprints*, where Cixous writes that she has 'a very great proximity with Derrida whom I have always considered to be my "other"' (80). Introducing one of her 1990 Wellek Library lectures in Critical Theory at the University of California, Irvine, which were published as *Three Steps on the Ladder of Writing*, he called her the greatest writer in the French language. 'For a great writer must be a poet-thinker, very much a poet and a very thinking poet' (*Three Steps*, front cover).

11    In her author's note, Cixous offers playfully subversive images appropriate to our nascent religious imaginary: 'You will of course have guessed that this portrait is to be somewhat unorthodox. UnCatholic in other words. What is a Young Jewish Saint [*Saint Juif*]? Given that its subject is Jacques Derrida, the inventor of *différance*, the poet who makes writing and hearing – and what an extraordinary sense of hearing he has – pair up and dance, this portrait is sotto voce and homophonically – do you hear? – that of a young *sainjuif*, I mean a Jewish monkey [*singe juif*], if there is such a thing, and why shouldn't there be a saintly monkey or a monkey of a saint?' (vii).

catena of moral events appropriate to the addressee's life' (10). The ultimate imperative of the Christian saint, to imitate Christ, is impossible, unrealizable, thus there are no rules for the creation of new texts and holy lives; instead they are created in the living of the life without rules, which is one of excess as it strives to bring into being one's own new transformative texts (xvi).

Is this not the space of imperatives that Cixous says she inhabits with Derrida? 'There is a relationship in writing in which I find my primary exigency, I would say, and which is his primary exigency' (*Rootprints* 84). Saint Jacques tells her a secret: 'one-step-more. When you arrive "at the end" (of a thought, of a description etc.) take one more step. When you have taken one more step, continue, take the next step' (84). The 'more' for Ignatius and for Cixous is not one of quantity but quality and intensity, as, for example, in the *Exercises* §319 in the first Rules for the Discernment of Spirits at a time of desolation, there is a recommendation not to insist upon more prayer but to 'insist more upon prayer'. Or, in this example from the autobiography: 'Whenever he made up his mind to do a certain penance that the saints had done, he was determined not only to do the same, but even more' (Ignatius, *A Pilgrim's Journey* 56).

And then there is the shared attention to the practice of writing. We know that Ignatius had 'attractive penmanship' and, at Loyola, wrote on 'polished and lined paper' (*A Pilgrim's Journey* 50). He sets out for Jerusalem carrying with him a notebook in which he has copied passages from his reading in convalescence.

> He took an account book – it was quarto in size and had three hundred pages – and in it he wrote our Lord's words in red ink, just as he had seen them in Ludolph's *Life of Christ*, but it was his own idea to record those of our Lady in blue. (*A Pilgrim's Journey*, Tylenda commentary 50, footnote 11)

He relates that the book 'afforded him much consolation' (*A Pilgrim's Journey* 63). He carried this book in his wanderings through Europe, scribbling notes constantly about his reading of the movements of his spirit, which made their way into letters to spiritual companions like Isabel Roser, his longtime friend, benefactress and, briefly, 'Jesuitess'.[12] Later, as superior general, he wrote thousands of letters from Rome (*Personal Writings* 113–15), another enforced immobility of sorts and an ironic destiny for one who wanted nothing more than to plant paths and walk them.

---

[12]  For background on Roser and correspondence between her and Ignatius, see Hugo Rahner's *Saint Ignatius Loyola: Letters to Women*.

As noted above, Cixous is also incredibly prolific. The seeds of this production are notes, notes as seeds, written on scraps of paper, in journals, anywhere and everywhere. 'I keep scores of little bits of paper, for I note at top speed what presents itself all the time, in a café at a minigolf, while walking along the street, I have small notebooks in my pockets, I scribble on a paper napkin' (*The Writing Notebooks* vii). Writing is a spiritual exercise. 'I try to organize it: beginning with silence. With the conditions of retreat, yes, the conditions of an interior voyage. With the least resistance possible' (*Rootprints* 105).

'The conditions of an interior voyage.' Indeed, Ignatius and Cixous are hermeneuts of the soul. I had had my doubts, but now I see reason to keep pursuing this linking. They illustrate why reluctance to engage postmodernism in theology and religious studies is an anathema and not the other way around. As Wyschogrod points out, 'the antiseptic atmosphere of modernism does not allow the saints to breathe' and failed 'to create a continuity with the past' (xiv, xvii). In its paradoxical refusal and embrace of language, its playful, excessive and reflexive nature, its acknowledgement of materiality and imagination, and its refusal of meta-narratives and acceptance of ambiguity, the postmodern is an atmosphere (a religious imaginary?) in which the saint may flourish. How so, specifically? Because 'the old does not simply disappear. It is displaced within specifiable discursive contexts – art, literature, philosophy – through critique' (xv).

Cixous's writing practices are critique enacted with as much body and soul as mind. Her continuous development of the idea of *écriture féminine*, with 'its willingness to defy the masculine and seek new relations between subject and the other through writing' (Sellers 5), may prove helpful as a lens into ways of reading anew hagiographies as narratives expressing, in Wyschogrod's words, 'the primacy of the other person and the dissolution of self-interest' (xiv). Cixous expresses an exquisite attentiveness to the other in her depictions of a life-changing reading encounter with the Brazilian writer Clarice Lispector.[13] The space of Cixous's immobility before this encounter and the creative movement that both impel are not as obvious as Ignatius's physical restriction. Though, like his, hers are formed out of intersections of life and body and text and writing, apropos, as she is proponent and practitioner of an aspect of *écriture féminine* mentioned above that she refers to as writing the body.

---

[13]    Clarice Lispector (1920–77) is one of the most important writers in twentieth-century Brazilian literature. Cixous began reading Lispector in the 1970s and helped bring her work to wider attention in Europe. Lispector is perhaps less well-known in the English-speaking world, though recently there has been a resurgence of interest, with a biography and new translations by Benjamin Moser (see Tóibín).

As Heather Walton writes, regarding the latter phrase:

> Cixous assumes Derrida's barely submerged mythology of writing as a female revolt against authority. Women's writing is a volcanic force, to shatter the framework of institutions, to blow up the law, to break up the truth with laughter. She incarnates this feminine writing in the symbolic figure of the woman who writes her body. (148)

Cixous's texts are dynamic, in constant movement, and it is difficult to make a claim for stillness at any point in her long and prolific career. Yet there are references to an immobilization she experienced followed by her encounter with Lispector. The most vivid depiction of this experience is expressed in an early experimental novel, *Vivre l'orange/To Live the Orange*, a text that is also an example of *écriture féminine*, which, because of Cixous's resistance to defining the practice, is perhaps best illuminated through her performance of it. The encounter is expressed in terms of a revelation:

> I wandered for ten glacial years in over-published solitude, without seeing a single human woman's face, the sun had retired, it was mortally cold, the truth had set, I took the last book before death, and behold, it was Clarice, the writing … The writing came up to me, she addressed to me, in seven tongues, one after the other, she read herself to me, through my absence up to the presence … I saw her face. My God. She showed me her face. I had my vision. (48)

The reader is reminded of the Book of Revelation: the number seven, sign of the divine, visions of God, a revelation by an angel, the dead who come to life, body made present in and through text. 'I know your affliction and your poverty, even though you are rich' (Rev. 2:8, New Revised Standard Version). In this apocalypse, God is she, and the meeting with her is holy.

Cixous has made the hermeneutical and spiritual shift to an embodied way of reading, a different mode of knowing, undertaken by Ignatius and suggested by Heidegger. I wonder what Cixous would make of Ignatius's prayer of the senses? Would she consider him a practitioner of writing the body, of *écriture féminine*, which she does not restrict by gender? In the Fifth Contemplation of the Second Week of the *Exercises*, the exercitant is asked at the end of the day of prayers and repetitions on the Nativity to apply the five senses 'with the aid of the imagination', to see, hear, touch, to 'smell the infinite fragrance, and taste the infinite sweetness of the divinity' (§101–25).

How does one respond to such vivid and felt prayer and writing? Have the two not shown evidence of being those who can reach into Heidegger's abyss and contribute toward a turning? Are not the reader and retreatant moved to awaken in another world, one of awe and wonder? The prayer of the senses is one of sinking, deepening, a hopefulness for the fruits of the day's contemplations to be made present. The response is no response. It is the gift of gracefully waiting.

## The Poet-Painter

Our path ends with Yves Bonnefoy. It was he who led me to see the transformative potential of immobility through the reading of his first major poetry collection, *On the Motion and Immobility of Douve*, an alternating series of prose and verse about the life, death and new life of a woman lover, Douve. His own immobility occurred as a result of a lack of art and literature in the provincial city of his childhood, which he has described as a place 'where what does not attract attention, where what is perpetuated without any real becoming, and without unsettling any established habit, was the law – and where the bookstores were empty' ('The Origins' 143). Then one day his philosophy teacher brings him a book from Paris, a collection of surrealists. He describes it as 'a real thunderbolt' and 'a whole world' ('The Origins' 143). He was attracted by the surrealist image, felt a kind of calling, that 'going toward' that Cixous spoke of above. In an interview in 1976, he recalls the moment:

> 'If only there were sun tonight,' I read, and it seemed to me that a road whose presence I had not even imagined opened in front of me, in this night I recognized as my own, and as deep as ever, but now suddenly murmuring, initiatory – the first step toward the first true light ... ('The Origins' 143–4)

Bonnefoy becomes disenchanted with surrealism out of a concern of distorted vision of the 'presence' that it initially revealed to him, but he keeps what becomes a lifelong interest in painting and sculpture, writing eloquently, perceptively and widely on such subjects as the paintings of the Italian Quattrocentro, the life and art of Alberto Giacometti, the work of Poussin, Hopper, Delacroix, Balthus and many others. His writing on art cannot be separated from his poetry, for it is his openness to and experience of the visual and the tactile, deeply reflected upon, that fuels an impossible desire to express the immediate and material in words. He finds in painting an immediacy unavailable to one who creates with words, but it is that very immediacy that illuminates that aspect of poetics that we have been circling around in this piece: the interior depths of the imagination where the creative act originates. That intense awareness of spiritual movements within oneself evident in the works of Ignatius and Cixous is also a quality of Bonnefoy, as can be seen, for example, in his perception of Edward Hopper:

> By means of the color he puts on the canvas, which becomes precision and intensity simply through hearing and assimilating the mysterious beauty of the world, the painter is able to bring about his own transmutation. He can, in sum, recompose his psychic being, turning his earlier anguish, born from doubts about the value of the physical world, into these pigments that are ablaze with joy. ('The Photosynthesis of Being' 146)

Like Cixous, what matters most to Bonnefoy in his critique is the affinity he feels for a work of art and/or an artist. Though he relies on art history, he is not an art historian. His concerns lie elsewhere, in sympathy with ours:

> I thought it made sense to imagine a relationship and a continuity between what one desires and the work of artists one loves the most: love being the sign of affinity as much as the key to knowledge. I desired the merging of poetic activity with criticism, at the most deeply personal level, rather than their dissociation through analysis. (Preface xviii)

Bonnefoy shares with Ignatius and Cixous a willingness to go into the depths, and invites us to go with him. The sparseness and beauty of his poems disguise their ability to disorient the reader and shift her thinking. In the midst of reading Douve, I realized I no longer recognized the landscape into which he had invited me. Yet I desired nothing more than to remain there, not as an escape but as the opposite: to wait in hope of a fleeting glimpse of the presence of something eternal held within those elemental and sacramental objects he writes into his poetry. I had awakened in a new world, perhaps the religious imaginary that this essay begins to seek.

We end in that poem, 'The Orangery', where we began, planting paths of thoughts and silence:

> So we will walk on the ruins of a vast sky,
> The far-off landscape will bloom
> Like a destiny in the vivid light.
>
> The long-sought most beautiful country
> Will lie before us land of salamanders,

Look, you will say, at this stone:

Death shines from it.

Secret lamp it is this that burns under our steps,

Thus we walk lighted. (Bonnefoy, *On the Motion* 119)

## Works Cited

Allen, Graham. *Intertextuality*. London: Routledge, 2011.

Barthes, Roland. *Sade, Fourier, Loyola*. Trans. Richard Miller. London: Jonathan Cape, 1976.

Bonnefoy, Yves. 'The Act and the Place of Poetry'. In *The Act and the Place of Poetry*, ed. John T. Naughton; trans. Jean Stewart and John T. Naughton. Chicago: University of Chicago Press, 1989, 101–17.

—— 'Interview with Yves Bonnefoy'. In *In the Shadow's Light*, trans. John Naughton. Chicago: University of Chicago Press, 1991, 161–79.

—— *On the Motion and Immobility of Douve*. Trans. Galway Kinnell. Newcastle upon Tyne: Bloodaxe, 1992.

—— 'The Origins and Development of My Concept of Poetry: An Interview with John E. Jackson (1976)'. In *The Act and the Place of Poetry*, ed. Naughton, 143–55.

—— 'The Photosynthesis of Being: Edward Hopper'. In *The Lure and the Truth of Painting: Selected Essays on Art*, ed. and trans. Richard Stamelman. Chicago: University of Chicago Press, 1995, 141–60.

—— 'Preface'. In *The Lure and the Truth of Painting: Selected Essays on Art*, ed. and trans. Stamelman. Print.

Caputo, John D. *The Mystical Element in Heidegger's Thought*. New York: Fordham University Press, 1990.

Cixous, Hélène. 'The Last Painting or the Portrait of God'. In *'Coming to Writing' and Other Essays*, ed. Deborah Jenson; trans. Sarah Cornell et al. Cambridge, MA: Harvard University Press, 1991, 104–31.

—— 'Poetry, Passion, and History: Marina Tsvetayeva'. In *Readings: The Poetics of Blanchot, Joyce, Kafka, Kleist, Lispector, and Tsvetayeva*, trans. Verena Andermatt Conley. Minneapolis, MN: University of Minnesota Press, 1991, 110–51.

—— *Portrait of Jacques Derrida as a Young Jewish Saint*. Trans. Beverly Bie Brahic. New York: Columbia University Press, 2004.

—— *Three Steps on the Ladder of Writing*. Trans. Sarah Cornell and Susan Sellers. New York: Columbia University Press, 1993.

—— *Vivre l'orange/To Live the Orange*. Trans. Ann Liddle and Sarah Cornell. Paris: Des Femmes, 1979.

—— *The Writing Notebooks of Hélène Cixous*. Ed. and trans. Susan Sellers. London: Continuum, 2004.

Cixous, Hélène and Mireille Calle-Gruber. *Hélène Cixous Rootprints: Memory and Life Writing*. Trans. Eric Prenowitz. London: Routledge, 1997.

Conley, Verena Andermatt. 'Introduction'. In *Reading with Clarice Lispector* by Hélène Cixous. Ed. and trans. Verena Andermatt Conley. London: Harvester Wheatsheaf, 1990, vii–xviii.

Detweiler, Robert. 'What Is Reading Religiously?' In *Breaking the Fall: Religious Readings of Contemporary Fiction*. New York: Harper and Row, 1989, 30–66.

Dulles, Avery. 'Preface'. In *The Spiritual Exercises of St Ignatius: Based on Studies of the Language of the Autograph*, trans. Louis J. Puhl, SJ. New York: Vintage, 2000, xiii–xxiii.

Eagleton, Terry. *How to Read a Poem*. Oxford: Blackwell, 2007.

Gilbert, Sandra M. 'Introduction: A Tarantella of Theory'. In *The Newly Born Woman* by Hélène Cixous and Catherine Clément. Minneapolis, MN: University of Minnesota Press, 1986, ix–xviii.

Heidegger, Martin. '"... Poetically Man Dwells ..."'. In *Poetry, Language, Thought*, trans. Albert Hofstadter. New York: Harper and Row, 1971, 209–54.

—— 'What Are Poets For?' In *Poetry, Language, Thought*, trans. Albert Hofstadter. New York: Harper and Row, 1971, 87–140.

Hölderlin, Friedrich. 'In Lovely Blueness ...'. In *Poems and Fragments*, trans. Michael Hamburger. London: Routledge, 1966, 601.

Ignatius of Loyola. *Personal Writings: Reminiscences, Spiritual Diary, Select Letters, including the text of 'The Spiritual Exercises'*. Trans. Joseph A. Munitiz and Philip Endean. London: Penguin, 1996.

—— *A Pilgrim's Journey: The Autobiography of Ignatius of Loyola*. Revised edition. Trans. Joseph N. Tylenda SJ. San Francisco: Ignatius Press, 2001.

—— *The Spiritual Exercises of St Ignatius, a New Translation Based on Studies in the Language of the Autograph*. Trans. Louis J. Puhl, SJ. Chicago: Loyola Press, 1951.

Ivens, Michael. *Understanding the Spiritual Exercises: Text and Commentary: A Handbook for Retreat Directors*. Leominster: Gracewing, 2008.

Jardine, Alice A. *Gynesis: Configurations of Woman and Modernity*. Ithaca, NY: Cornell University Press, 1985.

Jasper, David. *The Sacred Body*. Waco, TX: Baylor University Press, 2009.

Kearney, Richard. *Poetics of Imagining: Modern to Post-modern*. New York: Fordham University Press, 1998.

Rahner, Hugo. *Saint Ignatius Loyola: Letters to Women*. New York: Herder and Herder, 1960.

Sellers, Susan. *Hélène Cixous: Authorship, Autobiography and Love*. Cambridge: Polity, 1996.

Tóibín, Colm. 'Introduction'. In *The Hour of the Star*, trans. Benjamin Moser. New York: New Directions, 2011.

Walton, Heather. 'Hélène Cixous and the Mysteries that Beat in the Heart of the World'. In *Literature, Theology and Feminism*. Manchester: Manchester University Press, 2007, 144–66.

Wyschogrod, Edith. *Saints and Postmodernism: Revisioning Moral Philosophy*. Chicago: University of Chicago Press, 1990.

# PART IV
## Poets and Spiritual Experience:
## Mystical Gestures

# Chapter 12

# 'There Is a Verge of the Mind': Imagination and Mystical Gesture in Rilke's Later Poems

## Mark S. Burrows

> A true poet is not satisfied with an evasive imagination. He wants imagination to be a *voyage*. Thus each poet owes us his *invitation to the voyage*. With this invitation we register, in our inner being, a gentle impulsion which shakes us, which sets in motion beneficent reverie, truly dynamic reverie ... In the realm of imagination, every immanence takes on a transcendence. (Bachelard 21–3)

The artist, poet and printmaker William Blake announced in sweeping fashion that 'the imagination is not a State; it is the Human Existence itself'. Such a sweeping claim points to cultural and intellectual shifts occurring at the turn of the nineteenth century, in reaction to the narrow argumentation that had come to characterize Deist and Enlightenment rationalism. Romantics like Blake prized the imagination as the highest form of cognition, seeing it as a means of accessing dimensions of experience otherwise inaccessible. Rainer Maria Rilke, while no Romantic, stands as an heir to this long tradition. His poetry presumes that the act of seeing does not bring us, like spectators, to observe an external reality which is somehow 'outside' of us. Rather, our seeing is the experience by which we come to make reality, a form of imagination that finds expression in the poetic act. As he put it in an early poem:

> The hour bows down and stirs me
> with a clear and ringing stroke;
> my senses tremble. I feel that I can –
> and I seize the forming day.
> Nothing was yet done before I beheld it,
> and every becoming stood still;
> my ways of seeing are ripe, and, like a bride,
> to each one comes the thing each wills. (*Prayers* 35)

For Rilke, our 'ways of seeing are ripe', and actually determine what it is that we see. Thus, for the poet, seeing is not believing, as the common adage puts it, but rather the act of imagining is a way of seeing. It is the form of constructive perception by which we might say that seeing is making. For it is by means of poetic experience that we make the 'self', and at the same time find that we are 'making' the world. Or, to put it another way, Rilke sees the imagination as the fundamental way by which we learn to see and make reality, not as a form of perception that depends on what is seen. The imagination creates experience. It enables us to discover the world by making it, an interior process by which we give depth and texture to the world we inhabit, in and through the creative powers of the imagination. We 'seize' the day in its unfinished state, and 'make' it what will be, and thus, as he puts it, 'nothing was yet done before [we] beheld it'. Our ways of seeing, our manner of beholding, is itself the means by which we enact our 'becoming' in the world – and the world's 'becoming' within us. All of this points to how Rilke's poetics is a sustained invitation to embark on what Bachelard describes as the 'voyage' of the imagination.

This insight into the enduring power of this Romanticist epistemology suggests that we rightly read Rilke's poems as a distinctively modernist form of 'mysticism', a characterization that depends on appreciating Rilke's view of the imagination as the 'maker' of experience. Of course, the poet viewed that way of thinking as no longer tenable, turning from it as an abandoned site of conjecture that had become inconceivable and thus uninhabitable for modern artists and intellectuals. Beginning one of these fin-de-siècle poems which he writes as a musing upon this transition, he can claim that: 'One feels the radiance of a new page / on which everything could still come to be' (*Prayers* 42).

How then might we approach the question of 'the mystical' as a creative or imaginative 'journey'? Paul Mommaers points in this direction when he describes the mystic as 'one who experiences in an overpowering manner the presence of something that is beyond us, and more real than all that we otherwise characterize as reality' (24). George Steiner makes a similar claim for the aesthetic, which he describes in phenomenological terms as 'quicken[ing] into lit presence the continuum between temporality and eternity, between matter and spirit, between man and "the other"' (227). He goes on to suggest that this dimension of the arts can be best understood as 'the making formal of epiphany', an experience that recreates the artist's internal experience of what Steiner calls 'a shining through' (226). Strangely, Steiner sees the artist not as a creator but rather as a conduit of sorts, a medium for what I am here describing as 'mystical gestures'. It is this claim that the present essay explores, looking particularly at the late poetry of Rilke as found in his *Sonnets to Orpheus* (1922).

Rilke announces this characterization in his early novel, *The Notebooks of Malte Laurids Brigge*, a loosely structured memoir made up of often quite lengthy letters that he had earlier written to friends, together with journal entries made during his Paris years. In the early pages of the novel, Malte admits that:

> I am learning to see [*Ich lerne sehen*]. I don't know why it is, but everything enters
> me more deeply and doesn't stop where it once used to. I have an interior [*Ich habe*
> *ein Inneres*] that I never knew of. Everything passes into it now. I don't know what
> happens there. (5)

The entire novel, with all its strangeness, could be read as an extended meditation on creativity and the imaginative life, exploring the constructive powers of this *Inneres* as conveying what might be called a 'sense' of the mystical – at least as Mommaers and others have characterized it. At a later juncture in the book, Rilke's protagonist describes the origin and consequence of writing:

> World-consummator [*Weltvollendender*]: as that which comes down as rain over
> the earth and upon the waters, falling carelessly, at random – inevitably rises
> again, invisible and joyous, out of all things, and ascends and floats and forms the
> heavens: so our precipitations rose out of you, and vaulted the world with music.
> (76–7)

As Rilke came to understand it, poetry was an essentially constructive enterprise, an experience that consummates the world both for the poet and for the reader. Arising from *ein Inneres*, which Stephen Mitchell renders as 'an interior' though the word seems to suggest something closer to 'an innerness', the poem itself reflects in its form a cycle of falling and rising, beginning with a sort of randomness as experience 'falls' into language, but then rising into form with an apparent inevitability on its journey of becoming music. It is, in precisely this sense, the context for interpreting such poetry as a form of mystical gesture. The poet completes the world in this sense, and the very act of writing – or creating – comes to participate in a cycle he understands not in metaphysical but rather in phenomenological terms.

Viewed from this vantage point, the experience of this creative cycle mimics the *exitus/reditus* framework of neo-platonist cosmology. Art derives from the 'flow' of this cycle such that the poet's creative work embodies the movement of energy into form, and 'sense' into image and finally into lyric. This process points to what Ben Hutchison, in his study of Rilke's poetics, describes as 'a transition from "subjective" to "objektive Innerlichkeit"' (169). Rilke refuses to concede that the poet 'makes up' such images; rather, they seem to 'make him up', as it were. They are part of the real, and actually come to 'make' reality, even if perceptible principally through the imagination.

Conventional approaches to mysticism in the modern discussion still often follow William James's lead when he describes it as a peculiar 'mode of consciousness'. It actually comes to represent, he insists, the highest form of religious experience. To illustrate this he employs vivid metaphorical language to suggest that *there is a verge of the mind* which [music] haunt[s]; and whispers therefrom mingle with the operations of our understanding, even as the waters of the infinite ocean send their waves to break among the pebbles that lie upon our shores' (421; my emphasis). He defines this 'verge of the mind' in psychological rather than more narrowly religious terms, and claims it as the locus of the 'mystical'. As such, it is an experience that the 'once-born', to recall his categories, cannot begin to see, emerging only for those he describes as the 'twice-born', those whose lives have been broken through a failure that dispels a naïve trust in goodness.

Michel de Certeau begins his assessment of mysticism where James leaves off. He identifies what he calls '*la mystique*' – rendered in the English translation as 'mystics' – as a 'style' of thought and writing which began to emerge in the later Middle Ages. The intent of de Certeau's 'mystics', following Philip Sheldrake, was 'essentially radical and disruptive, both religiously and socially' (39). De Certeau suggests that 'mystics' represents more than a form of writing initiating the reader into a mode of experience, though it is surely this also. It also stands as a creative response to the 'global situation of crisis' affecting Western religious institutions in modernity ('Mystic Speech' 81). As de Certeau goes on to explain: 'The various strains of mystics, in their reaction to the vanishing of truths, the increasing opaqueness of the authorities and divided or diseased institutions ... institute a "style" that articulates itself into *practices* defining a *modus loquendi* and/or a *modus agendi*' (*Mystic Fable* 14).

At the close of *The Mystic Fable*, he presents 'mystics' as a poetics of experience, and locates its flourishing in modernity among outsiders to the ranks of the conventionally 'religious': in other words, artists and, among them, above all poets. According to de Certeau, this tradition of witness

> formed a solidarity with all the tongues that continued speaking, marked in their discourse by the assimilation to the child, the woman, the illiterate, madness, angels, or the body. Everywhere they insinuate an 'extraordinary': they are voices quoted – voices grown more and more separate from the field of meaning that writing had conquered, ever closer to the song or the cry. (*Mystic Fable* 13)

Unlike forms of mystical writings anchored in what were understood as the secure metaphysical foundations of an earlier age, de Certeau argues that 'mystics' no longer depends on 'a cosmos of divine messages (or "mysteries")' to be understood', taking the form of what he describes as 'itinerant practices which trace in language the indeterminate path of a mode of writing'. Such a *praxis* emphasizes departure rather than arrival, and favours longing – and even anguish – over satisfaction and darkness over light. The poetics at the heart of this 'mystics' offers itself, in de Certeau's language, as a 'liberating space' which refuses to 'lay down a meaning once and for all'. As an example of this posture, he points to Teresa of Avila's image of the 'interior castle' as a deliberate 'fable' or 'fiction' which 'opens up a free space in which to write (walk about), a space she can enter without permission, where she can find so many "treats"' (*Mystic Fable* 16). This description characterizes Rilke's writings with an equal force, particularly the later poetry of *The Duino Elegies* and *The Sonnets to Orpheus* (1922).

What remained of this 'mystics' after the crisis of Christianity in the modern West, aptly described by Erich Heller as 'an age dispossessed of all spiritual certainties' (170), are the energies and forms of poetry, according to de Certeau. This is so, not because of undergirding assumptions, measured either by metaphysical ideas or theistic convictions, but rather on account of the peculiar *diction* of such poetry. Again, de Certeau:

> The music [of poetry], come from an unknown quarter, inaugurates a new rhythm of existence – some would say a new 'breath', a new way of walking, a different 'style' of life [which] simultaneously captivates an attentiveness from within, disturbs the orderly flow of thought, and opens up or frees new spaces. (*Mystic Fable* 297)

This 'interior' is not simply a *tabula rasa* upon which the mind 'records' its impressions of the external world, as David Hume had suggested. Rather, it is the 'place' within us where poetry occurs by 'open[ing] up or free[ing] new spaces' within us, as de Certeau suggests. In this sense, the poet comes to represent what Rilke had addressed as the '*Weltvollendender*', whose art – again drawing on Malte's description of writing – 'transform[s] this capillary action all at once into the most convincing gestures, into the most available forms', seeking 'equivalents in the visible world for what ... had [been] seen inside' (*Notebooks* 83). In de Certeau's words, the poem 'comes without reason and does what it says: *it itself creates what it makes space for*' ('Mystic Speech' 202–3; my emphasis). In a word: *poiesis*.

It would be improper to introduce Rilke as a mystical theologian, since he distanced himself deliberately and forcefully from the horizon we think of as 'theology' in the proper sense of that word. But Rilke surely stands in the tradition of 'mystics', following de Certeau's lead, a point largely unnoticed in the critical reception of Rilke's writings. To illustrate this approach, I will focus on one of *The Sonnets to Orpheus* (II, 21; Burrows):

> Sing the gardens, my heart, that you don't know,
> like those poured into glass: radiant, unreachable.
> Fountains and roses from Ispahan or Shiraz,
> sing them into sanctity; praise them, each incomparable.
> Show, my heart, that you could never endure without them.
> That their ripening figs are meant only for you.
> That you linger with them among the blooming branches,
> like winds rising upon the face.
> Refuse the confusion that there is any want
> for one who resolves simply this: to be!
> As silken threads you were woven into the fabric.
> Whatever of these images you've joined in your heart,
> if only in a moment of the anguish we must face,
> sense how this points to the whole glorious tapestry.

The vivid metaphor with which this sonnet opens evokes James's notion of the mind's 'verge'. But in this case, the poet calls upon his heart to search not for what lies *beyond* this 'verge', but rather what is within – that is to say, the dimension of experience that the poet earlier described as 'an innerness'. His witness is not a yearning for transcendence as an escapist strategy, nor does he express it as a quest for invisibility. Rather, he sees it as a call to a peculiar form of immanence, of indwelling this world, and in this case as a longing for a kind of visibility – an immanence, as Bachelard put it, that 'takes on a transcendence' (23). This longing is a kind of gesture toward what we do not know but experience as a 'presence' that is always within us. This gesture of the imagination lures us toward the radiance of those 'gardens' we have not yet known, and which for this very reason become for us the source of an unattainable desire. The poem itself, one might say, is an allurement which reveals itself in the poet's praise, in the heart's 'worship' of such radiance. Within this interior 'sanctuary', Rilke calls us as witnesses to '*singe sie selig*', to 'sing them into sanctity' and 'praise them' because of their singular beauty – unreachable ('*unerreichbar*') and incomparable ('*keinem vergleichbar*').

What exactly do these gardens represent? Rilke would probably find this question misplaced: his interest is not in what these gardens suggested as external sites, but rather in what they incite within us – in other words, singing. He had already announced the importance of song in one of the earliest of the *Sonnets* (I, 3), addressing himself here directly to Orpheus:

> Song, as you teach it, is not desire,
> not a pleading for something finally achieved;
> song is being. An easy feat for the god.
> But when will we *be*?

It is crucial to notice what Rilke does not say: his call to singing is a gesture within us, not one toward something or someone, whether 'God' or 'a god'. To recall the opening line of this sonnet, 'A god can do it' (*Ein Gott vermags*). In this particular sense, singing for Rilke was anything but a duty, nor did he approach it as a moral responsibility. Song enacts 'being' itself. We discover our 'innerness', and become our true selves, when we sing. As such, song is its own gift. Thus, when Rilke calls us to 'sing [these gardens] into sanctity', we find ourselves implicated as readers in the 'making' of the world (*poiesis*). We ourselves, he implies, become 'world-consummators', those whose work it is to 'complete' the 'world'. And we do this chiefly through song. We 'sing' not only this *world* but our very *self* into 'being', for 'song is being' itself (*Gesang ist Dasein*, *Sonnets* I, 3).

As a sonnet intended for Orpheus, the muse who sought to lure Eurydice from the underworld, we hear the poet's invocation to 'sing what [we] do not know' as a call to a particular itinerancy: in the opening stanzas, one leading us from an 'outside' to the interiority of the heart's song, and then in the closing two stanzas to a particular *praxis*. The poem's flow moves us from the vivid intensities of imaginative experience – that is to say, 'whatever images you've joined yourself to within' – to emphasize the anguish of a particular moment – 'even if only in a moment of life's agony'. This suggestion evokes the tragic element in Orpheus's journey: one can almost hear whispers in the poem's unspoken margins warning us not to turn back, not to be distracted from the 'making' of song, and to continue onward.

The allusion to Orpheus thickens the poem's meaning, lending it the force of a 'mystical' gesture – or, rather, a cluster of gestures by which Rilke invites the reader to undertake what de Certeau calls an itineration. With Orpheus, we find ourselves lured by song to distinct practices of being, called to pay attention to all the 'moments' in our lives and particularly those that are the most difficult for us. Only in this way, Rilke suggests, will we come to know how the singular threads of our lives are part of 'the whole, glorious tapestry'.

Crucial to Rilke's poetic project is his call to 'make' our life by way of an imagination that sings and even praises the unknown. Here, the poet's vocation offers a way of redemption: in this case, by singing the 'gardens' that are always within us. As he laments in the first *Elegy*, our problem is existential and not geographical, since 'we are not reliably at home / in this managed world' of our making. We hear the same warning already in *The Notebooks*, where he reminds us that 'art means *not to know* that the world *is*, and, thus, to *make* one. Not to destroy what is already present, but rather *not to discover anything as fully completed*' (97).

Once again we hear his view that the poet's work is to 'make' the world, to give it shape through his singing, to 'enact' it in praise. He explains this vocation in a marvellous passage later in *The Notebooks* where he describes an adult whom he had admired as a child caught in the act of reading: 'I had the impression that the pages kept growing fuller beneath her gaze, as if she looked words onto them, certain words that she needed and that weren't there' (92). Such a reading – that is to say, that one makes what one needs beyond the givenness of what one finds – suggests the experience of 'overflowing' which Rilke associates with the arts generally and poetry in particular, that sense of being freed from the confines of the 'given' or 'written'. As de Certeau put it, such a 'mystics' functions by 'creat[ing] what it makes space for' ('Mystic Speech' 202–3). If poetry is this kind of singing, then song is this kind of being and 'acting' in the world (*modus agendi*).

The call to 'sing the gardens' that we do *not* know, such that the imagined 'outer' comes to enact the experienced 'inner', is what gives such vibrant energy to this sonnet. Rilke's metaphor of unknown 'gardens' suggests a kind of creative opening in our interior elaborated through a string of analogies. Thus, Rilke's language, despite the force of imperative verbs, voices not so much a declaration as an invitation: *Singe*, *Zeige* and *Meide* ('sing', 'show' and 'avoid', which I here render as 'refuse') invite just such an opening. In the eleventh line, which can be interpreted as the hinge on which this sonnet swings, we find the strange and wonderful claim – voiced by an implicit analogy – that the reader should consider herself as a 'silken thread' woven into the larger pattern of this 'fabric' (*Gewebe*). Indeed, the texture of this fabric gestures toward Rilke's reference, in the final stanza, to a *Teppich*, which literally means 'carpet' – a reference to a Persian rug, like those he had hung on the interior walls of his rooms in Muzot, with its symmetries only observable from a distance.

The sonnet thus 'sings' an invitation to a poetic life, as it were, voicing a distinct kind of music that 'haunts the mind' in such experience. It invites readers to become 'wanderers' in their hearts, itinerants who make their way beyond the bounds of their certainties by singing what they do not know but are able to imagine through the creative enactments of metaphor. Thus, the poem becomes a call to a distinct form of practice, one that Rilke describes in a luminous passage found in *The Notebooks of Malte Laurids Brigge*:

> In spite of my fear, I am still like someone standing in the presence of something great, and I remember that I often used to feel this happening inside me when I was about to write. But this time, I will be written. I am the impression that will transform itself. (53)

In the final pages of *The Mystic Fable*, de Certeau speaks of this form of 'mystics' in a sense that captures the poetics of Rilke's late writings, above all what we encounter in the *Sonnets*. He describes such a visionary as one who

> cannot stop walking and, with the certainty of what is lacking, knows of every place and object that it is *not that*; one cannot stay *there* nor be content with *that*. Desire creates an excess. Places are exceeded, passed, lost behind it. It makes one go further, elsewhere. It lives nowhere. (299)

This description captures the existential predicament that Rilke felt to be ours – in other words, as those who 'find ourselves in the position of one / who is always departing', as he put it in one of the *Elegies*:

> ... We are like the one
> standing on the farthest hill beyond his valley
> who, looking back one last time, pauses, lingers –
> so it is that we live always taking our leave. (no. 8)

But what is it, he wonders, that seduces us to look back, a reference that cannot but evoke Orpheus's fate? And what goal lures us forward? What radiance of unknown yet strangely familiar 'gardens' calls to us – which is to say, what future horizon beckons us to experience the 'innerness' of our lives? How do we come to 'know' these imagined 'gardens' as immanent to the heart's longings, even if such an imagination lies beyond our actual experience? In other words, how do we experience such 'gardens' in an 'overflowing' of the heart's longing, which de Certeau attributes to an 'excess created by desire' (*Mystic Fable* 299)? Such questions point back to the poet's confession, announced in *The Notebooks of Malte Laurids Brigge*, that 'I am learning to see. Yes, I am beginning' (6). They also offer a vivid illustration of Gianni Vattimo's suggestion that we must learn to interpret and experience 'artwork as prophecy, as a point of departure rather than a point of arrival', and thus learn to 'ask not what it means or what it refers to or what reality it should be referred to in order to be explained', but rather 'what it wants to say' (55).

The lure of this sonnet in its function as mystical gesture reminds us that Rilke's call is to a particular form of *poiesis*, a praxis of the imagination that shapes not only our 'interior' but the 'external' world we see – and, in that seeing, 'make'. As such, it stands as the means by which we set forth on a 'voyage' (Bachelard), one that occurs in and through the imagination. 'Sing the gardens, my heart, that you don't know ...' It legitimates the desire that 'makes one go further, elsewhere' because it 'lives nowhere' (de Certeau, *Mystic Fable* 299). In this sense, the sense of 'perpetual departure' that we find in Rilke's late sonnets is continuous with Rilke's voice echoing through *The Notebooks of Malte Laurids Brigge*, as if bringing to full circle Malte's confession that 'this time, *I* will be written. *I* am the impression that will transform itself'. That is, *poiesis* is finally not a matter of what the poet hopes to make through his work, but rather stands as a kind of gesture by which he 'makes' his life what it is. Such a mystical gesture, as Rilke reminds us persistently in his later poetry, is the primary purpose of art, both pointing to and enacting a 'voyage' of 'perpetual departure' – which is to say, a journey of the imagination, one by which we 'make' the world through our ways of seeing. In a word, *poiesis*.

Erich Heller captures this eloquently in his essay on 'The Hazard of Modern Poetry', arguing that:

> Poetry, at all times, is not merely descriptive and imitative in the Aristotelian sense. It is always also creative; creative indeed in the sense of making things that were not there before – and the derivation of the word 'poetry' points to just this kind of 'making'. But it is creative also in a profounder and more elusive sense. Poetry heightens and cultivates the creative element that is in experience itself. For experience is not in the impressions we receive; it is in *making* sense. And poetry is the foremost sense-maker of experience. It renders *actual* ever new sectors of the apparently inexhaustible field of *potential* experience. (279)

Thus, we find ourselves returning to the question we asked at the outset: is the enactment of Rilke's poetic creativity 'mystical'? Such a question depends, of course, on how we define the mystical. It surely is if, with de Certeau, we see it in its modernist forms as an invitation to 'a new way of walking, a different "style" of life [which] simultaneously captivates an attentiveness from within, disturbs the orderly flow of thought, and opens up or frees new spaces' (de Certeau, *Mystic Fable* 297). As such, they serve as a form of 'mystics', leading us as readers – or, perhaps better said, as 'singers' – into the uncharted depths of our own 'interior', awakening us to the 'gardens' which the poet calls us to 'sing ... into sanctity'. *Gesang ist Dasein.*

By such 'mystical gestures', Rilke's poetry calls us to know ourselves in all our fragmented 'moments' – and above all those that make up what he calls 'this life of anguish' – as part of 'the whole, the glorious pattern' of life. Or perhaps we should say with the poet that in our singing we ourselves become the 'song' that is 'being', experiencing not the poem but our very life as 'mystical gesture'. This is a realization that activates our 'innerness', inviting us as readers to join the poet in the 'voyage' of the imagination precisely at the 'verge' of the mind. As we join him on this journey, we find that the poems are themselves mystical gestures that lead us into our own 'innerness', a journey by which we 'complete' the world.

## Works Cited

Bachelard, Gaston. *On Poetic Imagination and Reverie*. Trans. and intro. Collette Gaudin. Dallas, TX: Spring, 1987.

Certeau, Michel de. *The Mystic Fable*, vol. 1. In *The Sixteenth and Seventeenth Centuries*, trans. Michael B. Smith. Chicago: University of Chicago Press, 1992.

—— 'Mystic Speech'. In *The Certeau Reader*, ed. Graham Ward. Oxford: Blackwell, 2007.

Heller, Erich. *The Disinherited Mind: Essays in Modern German Literature and Thought*. New York and London: Harcourt, Brace, Jovanovich, 1975.

Hutchison, Ben. *Rilke's Poetics of Becoming*. London: Legenda, 2006.

James, William. *The Varieties of Religious Experience: A Study in Human Nature*. New York: Random House, 1983.

Mommaers, Paul. *Was Ist Mystik?* Trans. Franz Theunis. Frankfurt am Main: Insel Verlag, 1979.

Rilke, Rainer Maria. *Die Sonette an Orpheus*. In *Gedichte 1910–1926. Kommentierte Ausgabe in vier Bänden*, ed. Manfred Engel, Ulrich Fülleborn, Horst Nalewski and August Stahl. Frankfurt am Main and Leipzig: Insel, 1996. [Unpublished translation of *The Sonnets to Orpheus* by Mark S. Burrows.]

—— *Duineser Elegien*. In *Gedichte 1910–1926. Kommentierte Ausgabe in vier Bänden*, ed. Manfred Engel, Ulrich Fülleborn, Horst Nalewski and August Stahl. Frankfurt am Main and Leipzig: Insel, 1996. [Unpublished translation of *The Duino Elegies* by Mark S. Burrows.]

—— *The Notebooks of Malte Laurids Brigge: A Novel*. Trans. Stephen Mitchell. New York: Random House, 1990.

—— *Prayers of a Young Poet*. Trans. Mark S. Burrows. Brewster, MA: Paraclete, 2013.

Sheldrake, Philip. 'Unending Desire: De Certeau's "Mystics"'. *The Way* 102 (2001): 38–48.

Steiner, George. *Real Presences*. Chicago: University of Chicago Press, 1989.

Vattimo, Gianni. *Art's Claim to Truth*. Ed. Santiago Zabala; trans. Luca d'Isanto. New York: Columbia University Press, 2008.

# Chapter 13

# 'The Pulse in the Wound': Embodiment and Grace in Denise Levertov's Religious Poetry

Sarah Law

Denise Levertov (1923–97) was a British-born poet who became a major voice in post-war American poetry. Her work pays great attention to the subtle musicality of language and the sensory details of the world about her. As Levertov herself observed, she was always drawn to the transcendent ('A Poet's View' 243), and later in her poetic career was drawn to the lives of spiritual figures, from biblical times to the present day. Often these figures (Brother Lawrence, Julian of Norwich, Thomas Merton) were contemplatives associated with Christian mysticism. But was Denise Levertov herself a mystic as well as a poet?

Initially, her own rebuttal would seem to disappoint such an enquiry. In a late interview, Levertov declared:

> I am certainly not a mystic! ... For a poet (and poets don't tend to be mystics: the poetic and mystic modes of experience are quite different, I think, though some mystics may also be poets), imagination (which, obviously, comes with the territory) is a prerequisite for faith, though all poets must have imagination and only some have faith. Poets are typically too mentally active and questioning to have the kind of faith that is an extension of trust ... if they do attain faith, it must involve the imagination. It is perhaps their substitute for the childlike direct assumptions of the naturally pure in heart. (Brooker 186)

These observations seem to suggest that exercise of the imagination somehow precludes mystical experience. However, I would argue that Levertov's own poetics do have much affinity with the mystical, contemplative tradition in Christianity, and indeed present a connection between mysticism, imagination and poetry itself.

Mysticism is, of course, a term fraught with definitions and misconceptions. It is certainly not confined to Christianity, although, since Levertov identified herself by the end of her life as Christian, I shall enquire within these parameters. In 1899, Dean Inge, a nineteenth-century Anglican authority on spiritual matters, observed that no word in our language – not even 'socialism' – has been employed more loosely than 'mysticism'. Sometimes it is used as an equivalent for symbolism or allegorism, sometimes for theosophy or occult science, and sometimes it merely suggests the mental state of a dreamer, or vague and fantastic opinions about God and the world (Inge 3).

The psychologist William James attempted, in *The Varieties of Religious Experience* (1902), to define mystical experience as having the four elements of passivity, transience, ineffability and noetic surety (a sense of knowledge gained). Inge's own tentative conclusion suggests that 'Religious Mysticism may be defined as the attempt ... to realise, in thought and feeling, the immanence of the temporal in the eternal, and of the eternal in the temporal' (5). This sounds like a good working definition for poets: to see eternity in a grain of sand, as Blake puts it. Indeed Inge's emphasis on the immanence of God, of a divine indwelling in the essence of the things of this world, is one with which Levertov has a considerable affinity.

This essay will look at Levertov's poetic trajectory in the light of her spirituality, and then at three main aspects of Levertov's 'mystical' poetics: her consideration of poetic inspiration as a form of contemplative prayer in itself; her use of poetic language, paying particular attention to her selection *The Stream and the Sapphire*; and finally (referring to the same selection) how her imaginative depiction of figures of faith not only lead to her own conversion, but also to her strengthened use of immanence and incarnational spirituality in the poetic image.

### Levertov's Pilgrimage

Levertov herself adopted the metaphor of life as a pilgrim's journey ('The Sense of Pilgrimage' 62–86). Although never describing herself as a mystic, she was aware of mystical ancestors on both her father's and mother's sides of the family: her father was descended from the Rav of Northern White Russia and her mother from Welsh mystical tailor and preacher Angel Jones of Molde. Her poem 'Illustrious Ancestors', from the 1958 collection *Overland to the Islands*, explores this heritage. While her ancestors 'used / what was at hand' (line 10) to flourish according to the obligations of their religious observances (the Rav) or craft (tailor Angel Jones), Levertov declares in this poem an early investment in not only integrating her heritage with theirs but in making the writing of poetry itself the means of revelation, allowing form and content to fuse with a mystery made tangible in language: she would like to make, she says, poems 'mysterious as the silence when the tailor / would pause with his needle in the air' (lines 16–18), utilizing the silence of white page as it meets and holds the enjambed poetic line.

Before her birth, Levertov's father converted from his Hasidic faith to Christianity and became an Anglican priest. Levertov writes of 'my father's Hasidic ancestry, his being steeped in Jewish and Christian scholarship and mysticism, his fervour and eloquence as a preacher' (Couzyn 75).[1] In addition, her childhood consisted of home-schooling, which had a strong sense of social action.

The only notably dream-like, visionary poetry of Levertov's early period is in her first book, *The Double Image*, published in Britain under the influence of the neo-Romanticism of the 1940s. On moving to America in 1947, Levertov lost her British poetic context and had to adjust to new accents, voices, phrasing and tradition. Under the new influences of objectivism, William Carlos Williams and the free verse poetics of the Black Mountain scene, her first US collections show an intense focusing on the world to hand. Critic Ralph Mills declared her work the 'poetry of the immediate' (98). Levertov admitted of her new American poetic context: 'What I did not find ... was an impulse of spiritual quest' ('Some Affinities of Content' 3), although she found a kindred spirit in the poetry of her friend Robert Duncan. Nonetheless poet Robert Pack identified her poetics as clearly spiritual: '[Levertov's] sense of the invisible spirit of things is rooted in what she sees, and through precise description, through intimation and evocation, she leads the reader to the brink of mystery' (Nelson 232). Levertov occasionally used liturgical terms in early work such as 'Matins', from *The Jacob's Ladder*, which nevertheless located the 'authentic' firmly in the actions of daily life. In that poem, the meditative strokes of a hairbrush lead to a revelation: 'the known / appearing fully itself' (Part 2: lines 9–12).

However, after what might be termed this early 'illuminative' phase (Underhill 232–65) came personal losses (the deaths of her mother and sister), and the horror of the Vietnam War: Levertov shifted poetic direction as she struggled in the 1960s and 1970s to come to terms with violent contemporary conflict, and much of her work became a poetry of protest. Her political fervour was not

[1]    Levertov's poetic drawing on Hasidic spirituality has been well documented; in particular, see Hallisey 5–11.

always accepted by critics who had previously celebrated her quiet, careful craft. Though she remained strong in her vocation as a poet and wrote urgent essays to justify her sense of political struggle, this was a difficult stage of her writing and her life. Subsequently, critics such as Lorrie Smith discerned a new level of poetic perception. 'She has lost irretrievably the innocent and easy epiphany of her early poems ... her [later] poems force us to see that both joy and terror are real in our world and challenge us to reconcile them for ourselves' (Smith 171). Not an easy reconciliation, and one in which the reader and poet seem to bear equal responsibility. However, Levertov went on to forge a powerful later poetics wrought by a 'dark' or difficult night.

## Poetry as Prayer

In her important essay 'Some Notes on Organic Form' in 1965,[2] Levertov compares poetic inspiration to contemplation: 'To contemplate comes from "*templum*, temple, a place, a space for observation, marked out by the augur." It means, not simply to observe, to regard, but to do these things in the presence of a god' (68). Although not specifically Christian here, Levertov uses the language of spirituality and prayer: not of traditional structured prayers – Levertov avoided traditional fixed poetic forms – but of contemplative prayer.

In a 1978 interview she explains: 'If you give to your material a kind of humble devotion, or attention, you will, if you have got any native talent to help you along, be *given* a good deal. And if you persist, then sometimes you are given the poet's special reward of the absolutely unpredictable' (Estees 96; my emphasis). Levertov names this process 'faithful attention' – waiting on the grace of words:

> I would say that for me writing poetry, receiving it, is a religious experience. At least if one means by this that it is experiencing something that is deeper, different from, anything that your own thought and intelligence can experience in themselves. Writing itself can be a religious act, if one allows oneself to be put at its service. I don't mean to make a religion of poetry, no. But certainly we can assume what poetry is not – it is definitely not just an anthropocentric act. (Estees 96)

In her early essay 'Origins of a Poem', she also discerns a priestly function to poetry: 'The poet – when he is writing – is a priest; the poem is a temple; epiphanies

---

2    Available both in text and online.

and communion take place within it' ('Origins of a Poem' 47). Levertov's divine here is ineffable: 'By divine I mean something beyond both the making and the needing elements, vast, irreducible' (47). Commenting on that essay, critic James Breslin believes that Levertov does not seek spiritual abstraction, but rather illumination through something more distinct and specific: 'she really means the incarnational metaphor, and a successful poem, for her, makes the word flesh in a language of magical realism' (58). Breslin suggests that Levertov's heightened apprehension of the transcendent in poetry is anchored in her use of image, language and detail. His phrase 'the incarnational metaphor' is a resonant one, reminiscent of Inge's definition of mysticism as an attempt to reveal the 'immanence of the eternal in the temporal' (5) and worth exploring further. It is also worth introducing Levertov's own selection of her poems on religious themes here, in which we can reflect on her spiritual and poetic journey towards a commitment both to the incarnational metaphor and the incarnation.

### *The Stream and the Sapphire*

This selection was published by New Directions in 1997, the year of Levertov's death. It contains poems 'on religious themes' from seven previous collections.[3] Only one, posthumous, collection was published subsequently (*This Great Unknowing*). We have in effect a summing-up of Levertov's religious journey in poetry, although the selection is ostensibly reader-oriented: Levertov wished to meet the needs of 'readers who are themselves concerned with doubt and faith, and ... like to have a focused single volume at times, to stuff in a pocket or place at their bedside' (*The Stream and the Sapphire* viii). Her comment indicates certain poetic qualities: simple language but serious themes ('concern[s] with doubt and faith'); a grasp of the practical and daily (a pocket or bedside book); and that powerful adjective 'focused'.

*The Stream and the Sapphire* is divided into sections. The first section, 'The Tide', explores the hesitancy of human response to the Divine. It oscillates, honestly, between doubt and spontaneous faith, between apathy and commitment. 'Flickering Mind' (*A Door in the Hive*)[4] explains that the speaker

---

[3]    *Life in the Forest* (1978), *Candles in Babylon* (1982), *Oblique Prayers* (1984), *Breathing the Water* (1987), *A Door in the Hive* (1989), *Evening Train* (1992) and *Sands of the Well* (1996). All first published by New Directions Press, New York.

[4]    Within this essay, I state the collection in which poems mentioned were originally published.

stops to contemplate God, only to find that her mind 'at once / like a minnow darts away' (lines 14–15).

With its alternating short and longer lines, the shape of the poem echoes the flickering evoked by its title and is a good example of Levertov's use of open form. Language, although conversational and understated in most of Levertov's work, is nonetheless extremely important, as is its placing. Levertov developed her own poetics of 'organic form', deriving inspiration from William Carlos Williams's 'variable foot' and the subsequent 'breath' theories of Charles Olson's 'Projective Verse'. In this poetics, vocabulary, line length and line break must be unique to the particular poem under creation. The poem does not owe its lineation and layout so much to the physical pattern of breath (which Olson extolled) as to the inner 'inspiration' which one receives, having paid attention to the emergent sounds and senses of the lines. This is the hallmark of Levertov's own poetry.

In her poem the sense of divine constancy ('the unchanging presence, in whom all / moves and changes' [lines 27–8]) is innate to the natural world. The least embodied noun is qualified by a descriptor indicating life: the 'pulsing' shadow of line 26. It is the poet whose attention is lacking, 'absent' (line 1), indicating the difficulty in giving the 'faithful attention' so required of the poet-contemplative. Present too in this first section are the themes of imagination and incarnation which are hallmarks of Levertov's developing faith-poetics. Imagination is employed here not in the sense of depicting a biblical scene or holy life, but with the thought, prevalent in Levertov's early poetry, that as human beings we do not know our own spiritual and creative power: we have wings which cause our shoulders to ache. For example, in 'The Wings' (*The Sorrow Dance*) she wonders whether, camel-like, she carries 'pure energy ... / ... humped and heavy?' (lines 17–18).

'Standoff' (*Breathing the Water*) contains the powerful image of 'God crucified on the resolve not to displume / our unused wings' (lines 4–5) and ends wondering when we will ever dare to fly. Also in this section, 'On the Mystery of the Incarnation' (*A Door in the Hive*), suggests that it is precisely 'compassion for our ugly / failure to evolve' (lines 9–10) which led to God's 'entrusting' his 'Word' (lines 11–12). 'Word' is capitalized to signify the New Testament reference to St John's gospel. In the text of a poem it also holds connotations of language itself entrusted; not as a cerebral function but as awe which speaks to the heart directly. Poetic language itself bypasses the efforts of the intellect and forms the 'pulse' in the heart.

*'Believers'*

Although known as a poet of 'the immediate', Levertov became a poet much praised for her use of her imagination, with critic Harry Martens observing that Levertov became 'increasingly convinced that exercise of the imagination moves one toward faith' (Wagner-Martin 196). In her essay 'A Poet's View', Levertov connects imaginative power and religious faith: 'To believe, as an artist, in inspiration or the intuitive, to know that without Imagination ... no amount of acquired craft or scholarship or of brilliant reasoning will suffice, is to live with a door of one's life open to the transcendent, the numinous' (241). Subsequently in this essay she writes: 'Imagination ... is the perceptive organ by which it is possible, though not inevitable, to experience God' (246). We can see Levertov's growing belief that, for poets, this is the path to spiritual insight, as voiced in her late interview quoted at the start of this essay.

Levertov declared that she was not influenced by the increasingly popular 'confessional' movement in US poetry: 'I'm certainly very tired of the me, me, me kind of poem' (O'Connell). Always wary of the public display of private agonies, she warns in a retrospective piece following the death of Anne Sexton: 'The manifestations – in words, music, paint, or what have you – of private anguish are exploited by a greedy public, a public greedy for emotion at second hand because starved of the experience of community' ('Anne Sexton' 189). In place of this popular but unhealthy confessional concern with the poet's self, particularly in her later work, Levertov employed a heightened use of her imagination in the presentation of other human stories, from both biblical and historical settings. In this way, human experience becomes the bridge between the world and the transcendent: in *Oblique Prayers*, 'Vocation' evokes her admiration for 'the nameless great', those who, through circumstance and loss, she perceives as morally and spiritually greater than herself. It is through them, she suggests, that 'we keep our title, human, / Word like an archway, a bridge, an altar'(lines 18–19).

Although in 'Vocation' the martyrs are unnamed, in other poems, specifically those gathered in *The Stream and the Sapphire*, Levertov meditates on the lives of specific people who offer qualities of the 'archway ... bridge ... altar' to the divine. They provide an ahistorical community of the faithful.

This imaginative reconstruction of a human experience leading to an experience of the divine has its connections with traditional spiritual practice, something that Levertov was delighted to discover. In her foreword to *The Stream and the Sapphire*, Levertov describes her developing poetic practice: as 'do-it-yourself theology' which 'seemed at the time of writing to risk presumption, but

I later discovered it was much like what Ignatius of Loyola recommended in the "Exercises"' (vii). She explains more in her last interview:

> I was really amazed at how close the exercises of St Ignatius of Loyola were to a poet or novelist imagining a scene. You focus your attention on some particular aspect of the life of Christ. You try to compose that scene in your imagination, place yourself there ... You establish who you are and where you stand and then you look at what you see. (O'Connell)

In *The Stream and the Sapphire*, Levertov's poems of biographical focus feature in the section 'Believers'. In her biographically inspired poetic writing, she always strove for authenticity of insight rather than clichéd situations, even of holiness – elsewhere she had castigated 'those blond, bland, Holy Families of undertakers' Christmas calendars' ('Some Affinities of Content' 13). The figures in 'Believers' are placed in roughly chronological order of subject presented, starting with two poems about the New Testament St Peter: 'Poetics of Faith' (*Sands of the Well*) and 'St Peter and the Angel' (*Oblique Prayers*). These are followed by 'Caedmon' (*Breathing the Water*), the monk whose story is first told by Bede in his *History of the English People*. Caedmon, like St Peter, is visited by an angel; but while Peter is released to resume 'the ecstatic, dangerous, wearisome roads / of what he still had to do' ('St Peter and the Angel' lines 15–16), Caedmon is given more explicit poetic fire in the sudden gift of speech and language, as a divine hand 'touched my lips and scorched my tongue / into the ring of the dance' (lines 32–3).

'Caedmon' is a poem written in the first person, indicating the poet's particular identification with this gift of inspired language. The body is also prominent in all three of the poems: 'Poetics of Faith' explores the moment when Peter walks on water, leaving his dreaming toes to remember the sensation. Words themselves are dancing, as though embodied, at the conclusion of 'Caedmon'. Interestingly too, the image of the 'ring of the dance' recurs in 'Dom Helder Camara at the Nuclear Test Site' (*Sands of the Well*), a later poem in this selection of 'Believers': Dom Helder Camara was the twentieth-century Brazilian priest author of *The Spiral of Violence* (1971). In Levertov's poem, instead of a spiral of violence, peace and solidarity are enacted by circles of dance: 'instinct pulls us into the ancient / rotation, symbol of continuance' (lines 24–5).

In this poem we have two recurring images in Levertov's work. The first is that of pilgrimage as a life's journey. Dom Helder is presented at the start of his poem as an 'octogenarian wisp'(line 1), at the end of his long life of social action: his pilgrimage is not geographical but the uphill struggle of consciousness-raising and alleviating the causes of poverty. Secondly we have the image of the ring, circle or, by association, sphere as a 'symbol of continuance'. This became an increasingly important image in Levertov's final poetry.

Levertov was drawn to the mystics even though she did not consider herself to be one. Unsurprisingly this interest included Brother Lawrence, the seventeenth-century lay Carmelite friar who, like Levertov herself, found traces of the numinous in the daily round of domestic duties: the *Practice of the Presence of God* (to use the title of his tract) 'touched / your dullest task, and the task was easy' ('Conversion of Brother Lawrence' Part 2: lines 36–7, in *Sands of the Well*). However, Levertov's engagement with an earlier medieval mystic was deeper still: she found in the fourteenth-century mystic Julian of Norwich a written testimony of visionary experience which spurred her into both imaginative reconstruction and a sequence in which she not only depicts but addresses Mother Julian as the subject of her meditations.[5]

Levertov's sequence 'The Showings: Lady Julian of Norwich (1342–1416)' (*Breathing the Water*) illustrates great empathy for Julian, the only female mystical figure about whom she writes, and within her Julian poems there is illustration not only of classic and recent definitions of mysticism, but also of Levertov's own evolving spiritual poetics.

Levertov's first concern in the 'Showings' sequence is one of the ineffability of a mystical experience which cannot be wholly articulated. We are incapable of articulating such experiences, which, like black holes, are 'both dense and vacant' (Part 1: line 2). The dense language of these lines is leavened by the literal vacancy of the line of white space following the word which announces it ('vacant'). Through its organic form, the poem evokes what words alone can only point to. Levertov's line breaks always indicate a pause, an extra emphasis on end-of-line words, and here 'unutterable' signals a break from communicable language to a mere 'swarming of molecules' (line 5). Yet the predominant note is one of wonder: Pascal's imaginative power, albeit imagining what he could not imagine, was greater than his dread, Levertov notes in lines 5–7.

Imagination, even if it is functioning in a negative capacity, stimulates awe. In her 'Some Notes on Organic Form', Levertov had written: 'A religious devotion to the truth, to the splendour of the authentic, involves the writer in a process rewarding in itself. When, however, that devotion brings us to undreamed abysses and we find ourselves sailing slowly over them and landing on the other side –

---

5    In 'In a Hazelnut', I have discussed Levertov's Julian poetry in the context of four contemporary women poets who depict Julian of Norwich in their poetry. However, my reading of the Julian poems here is new and has been refocused on the questions of mysticism and immanence discussed in this chapter.

that's ecstasy' (73) – a journey echoed by Levertov's 'Showings' poems, from the 'vast gaps we call black holes' (line 1) to the lyricism of Julian's experiences.

Juxtaposed against this opening section comes Levertov's hallmark engagement with the specificity of daily life: the 'earth of our daily history' (line 8), its presence cited in beautiful particulars.

This sensitive beholding certainly still echoes the poetics of William Carlos Williams: no ideas but in things. But these are illuminated things. In this poem we also find an intense awareness of the human condition: 'beat of our hearts now, good or bad, / dying or being born, eroded, vanishing ' (lines 13–14); the subsequent space break emphasizing our fragility. The smaller, more insignificant an object is, the more Levertov presents its spiritual resonance. The things of the world are fused with holiness. 'Hers is a sacramental notion of life,' suggests critic Albert Gelpi, 'experience is a communion with objects which are in themselves signs of their own secret mystery' (92). Levertov herself often quoted Thoreau: 'You must love the crust of the earth on which you dwell. You must be able to extract nourishment out of a sandheap' (epigraph to 'Joy', in *The Sorrow Dance* 33). She finds a partner in Julian who, for all her graphic visions, had as the most mysterious a seemingly insignificant object which could be held in the palm of a human hand. In chapter five of her *Revelation of Love*, Julian tells how she was shown 'a littil thing, the quantitye of an hesil nutt in the palme of my hand; and it was as round as a balle. I lokid thereupon with eye of my understondyng and thowte: "What may this be?" And it was generally answered thus: "It is all that is made"' (7).

She marvels at its existence and its vulnerability, and is given the reassurance that it exists because God loves and keeps it safe: 'I mervellid how it might lesten, for methowte it might suddenly have fallen to nowte for littil. And I was answered in my understondyng: *It lesteth, and ever shall for God loveth it*' (7). Levertov depicts this mystery in her poem, interweaving her own dialectic of doubt and faith, addressing Julian in the way that Julian addressed God.

This moment in the poem, with its symmetry and use of quotation from Julian herself, contains the kernel of Levertov's spiritual poetics. The world, and all that is, is indeed 'a little thing, the size of a hazelnut / held safe in God's pierced palm' (lines 26–7). It echoes the sense Levertov expresses elsewhere that our vulnerable world, and our own existences, are reliant on and encompassed by the sustaining grace of God, for example, in the poems 'Suspended' (*Evening Train*) and 'The Avowal' (*Oblique Prayers*).

The poem also offers a sacramental sense of transformation. The little thing is 'all that is made', yet retains its insignificant outward form.

The third and fourth poems of Levertov's 'Showings' imagine a precursory childhood experience where Julian's mother places 'into her two cupped palms / a newlaid egg, warm from the hen' (Part 4: lines 7–8). Levertov uses the maternal imagery of both human mother and warm egg. It intensifies the subsequent insights offered by the 'hazelnut' vision: God entrusts to a 'five-fingered / human nest / the macrocosmic egg' (Part 4: lines 15–17). Here, Julian's hand is the nest; another nurturing image. Poignantly, it is God's hand, here and in the earlier 'Showings' poem, which is wounded: 'God's wounded hand' (Part 4: line 1); 'God's pierced palm'.

In fact, the image of a small object held in the palm is not new to Levertov. An earlier poem, 'Pleasures' (*With Eyes at the Back of Our Heads*), describes how the poet is enchanted by a fruit (a mamey fruit) 'large enough to fill / the hungry palm of a hand' (lines 12–19). In this poem, the speaker's hand is hungry for sensation and knowledge, rather than wounded, as is God's, or the vibrant nest of the young Julian's hand. The image of the open palm, receiving a mystery or something of wonder, is clearly an important one for Levertov. It even appears in the sequence of mainly political protest, 'Staying Alive' (*To Stay Alive*), where the poet seeks to preserve individual memories, longing to hold 'moments and their processions in palm / of mind's hand' ('Staying Alive': 'Entracte' Part V: lines 2–3). By the time Levertov writes the 'Showings' poems, the image of the little thing containing all that is has gained in spiritual resonance: there is a Eucharistic echo in such a vulnerable object, given by a wounded God into the palm of a human hand.

Finally, this recurring image seems to offer a symbol of poetry: the 'little thing' that is the outward form of a lyric poem can somehow seem to encompass 'every awareness our minds contain' ('The Showings', Part 1: line 20). Like a worry stone, a poem is also a little thing which can be metaphorically held in the palm of the hand. Held and read with reverence, a poem itself has a sacramental depth.

Julian of Norwich was given reassuring, albeit mysterious, visions, but also witnessed the suffering Christ. Levertov's poem 'On a Theme from Julian's Chapter XX' (*Breathing the Water*) meditates on Christ's connection to all suffering ('torture then, torture now, / the same, the pain's the same' [lines 9–10]) and yet also his suffering's uniqueness, infused with 'utmost Imagination' (line 40). God is present 'within the mesh of the web' (line 48) of the world, and within the mesh of the poetic text.

However, Julian's original text is also suffused with joy. In one vision she witnesses Christ's agony on the cross transformed inexplicably into cheerfulness. In another vision Julian learns to laugh at the devil. Levertov identifies this irrepressible breakthrough of spiritual *jouissance* in her sixth 'Showings' poem: 'Julian laughing aloud, glad, / with a most high inward happiness' (Part 6: lines 1–2). She praises Julian's tenacious faith: 'you clung to joy ... clung like an acrobat' (lines 31, 35). Certainty of faith comes to Levertov herself through her later writing, particularly that using the framework of the liturgy. A moment of transition from doubt to faith is precisely what she evokes in 'The Servant-Girl at Emmaus' (*Breathing the Water*), an ekphrastic meditation on Veslasquez's painting of the same name. The servant girl hesitates over her act of recognition, yet is the first to know: she 'swings round and sees / the light around him' (lines 19–20).

Levertov sees imagination as interfused with the physical world, and her faith is likewise dependent on the world and the body: particularly the resurrected body. In the antepenultimate section of *The Stream and the Sapphire*, this belief in the fusing of spirituality with flesh sustains her: in order to attain faith 'we must feel / the pulse in the wound' ('On Belief in the Physical Resurrection of Jesus' lines 37–9 [*Sands of the Well*]). Similarly, in the voice of 'St Thomas Didymus' (*A Door in the Hive*): 'I needed / blood to tell me the truth' (lines 67–8).

The 'St Thomas Didymus' poem anthologized in *The Stream and the Sapphire* blends physicality with Levertov's motif of spiritual light: the illuminative with the immanence of the body. In this poem she adopts the strategy of once again writing in the first person as dramatic monologue: 'my fingers encountering / rib-bone and pulsing heat' (lines 82–3). Levertov adopts a fragmented lineation in this poem; owing something to William Carlos Williams's variable foot, it also has the pulse of Levertov's faith to it; an antiphonal progress through doubt to touch to trust. The question of suffering is not answered but given its place in the vast design; the 'knot' (line 92) (or 'not') in the heart is transformed into co-operation with the 'risen sun' (line 99) (or 'son').

Levertov identifies her longer 'Mass for the Day of St Thomas Didymus' (*Candles in Babylon*) as the particular poetic sequence which led to her conversion. This poetic sequence is not in *The Stream and the Sapphire* but important when considering Levertov's religious commitment. She began the composition as an agnostic:

> I thought to myself that it might be possible to adapt this framework [of the Mass] to the creation of a poem ... I thought of the poem as 'an agnostic Mass' ... But a few months later, when I had arrived at the Agnus Dei, I discovered myself to be in a different relationship to the material and to the liturgical form from that in which I had begun. The experience of writing the poem – that long swim

through waters of unknown depth – had been also a conversion process, if you will. ('Work that Enfaiths' 250)

It is the act of writing, the act of a poet's 'work' that 'enfaiths' Levertov during this process: her faith finds its pulse, just as St Thomas touched the resurrected Christ. Appropriately enough, this poetic sequence draws on the structure of the Mass, a liturgy which celebrates the mystery of incarnation and transubstantiation: the two concepts that crystallize Levertov's faith pilgrimage.

The 'Sanctus' celebrates the power of the imagination: 'all that Imagination has wrought, has rendered' (lines 4–5); in the 'Benedictus', 'flesh and / vision' (lines 11–12) are fused. Flesh and vision together form the essence of Levertov's poetics, a 'sacramental' perspective that allows for a fusion of the ineffable and the tangible.

However, the god of the St Thomas Didymus sequence is vulnerable: a 'shivering god' ('Agnus Dei' line 46) to whom we must respond in the hope that 'something human still / can shield you' (lines 52–3). This final image shifts Levertov's spirituality towards a mysticism of responsibility and engagement. Levertov stepped back from her proactive political involvement but she was still prepared to take poetic risks, believing that the world needed a spiritual perspective on a grossly materialistic and overly technologized culture. In her last interview, she commented:

> When I started writing explicitly Christian poems, I thought I'd lose part of my readership. But I haven't actually. I think interest in religion is a counterforce to the insane, rationalist optimism that surrounds the development of all this new technology ... Our ethical development does not match our technological development. (O'Connell)

## Conclusion

Finally, can we say whether Denise Levertov was a mystic? Of course theologically, this cannot be confirmed, except perhaps by an experienced spiritual director. We can certainly say that Levertov was drawn to the mystics: it was a major factor in her becoming Roman Catholic in 1989: 'The Catholic liturgy and mystical tradition are what I feel most nourished by among the different kinds of churches that there are' (Gish 180). We can at least identify some qualities associated with mysticism according to classic definitions, while knowing that our understanding of mysticism might vary, and that definitions of mysticism are frequently broad and even contradictory. The classic (William) Jamesian qualities of ineffability and passivity both have some connection to Levertov: her waiting for the grace of poetry very much resembles that active passivity of contemplative prayer. Although certainly a wordsmith, her increasing awareness that there are 'vast gaps' and a 'dizzying multiplication' to the world indicate her sense of the wonder behind creation. Her acknowledgement of the transience (another Jamesian term) of the spiritual experience is indicated in poems such as 'Human Being' where a sense of wonder alternates with doubt and fear. 'Noetic surety' comes later, with floods of light, and conversion, through St Thomas Didymus.

Levertov's 'Variation and Reflection on a Theme by Rilke', at the conclusion of *Breathing the Water*, illustrates her own sense of humanity's connection with the Divine which is both without and within the 'pulse of flesh' (Part 2: line 2).

Dean Inge's concept that 'Mysticism [is] the attempt ... to realise, in thought and feeling, the immanence of the temporal in the eternal, and of the eternal in the temporal' (5) becomes more resonant to Levertov as her poetry develops, particularly with her understanding of Julian of Norwich's hazelnut image. The maternal imagery in the 'Showings' sequence is strong too, challenging any notion of Levertov as a poet who ignores her own female gender. Finally, no one can accuse Levertov of not being a 'poet in the world'; protest and political action were part of her life and her poetry. Even in the later 'post-protest' poetry, it is left for poet and reader to take action in accepting and cherishing a 'shivering god'. It is human activity which continues to be the pulse in the wound of the world, and it is only an incarnational mysticism which allows for the reception, and beholding, of mystery.

## Works Cited

Breslin, James. 'Denise Levertov'. In *Denise Levertov: Selected Criticism*, ed. Albert Gelpi. Michigan: University of Michigan Press, 1993, 55–90.

Brooker, Jewel Spears, ed. *Conversations with Denise Levertov*. Jackson, MS: University of Mississippi Press, 1998.

Couzyn, Jeni, ed. *Contemporary Women Poets*. Tarset: Bloodaxe, 1985.

Estees, Sybil. 'Denise Levertov'. In *Conversations with Denise Levertov*, ed. Spears Brooker, 87–100.

Gelpi, Albert. 'Two Notes on Denise Levertov and the Romantic Tradition'. In *Denise Levertov: Selected Criticism*, ed. Gelpi, 91–5.

Gish, Nancy K. 'Feminism, Poetry and the Church'. In *Conversations with Denise Levertov*, ed. Spears Brooker, 171–81.

Greene, Dana. *Denise Levertov: A Poet's Life*. Illinois: University of Illinois Press, 2013.

Hallisey, Joan. 'Denise Levertov's Illustrious Ancestors: The Hassidic Influence'. *Melus* 9.4 (1982): 5–11.

Inge, Ralph William. *Christian Mysticism*. London: Methuen, 1899.

James, William. *The Varieties of Religious Experience*. London: Longmans, 1902.

Julian of Norwich. *A Revelation of Love*, ed. Marion Glasscoe. Exeter: University of Exeter Press, 1993.

Law, Sarah. 'In a Hazelnut: Julian of Norwich in Contemporary Women's Poetry'. *Literature and Theology* 25.1 (2011): 92–108.

Levertov, Denise. 'Anne Sexton: Light up the Cave' (1974). In *New and Selected Essays*. New York: New Directions, 1997, 186–93.

—— *Breathing the Water*. New York: New Directions, 1987.

—— *Candles in Babylon.* New York: New Directions, 1982.

—— *A Door in the Hive*. New York: New Directions, 1989.

—— *The Double Image.* London: The Cresset, 1946.

—— *Evening Train*. New York: New Directions, 1992.

—— *The Jacob's Ladder.* New York: New Directions, 1958.

—— *Life in the Forest*. New York: New Directions, 1978.

—— *New Selected Poems.* Tarset: Bloodaxe, 2003.

—— *New and Selected Essays.* New York: New Directions, 1992.

—— *Oblique Prayers.* New York: New Directions, 1984.

—— 'Origins of a Poem'. In *The Poet in the World*. New York: New Directions, 1973, 43–56.

—— *Overland to the Islands.* Highlands, NC: Jargon, 1958.

—— *The Poet in the World.* New York: New Directions, 1973.

—— 'A Poet's View.' In *New and Selected Essays*, 239–46.

—— *Sands of the Well.* New York: New Directions, 1996.

—— 'The Sense of Pilgrimage'. In *The Poet in the World*, 62–86.

—— 'Some Affinities of Content' (1991). In *New and Selected Essays*, 1–21.

—— 'Some Notes on Organic Form' (1965). In *New and Selected Essays*, 1992, 67–73.

—— *The Sorrow Dance.* New York: New Directions, 1967.

—— *The Stream and the Sapphire: Selected Poems on Religious Themes.* New York: New Directions, 1997.

—— *Tesserae: Memories and Suppositions.* New York: New Directions, 1995.

—— *This Great Unknowing: Last Poems.* New York: New Directions, 2000.

—— *To Stay Alive*. New York: New Directions, 1965.

—— *With Eyes at the Back of Our Heads*. New York: New Directions, 1960.

—— 'Work that Enfaiths' (1990). In *New and Selected Essays*, 2, 247–58.

Mills, Ralph. 'Denise Levertov: Poetry of the Immediate'. In *Critical Essays on Denise Levertov*, ed. Linda Wagner-Martin. New York: Hall, 1991, 98–110.

Nelson, Rudolph. 'Edge of the Transcendent: The Poetry of Levertov and Duncan'. In *Critical Essays on Denise Levertov*, ed. Linda Wagner-Martin, 1991, 225–35.

O'Connell, Nicholas. 'Levertov's Final Interview: The Poet's Valediction'. *Modern American Poetry*. Accessed 6 May 2011. <http://www.english.illinois.edu/maps/poets/g_l/levertov/oconnell.htm>. [From Nicholas O'Connell, *At the Field's End: Interviews with 22 Pacific Northwest Writers*. Seattle, WA: University of Washington Press, 1998; reprinted in *Poets and Writers Magazine* (May/June 1998).]

Smith, Lorrie. 'Songs of Experience: Denise Levertov's Political Poetry'. In *Critical Essays on Denise Levertov*, ed. Linda Wagner-Martin, 156–72.

Underhill, Evelyn. *Mysticism: The Nature and Development of Spiritual Consciousness* (1911). London: Oneworld, 1999.

Wagner-Martin, Linda. 'Levertov: Poetry and the Spiritual'. In *Critical Essays on Denise Levertov*, ed. Linda Wagner-Martin. New York: Hall, 1991, 196–204.

# PART V
## Poetry, Religious Imagination and Religious Belief

# Images of the Virgin in the Late Sixteenth Century: The Catholic Devotional Poetry of Henry Constable

Lilla Grindlay

I shall begin this essay with two very different descriptions of the same biblical woman, the Virgin Mary. In the first, she is humble, acquiescent and obedient to God's will, the handmaid of the Lord, while in the second she is enthroned in splendour, the Queen of Heaven, interceding before God for man. The image of the Virgin, polyvalent and often paradoxical, has over the centuries fascinated writers, musicians and artists. In late sixteenth-century England, the interchange between representations of the Virgin and the creative imagination was particularly significant. We find ourselves in a time when, following the pendulum swings of England's earlier Reformation, Protestantism can be viewed as the established religion of the state. This led to an eradication of what was deemed an excessive devotion to the Virgin from state-authorized worship, particularly veneration of the Virgin in her resplendent guise of Queen of Heaven. In Protestant writing, we find the Virgin is almost exclusively described as a humble and submissive handmaid. Many Catholic writers sought to counteract this by representing Mary in triumphant and often militaristic terms as the Queen of Heaven.

The poetry of Henry Constable gives us a powerful example of how, in this period of confessional complexity, imaginative writing that deployed the image of the Virgin often did so in a controversial way. Constable was an Elizabethan courtier and gentleman poet, who in the 1580s wrote a sequence of secular sonnets. In these, he frequently adopted the position of the servile lover seeking favour from a cruel mistress. His conversion to Catholicism in 1591 was a stimulus for a change in poetic voice. In 17 'Spirituall Sonnettes', the focus of Constable's adoration shifted from the mistress of the secular sonneteering tradition to the Virgin Mary. Perhaps because he was so steeped in a poetic tradition that elevated the mistress – and because a number of his secular sonnets had been written to Queen Elizabeth herself – he chose to represent the Virgin almost exclusively as the Queen of Heaven. The result is a triumphalist apologia for the Virgin delivered by a poetic voice seeking heavenly rather than earthly patronage.

After a brief exploration of the history of the image of the Queen of Heaven, this essay will give readings of three of Constable's poems. The first is an example of a secular sonnet written to the Queen; in this, Constable uses Petrarchan language as a mask for the quest for preferment. This sonnet also reveals Constable to be an exponent of a particularly intriguing poetic fashion of using sacred – particularly Catholic – language to describe the erotic. The next two poems are sacred verses written to the Virgin as Queen of Heaven. In these, Constable creates a dialogue with his secular poetic voice. He uses his sacred poetry to criticize his own and others' erotic verse, particularly verses written to Elizabeth. His depiction of the Virgin as the Queen of Heaven outshining all earthly queens in both beauty and power can also be seen as a riposte to post-Reformation Protestant representations of the Virgin as humble handmaid. Through a close examination of the cultural context of Constable's use of one image, that of the *Virgo lactans*, I will show just how confrontational his sacred poetic voice was.

Constable was writing in the closing decades of the sixteenth century, a time which also formed the closing decades of Queen Elizabeth's reign. Although England was on the surface a Protestant nation by this time – its Queen excommunicated by the Pope – the religious landscape remained a variegated one. Thanks to the work of historians such as Eamon Duffy, Patrick Collinson and Christopher Haigh, we have become accustomed to a view that England's Reformation cannot be regarded simply as a shift from Catholic to Protestant. To use John Bossy's phrase, the 'Catholic community' in England remained a small but significant unit, while as Alexandra Walsham has observed, many non-recusant Catholics outwardly conformed by attending Protestant churches to avoid fines. This is not to deny the ultimate success of the Reformation – during Elizabeth's reign Catholicism was frequently demonized – but the sense of confessional complexity that this historical scholarship has left us with is a profound one.

Constable's own confessional story is a testament to the wavering belief systems of many in this period. Prior to his conversion he was a prominent figure at court, and during this time in his life he carved for himself a reputation not only as a poet but also as a Protestant polemicist (Grundy 15). In 1591, Constable left England for France on an expedition led by the Earl of Essex. He never returned during Elizabeth's reign; at some point after his arrival in

France, he publicly announced his conversion to Catholicism. It is thought that this occurred in 1591, and that Constable's father's death, in the same year, may have been related to the shock of his son's decision (Bossy, 'A Propos of Henry Constable' 231–2). Upon leaving England, Constable spent time in Paris and Rome, and undertook a mission to Scotland in 1599 in an attempt to convert James to the Catholic faith. He returned to England on James's accession, but his attempts to sway the King to Catholicism once more were thwarted by Robert Cecil, leading to his imprisonment and ultimate exile, again in France. He died in Liège in 1613. Constable's conversion thus led to exile, imprisonment and the loss of his inheritance. It is a personal history of apostasy that warns us that, in a study of confessional standpoints in post-Reformation England, we frequently find ourselves in muddy waters.

## The History of the Queen of Heaven

In representing the Virgin as the Queen of Heaven, Constable was tapping into an aspect of Marian iconography that was as rich as it was controversial. From as early as the fifth century, stories of the coronation of the Virgin as Queen of Heaven were in currency (Warner 104–5). Iconography of the Virgin as Queen of Heaven is intertwined with the extra-scriptural tradition of her assumption, as the Virgin rises to heaven to reign triumphantly by Christ's side as his Queen. The coronation of the Virgin and her place in heaven confirmed her hierarchical significance as above the angels and the saints, and was bound to her role as man's mediatrix, interceding for sinners. In the Middle Ages, the images of the Virgin enthroned and crowned in splendour were ubiquitous in both statues and pictures; from the tenth century statues known as 'Virgin in Majesty' or 'Seat of Wisdom' became popular (Boss 161). There was often a political dimension to Mary's queenship, as in the eleventh and twelfth centuries Mary was increasingly viewed as a type of the Church, or *Maria Ecclesia* (de Visscher 180). The cult of Mary's queenship was amplified by the increasing popularity of the Marian antiphon the *Salve Regina* in the Western Church from early in the twelfth century (Warner 115).

Prior to the Reformation, iconography of the Virgin as the Queen of Heaven was not set in conflict with the humble and acquiescent handmaid of the annunciation. Instead, both humble mother and heavenly queen appeared to co-exist within the same imaginative space. As the anthropologist Victor Turner comments, the image of Mary can be seen as 'a signifier meant to represent not only the historical woman who once lived in Galilee, but the sacred person who resides in heaven, appears at times to living persons, and intercedes with God for the salvation of mankind' (143). The Reformation polarized these two aspects of the Virgin's image. In Reformist writing, the Queen of Heaven was perceived as the 'Catholic' model of Mary and the humble handmaid as the 'Protestant' model.

It would be over-simplistic to state that the Reformation was wholly responsible for curtailing the popularity of the image of the Virgin as the Queen of Heaven. Towards the end of the Middle Ages, there is evidence of an increasingly Christocentric piety (Bynum 16–17; Peters 60–96), and as Diarmaid MacCulloch has indicated, there might indeed have been an alternative, more Christocentric, future for Catholicism, had the Reformation not occurred (195–6). However, there is little doubt that the Reformation led to a radical shift in the way in which the Virgin was perceived. Beth Kreitzer has charted in Lutheran sermons a transformation of the Virgin's role from active *Maria Regina* interceding on mankind's behalf to a humble, submissive and obedient peasant girl, who can be viewed almost as a passive personification of justification by faith. Lutheran Mary thus becomes the perfect godly Protestant woman, who can serve as a behavioural model to a pastor's female flock. As Bridget Heal has observed, this reworked old established symbols rather than abolishing them, stripping Mary of her salvific power and instead exalting her as a model of right belief and conduct (*Cult of the Virgin Mary* 114–15).

This ideological shift, described by Merry Wiesner-Hanks as 'a reduction of the female ideal from heavenly to housebound', had a profound effect upon the fate of the image of the Virgin in post-Reformation culture (295–308). Any writer deploying the image of the Virgin as Queen of Heaven was entering into a discourse that had become polemical, as the Queen of Heaven became a site of resistance rather than a beloved symbol. In the pulpits of Elizabethan England, sermon after sermon vilified the Queen of Heaven as a morally dubious figure created by Catholic vanity. A 1584 English translation of Calvin's *A Harmonie Upon the Three Evangelists, Matthew Mark and Luke* gives an exegesis of St Luke's Magnificat which is illustrative of the paradigms of the humble Protestant Virgin Mary and the Catholic Queen of Heaven. It presents Mary as a humble and lowly figure who casts herself down and exalts God, an action which makes titles such as 'Queen of Heaven' wholly inappropriate:

> Whereby we perceive how much the papists differ from her, for what good things
> soever she had of God, they made small accompt of and unadvisedly they set her
> foorth wyth their owne vaine inventions: They aboundantly heape up together
> for her magnifical & more then proud titles, as that she shuld be the Quene of
> heaven. (35)

The diminishing of the Virgin's role in Protestant writing led in many ways to a Catholic retrenchment. In Counter-Reformation Europe the Virgin became, in Bridget Heal's words, 'a symbol of militant recatholicisation', and was frequently seen in the empowered guise of Queen of Heaven ('Marian Devotion' 225). As Trevor Johnson has observed, Counter-Reformation writers such as the Jesuit Peter Canisius brought Marian piety to the forefront, sparking 'Marian fervour throughout Catholic Europe, at both elite and popular levels' (363–5). Canisius's apologia, *On the Incomparable Virgin Mary* (1577), represented the Virgin as a majestic Queen of Heaven honoured by constant song from three choirs of angels. Constable's sacred verse can be read therefore not only as devotional writing to the Virgin, but also as poetry which forcefully reclaims and reaffirms iconography of the Virgin which Protestantism sought to eradicate.

## Constable's Secular Voice

Before we turn to Constable's deployment of the image of the Queen of Heaven, it is important to gain some sense of his secular voice. Prior to his conversion to Catholicism, Constable was in many ways the archetypal Elizabethan gentleman poet and courtier. The main body of his extant secular work is a series of 63 sonnets which were circulated both in manuscript and print. Constable was one of the first proponents of the sonnet form in England, and his influence is felt in the works of many other writers of his age, including the poetry of Shakespeare, Drayton and Daniel (Grundy 60–3). His secular sonnets are a series of elegantly crafted and rhetorically adept poems which reveal that their writer is a man of fashion. In Constable's secular verse, one finds a number of the Petrarchan motifs which characterize so much of Elizabethan love poetry. His repeated representation of the beloved as an idealized archetype of beauty follows all the rules. She needs no weapons but her eyes; she is white-skinned and has decorously blushing cheeks. Constable's lady is cruel and tyrannical as well as sweet: a series of sonnets project the speaker's anguish as he complains of tormented devotion to an idealized and unattainable beloved.

But as Arthur Marotti has observed, love in the Elizabethan sonnet is not always love; instead, it can be seen as a metaphor for political ambitions (396). Constable wrote his secular sonnets to a number of female addressees, but perhaps the most interesting of his sonnet mistresses is the Queen herself. Constable's secular verse thus exemplifies a tradition in both poetry and pageantry that portrayed the Queen as a beautiful but cruel Petrarchan mistress. His poems to the Queen were written to a woman who understood that the language of love was frequently a codified expression of the language of ambition, and who manipulated her role as the sonneteer's muse (Bates 7; Bell 108–13). It is highly significant that during Elizabeth's reign the word 'courtship' took on the meaning of wooing a woman as well as behaving like a courtier, in what Ilona Bell has described as 'a telling concatenation of meanings' (2). One can view Constable as a writer who was steeped in a tradition that viewed a poem as a politicized structure.

One secular sonnet, entitled 'To the Queene touching the cruell effects of her perfections', exemplifies this:

> Most sacred prince why should I thee thus prayse
> Which both of sin and sorrow cause hast beene
> Proude hast thow made thy land of such a Queene
> Thy neighboures enviouse of thy happie dayes.
> Whoe never saw the sunshine of thy rayes
> An everlasting night his life doth ween
> And he whose eyes thy eyes but once have seene
> A thowsand signes of burning thoughts bewrayes
> Thus sin thow causd envye I meane and pride
> Thus fire and darknesse doe proceed from thee
> The very paynes which men in hell abide
> Oh no not hell but purgatorie this
> Whose sowles some say by Angells punish'd be
> For thow art shee from whome this torment is.[1] (138)

Here is all the Petrarchan hyperbole of the rejected lover, as those denied the light of the Queen's gaze dwell in 'everlasting night'. Meanwhile, those on whom the Queen's gaze has alighted are plunged into the 'fire and darknesse' of tortured love, wracked with envy. This sonnet speaks very strongly, however, of love as a political exchange: in the first quatrain, the speaker uses the gender-neutral term 'prince' to describe the Queen as a monarch who has made her realm proud. However, in the sonnet's final lines, the speaker's state of jealous torment shows all the self-abnegation of the secular sonneteer, with the Queen in the familiar position of the *belle dame sans merci* (Doran 35–6).

One particularly arresting metaphor towards the end of this sonnet may cause the reader to pause. Constable describes his state of rejection as a secular

---

[1]    All references to Constable's poetry are from Joan Grundy's edition. I have retained original spellings, with the exception of i/j and u/v, which have been modernized.

purgatory, with the Queen as his punishing angel. When one considers the poet's own personal history of apostasy, this can create an extraordinary moment of tension. In the speaker's use of the word 'purgatory', is there perhaps a muffled reference to Constable's own religious torment en route to conversion? In reality, this is an image that tells us everything and nothing. We have ascertained from Constable's use of Petrarchan language that he was a man of poetic fashion, and his use of sacred imagery is an example of another poetic trend. In the latter years of Elizabeth's reign, the use of sacred – particularly Catholic – language to express erotic feeling became fashionable (Hackett, 'Art of Blasphemy' 42). The Catholic signifier 'purgatorie' is one of many examples of sacred language used to configure the erotic in Constable's verse, and may exist here simply for aesthetic purposes. Constable's lover-speaker often expresses his agony in terms of martyrdom, for example. In one poem, 'To his Ladies hand upon occasion of her glove which in her absence he kissed' (131), a glove of the lady's is fetishized into a relic, as he places himself in the position of Christ. Her hand has given him, like Christ, five wounds, and these secular stigmata, he observes, cause him to feel pain at a greater intensity than Saint Francis:

> Now [as Saint Francis] if a Saint am I
> The bow which shotte these shafts a relique is
> I meane the hand which is the reason why
> So many for devotion thee would kisse
> And I thy glove kisse as a thinge devine
> Thy arrowes quiver and thy reliques shrine. (Lines 9–14)

The confessional complexities of post-Reformation England make this poetic trend a particularly perplexing one. In the case of an apostate such as Henry Constable, it is difficult to tell whether one should read his own personal confessional anxiety into his use of sacred language to configure the erotic. John Carey's 1981 study of John Donne's poems showed how personal confessional details can be read into the interchange of sacred and erotic imagery (37–59), sparking what Paul J.C.M. Franssen has termed 'The Resurrection of the Author' (153). As Helen Hackett and Alison Shell have observed, this approach to Constable can be applied productively to his verse (Hackett, 'Art of Blasphemy' 40–8; Shell 122). Certainly, it is hard not to feel that Constable's apostasy freights his use of imagery such as 'purgatorie' in his secular verse with a certain significance. Was he leaning towards Catholicism when he wrote these words, or was he simply following the fashion of the times?

## Constable's Sacred Parody

Constable's secular sonnets thus afford us tantalizing glimpses of theological instability and tension, but his sacred sonnets tell a very different story. Although we cannot pin a precise date on Constable's 'Spirituall Sonnettes', their Catholic tone and the fact that in many of them Constable appears to be atoning for his previous, secular, voice indicate, as Alison Shell has concluded, that he wrote them after his conversion (107). In these poems, we find a dramatic change in poetic voice, from secular love sonneteer to Catholic devotional poet. We have established that Constable's secular verse often used sacred language to connote the erotic. In his sacred poetry, we can see a transformation: instead of the sacred used to configure the erotic, we have erotic and sensual language used to express spiritual love. Constable here juxtaposes his sacred voice against his own earlier secular voice. His spiritual poems thus create what Louis Martz has termed 'sacred parodies', responding directly to trends in secular verse (184–93). An example of a sacred parody can be found in the work of Robert Southwell who, in his poem 'Dyers Phancy Turned to a Sinners Complaint', turned a secular love poem by Sir Robert Dyer about unrequited love into a sacred poem about sin and repentance (Southwell 32). What is particularly interesting about Constable is that his sacred verse is situated in a dialogue with his own, rather than other, secular works. The result, however, is the same: the use of the language of secular love poetry in Constable's sacred works expresses a love that is perceived as infinitely superior to profane love.

Constable wrote four sonnets addressed directly 'To Our Blessed Lady', and in all four he represented the Virgin as Queen of Heaven. The image of the Virgin itself forms one of the most evocative *topoi* in the interrelation of sacred and secular; the roots of this are in the medieval tradition of courtly love which often redeployed imagery of Mary as a way of connoting erotic devotion. This was a two-way exchange, as the Virgin was frequently described in sacred verse in terms reminiscent of those used to describe the mistress (Atkinson 130–1; MacDonald 33). As Julia Kristeva has observed, 'both Mary and the Lady were focal points of men's aspirations and desires' (106). In Elizabethan England, the image of the Virgin Mary was, both explicitly and implicitly, part of the Catholic language that became fashionable in literature written towards the end of the Queen's reign, and imagery connected with the Virgin was used by some courtly poets in more extravagant panegyric to the Queen (Hackett, *Virgin Mother* 146– 51). The relationship between Elizabeth the Virgin Queen and Mary the Queen of Heaven has its own place in discourses on the interrelationship between sacred and secular iconography. An influential body of scholarly opinion, pioneered by Frances Yates and Roy Strong, has argued that, as the Virgin was eradicated from cultural consciousness, Elizabeth I filled the psychological and cultural gap that she had left behind. More recent research by scholars including Helen Hackett and Louis Montrose has warned us to approach this interchange with a degree of caution and qualification, while acknowledging that there is some degree of cultural relevance to the connection between the Queen of Heaven and the Queen of England.

Although Constable did not directly engage in the use of images connected with Mariology to describe the Queen in his secular verse, his sacred works play a significant part in discourses which connect Queen Elizabeth with the Virgin Mary. Unusually, this is from a standpoint of censure rather than of praise. His representation of the Virgin as both Queen and object of affection in his 'Spirituall Sonnettes' is extremely similar to representations of Elizabeth in encomiastic poetry. Constable's sacred poems thus function in a number of ways. They are an apologia for the Virgin in her Catholic, oppositional guise of Queen of Heaven, and an encoded criticism not only of Queen Elizabeth herself, but also of the extravagant love poetry written about her.

The use of sacred verse to criticize the secular can be seen through an examination of one of the four sacred sonnets which Constable addressed to the Virgin as Queen of Heaven. Like the idealized Petrarchan beloved of his secular sonnets, Constable's Virgin is represented as beautiful, but as this sonnet demonstrates, this is a beauty that outshines that of the earthly mistress. In this poem, Mary leads a hierarchy of queens. We also find a personal sense of atonement on Constable's part for the former wrongs of his sonnets written in praise of Queen Elizabeth:

> Sovereigne of Queenes: If vayne Ambition move
> my hart to seeke an earthly prynces grace:
> shewe me thy sonne in his imperiall place,
> whose servants reigne, our kynges & queenes above.
> And if allurying passions I doe prove,
> by pleasyng sighes: shewe me thy lovely face:
> whose beames the Angells beuty do deface:
> and even inflame the Seraphins with love.
> So by Ambition I shall humble bee:
> when in the presence of the highest kynge
> I serve all his, that he may honour mee.
> And love, my hart to chaste desyres shall brynge,

when fayrest Queene lookes on me from her throne
and jealous byddes me love but her alone. (189)

Here is a poem functioning as a sacred parody, its use of the language of the lover, so familiar from Constable's earlier secular sonnets, denoting sacred devotion. The opening of this sonnet places us firmly in the lexicon of monarchy, patronage and power: all the language that Constable has earlier used in relation to the sonnet mistress is here deployed by a speaker who focuses on heavenly rather than earthly rewards. The Virgin is represented as powerful, as opposed to meek and submissive. Her role here is of mediatrix: through her, the speaker can see Christ. The Virgin is also presented as an archetype of beauty, whose face has the power to emit light, and whose beauty is above the angels. In an earlier secular sonnet, 'Of the excellencye of his Ladies voyce' (124), Constable had similarly compared his mistress to angels: 'The basest notes which from thy voyce proceed / The treble of the Angells doe exceed' (lines 9–10). Here, in a poem written to the Virgin, the motif of a beloved who is above the angels is used for sacred rather than erotic purposes.

The use of imagery so explicitly connected with the love poems of the secular sonneteer serves as a reminder of the poetic style that the speaker has rescinded. His love for the Virgin ennobles him, turning him away from 'allurying passions' and towards 'chaste desyres'. There is an echo here of the secular Petrarchan sonneteer, who also claimed to be spiritually elevated by devotion to his unattainable mistress; however, this was often delivered with a knowing sense of hypocrisy, masking sexual desire as well as political subtext. In Sidney's sonnet 71, for example, Astrophil's 'chaste desyres' for Stella collapse into the carnal, as he cries out 'But ah, desire still cries: "Give me some food"', hankering after physical pleasure (Sidney 182). In Constable's sonnet, the speaker's earthly ambitions for self-aggrandizement and sexual love are both transcended by the Virgin's radiant presence, perhaps to emphasize that it is only the Virgin who can inspire truly 'chaste desyres'.

The duality of Constable's representation of Mary as Queen of Heaven – in both her own right and as a vehicle to criticize the Queen – is seen in the extraordinary shift which occurs in this sonnet's final rhyming couplet. Who is the 'fayrest Queene' that Constable refers to? Within Constable's vision of heaven, this is the Virgin herself, an awe-inspiring figure who shows justifiable anger at the speaker for seeking earthly love. Constable is here countering the Protestant representation of Mary as a humble handmaid via a representation of the Virgin that is both active and empowered. But the image also evokes representations of Elizabeth. This means that the lines can be read as a criticism not only of the Queen, but also of the poetry written about her, which, like Constable's own, often presented her as the cruel Petrarchan mistress.

## Constable's *Virgo Lactans*

In a second sonnet to the Virgin, we find overarching motifs that Constable repeatedly explores in his sacred verse. The Virgin's representation as Queen of Heaven holds within it echoes of the speaker's contempt both for earthly Queens and for his own former amorous dalliances, in a sonnet which at its core is about seeking pleasure in heaven alone:

> Why should I any love O queene but thee?
> if favour past a thankfull love should breede?
> thy wombe dyd beare, thy brest my saviour feede;
> and thow dyddest never cease to succour me.
> If Love doe followe worth and dignitye?
> thou all in [thy] perfections doest exceede:
> if Love be ledd by hope of future meede?
> what pleasure more then thee in heaven to see?
> An earthlye syght doth onely please the eye,
> and breedes desyre, but doth not satisfye:
> thy sight, gyves us possession of all joye,
> And with such full delyghtes ech sense shal fyll,
> as harte shall wyshe but for to see thee styll,
> and ever seyng, ever shall injoye. (190)

A familiar distaste is here expressed for the pleasures of secular love. The imagery of this sonnet culminates in the pejorative description of secular pleasure, tainted by the limits of 'earthlye syght' which only 'breedes desyre'. Here, the image of breeding is given unpleasant and spiritually sterile associations of lust. In gazing upon an earthly mistress the speaker is using only one sense, and the paucity of this is underlined by the fact that, in gazing upon the Virgin, he achieves a state of rapture in which all of his senses are engaged and satisfied.

In this sonnet, Constable invests the image of the Virgin with power as well as sensual beauty. She is here represented not only as the Queen of Heaven, but as the *Virgo lactans*: 'thy brest [dyd] my saviour feede'. The poem describes her as fecund and full, spiritually nourishing the speaker as she physically nourishes Christ, a sacred reappropriation of the language of the secular sonneteer who seeks patronage, service and hospitality. The whole tone of the sonnet is one of satisfaction and repletion, seen through its repeated imagery of gestation, suckling and feeding. In it, the Virgin's power is located in her breasts, which both physically and spiritually nurture. If Constable is reproaching the Queen Elizabeth here, it is for her failure to provide an heir.

Constable's embodiment of the Virgin as *Virgo lactans* is a particularly confrontational one, as the image of the Virgin suckling Christ held at this time complex and often conflicting meanings. Initially adapted from pagan images of suckling goddesses, in particular the Egyptian god Isis nursing Horus, the *Virgo lactans* was a part of Marian iconography from the fourth century, and reached its height of popularity in the fourteenth and fifteenth centuries (Warner 192–4). Conceptually, there are strong links between the Virgin's nurturing role and her role as the intercessory Queen of Heaven. The links between the *Virgo lactans* and the Virgin as Queen of Heaven were strongly forged in the Middle Ages. The image of the Virgin's milk nourishing the souls in torment in purgatory was a common one, while representations of the Virgin at the Last Judgement often showed her baring her breast to Christ, as if to remind him of his infant dependency upon her (Rouse 60). There were even elements of a power struggle in some late medieval iconography, which often showed the Virgin suckling Christ to appease his anger, so that he might show mercy on humanity in the Last Judgement (Ryan 59–74). A number of medieval representations of the *Virgo lactans* show her enthroned and crowned. An example of this can be found in the popular pilgrimage site of Halle in the southern Netherlands where a thirteenth-century statue of the *Virgo lactans* as Queen of Heaven was said to have performed many miracles.

Iconography of the suckling Virgin disappeared, however, as the Reformation gathered pace. There are a number of reasons for this. The disappearance of the *Virgo lactans* can be seen in the context of the anxiety of reformers about idolatrous attention to the Virgin's body. It was also concurrent with a trend charted by both Marilyn Yalom and Margaret Miles, who observe that there was from the Reformation onwards a subtle shift in the way images of the breast were perceived, moving from sacred to erotic (Yalom 49–90; Miles 10–19). Perhaps the most potent reason for the Reformation mistrust of the image of the *Virgo lactans* is that it can be seen as one of the most empowered representations of the Virgin. In the image of the Virgin breastfeeding her child, we see the infant Christ powerless before his mother, needing her milk for nourishment and survival. Although the *Virgo lactans* can, paradoxically, be viewed as an image which connotes the Virgin's humility (Spurr 27; Warner 202–5), post-Reformation debates over Mariolatry constructed the suckling mother as a very powerful figure, capable of producing impassioned responses that were both positive and negative (Morrison 33; Dolan 112).

Further accentuating the power of the image of the nursing woman was the commonplace belief that breast milk carried with it a sense of psychological and moral, as well as physical, nourishment. This led to widespread concern. What if, via suckling the child, the mother or the nurse was passing on negative and immoral personality traits? This firmly embedded link between breast milk and moral rigour led to the breast becoming a site of theological as well as psychological instability in post-Reformation discourse (Yalom 37). Feeding and theological instruction fused. Breast milk can be seen to represent the passage from one generation to the next, and in a world where parents were often raised on a different system of beliefs from their children, it came to be associated with dangerous religious values. In the *Homily against Peril of Idolatry*, read out in all churches during Elizabeth's reign, we find a description of the 'rabblement of the popish church' which has 'drunk in idolatry almost with their mothers milk' (Griffiths 187).

A number of negative representations of the *Virgo lactans* can be found in Protestant writing. An extreme example of this is in *The Jesuites Gospell* (1610) which was written by William Crashaw, the Protestant polemicist and father of Catholic poet Richard.[2] Crashaw's text is drenched with thunderous fear about the threat of the figure of Mary as a nursing mother. In it, a perceived over-inflation of the value of Mary's milk speaks metonymically for the idolatrously over-inflated value of the Virgin herself, as Crashaw's text conflates anxiety about the empowered Virgin suckling Christ with anxiety about her empowered role as Queen of Heaven. His complaint is that this diminishes Christ's power, making him a disturbingly dependent infant, and his mother into an idolatrously all-powerful figure:

> Speaking unto Christ, God coaequall with the father, and whose very humanity raigneth now in glory at Gods right hand ... as to a poore childe sucking his mothers brests: such conceits are common, and such words and writings rife with them, of our blessed Saviour, who never speake of the Virgin Mary, but with the title of Queene of heaven, Lady of angels, the gate of Paradise ... fitting none but him that is God, or at the last she is always a comaunding Mother, and he an infant governed and an obedient childe. (W. Crashaw sig. 13r)

---

[2]    In an essay which is underpinned by a psychobiographical approach, Richard Crashaw's own striking use of *Virgo lactans* imagery is worthy of note. In his extraordinarily sensual poem 'Blessed Be the Paps which Thou Hast Sucked', the reader is placed in the position of the *Virgo lactans* (R. Crashaw 14).

The image of Christ as a helpless infant intertwines with the image of Christ the obedient servant to the Queen of Heaven.

Armed with this context of the often bitter controversy surrounding iconography of the *Virgo lactans*, let us return to the first four lines of Constable's poem: 'Why should I any love O queene but thee? / if favour past a thankfull love should breede? / thy wombe dyd beare, thy brest my saviour feede; / and thow dyddest never cease to succour me.'

In a sonnet that is replete with images of nurturing and satisfaction, Constable here represents the Virgin as a figure who nurtures man both physically and spiritually. What is particularly striking about this image is that, as Constable's *Virgo lactans* nourishes both Christ and the speaker, she does so in her queenly guise. The poem thus functions as a defiant reiteration of the significance of the Queen of Heaven. It is an image that is worthy of note for more than its medieval resonances, providing a cultural expression of the *Virgo lactans* that, when read in the context of post-Reformation discourses on the religious significance of breastfeeding, becomes as confrontational as it is arresting.

Our exploration of the life and work of Henry Constable has given us an insight into both the confessional complexity of post-Reformation England, and the often controversial way in which iconography of the Virgin was deployed by many writers. In the work of an apostate such as Constable, the relationship between poetry and the religious imagination is a particularly fascinating one. As a secular sonneteer, Constable frequently used sacred language to express the erotic. When his later conversion is taken into consideration, this creates within his secular work moments of extraordinary tension and power. Constable's sacred sonnets can be set in direct, confrontational, dialogue with his secular voice. Erotic language is now used devotionally to represent the Virgin as the object of true sacred desire; this forms a striking juxtaposition to the false erotic expressions of desire used to flatter Queen Elizabeth. Constable's deployment of iconography of the Queen of Heaven is thus integral to the creation of sacred parody in his verse, but it functions in another, highly significant, way. As a secular sonneteer, Constable learned to use a poem as a political construct, deploying its expressions of love as a tool to gain patronage and service. In a different way, his sacred poems are also politicized as, throughout his 'Spirituall Sonnettes', Constable's repeated representation of the Virgin as Queen of Heaven can be seen as a way of counteracting Protestant depictions of the Virgin as a humble handmaid. As our exploration into historical and ideological context has shown, Constable's image of the Virgin as the empowered *Virgo lactans* was perhaps the most controversial of all of his representations of the Queen of Heaven.

As a devotional poet, Constable makes a striking contribution to the Catholic aesthetic in post-Reformation England, through his re-imagining of the image of the Virgin Mary as Queen in splendour, as opposed to humble and submissive Protestant girl.

## Works Cited

Atkinson, Clarissa W. *The Oldest Vocation: Christian Motherhood in the Middle Ages*. Ithaca, NY: Cornell University Press, 1991.

Bates, Catherine. *The Rhetoric of Courtship in Elizabethan Language and Literature*. Cambridge: Cambridge University Press, 1992.

Bell, Ilona. *Elizabethan Women and the Poetry of Courtship*. Cambridge: Cambridge University Press, 1998.

Boss, Sarah Jane. 'The Development of the Virgin's Cult in the High Middle Ages'. In *Mary: The Complete Resource*, ed. Sarah Jane Boss. Oxford: Oxford University Press, 2007, 149–72.

Bossy, John. 'A Propos of Henry Constable'. *Recusant History* 6 (1962): 228–37.
—— *The English Catholic Community, 1570–1850*. London: Darton, Longman and Todd, 1975.

Bynum, Caroline Walker. *Fragmentation and Redemption: Essays on Gender and the Human Body in Medieval Religion*. New York: Zone, 1991.

Calvin, John. *A Harmonie Upon the Three Evangelists, Matthew Mark and Luke*. Trans. E.P. London: [n.pub.], 1584.

Carey, John. *John Donne: Life, Mind and Art*. London: Faber and Faber, 1981.

Collinson, Patrick. *The Religion of Protestants*. Oxford: Oxford University Press, 1982.

Constable, Henry. *The Poems of Henry Constable*. Ed. Joan Grundy. Liverpool: Liverpool University Press, 1960.

Crashaw, Richard. *The Complete Poetry of Richard Crashaw*. Ed. George Walton Williams. New York: New York University Press, 1972.

Crashaw, William. *The Jesuites Gospel*. London: E.A. for Leonard Becket, 1610.

Dolan, Frances. *Whores of Babylon: Catholicism, Gender, and Seventeenth-Century Print Culture*. New York: Cornell University Press, 1999.

Doran, Susan. 'Why Did Elizabeth Not Marry?' In *Dissing Elizabeth: Negative Representations of Gloriana*, ed. Julia M. Walker. Durham, NC: Duke University Press, 1998, 30–59.

Duffy, Eamon. *The Stripping of the Altars*. 2nd edition. New Haven: Yale University Press, 2005.

Franssen, Paul J.C.M. 'Donne's Jealous God and the Concept of Sacred Parody'. In *Sacred and Profane: Secular and Devotional Interplay in Early Modern British Literature*, ed. Helen Wilcox, Richard Todd and Alasdair MacDonald. Amsterdam: VU University Press, 1996, 150–62.

Griffiths, John, ed. *The Two Books of Homilies Appointed to be Read in Churches* (1560). Vancouver: Regent College Publishing, 2008.

Grundy, Joan. 'Introduction'. In *The Poems of Henry Constable*. Liverpool: Liverpool University Press, 1960, 15–105.

Hackett, Helen. 'The Art of Blasphemy? Interfusions of the Erotic and the Sacred in the Poetry of Donne, Barnes and Constable'. *Renaissance and Reformation / Renaissance et Réforme* 28.3 (2004): 27–51.

—— *Virgin Mother, Maiden Queen: Elizabeth I and the Cult of the Virgin Mary*. Basingstoke: Palgrave, 1995.

Haigh, Christopher. 'The Continuity of Catholicism in the English Reformation'. *Past and Present* 93 (1981): 37–69.

Heal, Bridget. *The Cult of the Virgin Mary in Early Modern Germany: Protestant and Catholic Piety, 1500–1648*. Cambridge: Cambridge University Press, 2007.

—— 'Marian Devotion and Confessional Identity in Sixteenth-Century Germany'. In *The Church and Mary*, ed. R.N. Swanson. Woodbridge: Ecclesiastical History Society, 2004, 218–27.

Johnson, Trevor. 'Mary in Early Modern Europe'. In *Mary: The Complete Resource*, ed. Sarah Jane Boss. Oxford: Oxford University Press, 2007, 363–84.

Kreitzer, Beth. *Reforming Mary: Changing Images of the Virgin Mary in Lutheran Sermons of the Sixteenth Century*. Oxford: Oxford University Press, 2004.

Kristeva, Julia. 'Stabat Mater'. In *The Female Body in Western Culture: Contemporary Perspectives*, ed. Susan Rubin Suleiman. Cambridge, MA: Harvard University Press, 1986, 99–118.

MacCulloch, Diarmaid. 'Mary and Sixteenth-Century Protestants'. In *The Church and Mary*, ed. R.N. Swanson. Woodbridge: Ecclesiastical History Society, 2004, 191–217.

MacDonald, A.A. 'Contrafacta and the *Gude and Godlie Ballatis*'. In *Sacred and Profane: Secular and Devotional Interplay in Early Modern British Literature*, ed. Helen Wilcox, Richard Todd and Alasdair MacDonald. Amsterdam: VU University Press, 1996, 33–44.

Marotti, Arthur. '"Love is Not Love": Elizabethan Sonnet Sequences and the Social Order'. *English Literary History* 49.2 (Summer 1982): 396–428.

Martz, Louis L. *The Poetry of Meditation* (1954). New Haven: Yale University Press, 1962.

Miles, Margaret. *A Complex Delight: The Secularization of the Breast, 1350–1750*. Berkeley, CA: University of California Press, 2008.

Montrose, Louis. *The Subject of Elizabeth: Authority, Gender and Representation*. Chicago: University of Chicago Press, 2006.

Morrison, Susan Signe. *Women Pilgrims in Late Medieval England*. London: Routledge, 2000.

Peters, Christine. *Patterns of Piety: Women, Gender and Religion in Late Medieval and Reformation England*. Cambridge: Cambridge University Press, 2003.

Rouse, Clive E. *Medieval Wall Paintings* (1968). Princes Risborough: Shire, 1991.

Ryan, Salvador. 'The Persuasive Power of a Mother's Breast: The Most Desperate Act of the Virgin Mary's Advocacy'. *Studia Hibernica* 32 (2002/2003): 59–74.

Shell, Alison. *Catholicism, Controversy and the English Literary Imagination, 1558–1660*. Cambridge: Cambridge University Press, 1999.

Sidney, Philip. *The Major Works*. Ed. Katherine Duncan-Jones (1986). Oxford: Oxford University Press, 2002.

Southwell, Robert. *Collected Poems*. Ed. Peter Davidson and Anne Sweeney. Manchester: Carcanet, 2007.

Spurr, Barry. *See the Virgin Blest: The Virgin Mary in English Poetry*. Basingstoke: Palgrave Macmillan, 2007.

Strong, Roy. *Gloriana: The Portraits of Queen Elizabeth I*. London: Thames and Hudson, 1987.

Turner, Victor and Edith Turner. *Image and Pilgrimage in Christian Culture*: *Anthropological Perspectives*. Oxford: Blackwell, 1978.

Visscher, Eva de. 'Marian Devotion in the Latin West in the Late Middle Ages'. In *Mary: The Complete Resource*, ed. Sarah Jane Boss. Oxford: Oxford University Press, 2007, 177–201.

Walsham, Alexandra. *Church Papists: Catholicism, Conformity and Confessional Polemic in Early Modern England*. Woodbridge: Boydell, 1993.

Warner, Marina. *Alone of All Her Sex: The Myth and the Cult of the Virgin Mary* (1976). New York: Vintage, 1983.

Wiesner-Hanks, Merry E. 'Luther and Women: The Death of Two Marys'. In *Disciplines of Faith: Studies in Religion, Politics and Patriarchy*, ed. Jim Obelkevich, Lyndal Roper and Raphael Samuel. London: Routledge, 1987, 295–308.

Yalom, Marilyn. *A History of the Breast*. London: Harper Collins, 1997.

Yates, Frances A. 'Queen Elizabeth as Astraea'. *Journal of the Warburg Institute* 10 (1947): 27–82.

# Index

Abrams, M.H. 156
absence (of God) 18, 59, 61
action 55–7, 64, 72, 73, 82, 117, 124, 129,
    168, 172–3, 223, 234
Adam 79, 114, 154, 171
adoration 6, 74, 75, 76, 77, 84, 135, 239
*Adoro te Devote* 4, 74–6, 84
    interpretation of 76–83
aesthetics 18–21, 25, 33, 28–40, 43, 55, 56,
    67–9, 91, 131–5, 141–5, 209–10,
    239–40, 243–53
affectivity 55, 57, 76, 92, 94, 99, 195,
    197
Albert the Great 82, 105
Alter, Robert 15
Altizer, Thomas 12
Amis, Martin 25
analogy 15, 17, 19, 46, 54, 73–4, 79
anthropomorphism 130–5
apophaticism 70, 73, 137, 229
Aquinas; *see* Thomas Aquinas
Arendt, Hannah 104
Aristotle 10, 16, 22, 67, 76, 79, 80–1, 85,
    118
Arjuna 172–3
Arnold, Matthew 11, 12, 23, 26, 27
art 18–19, 23, 24, 26, 43, 44, 45, 59–64,
    65, 67–8, 85, 91, 130, 132–3, 139,
    142, 144, 146, 154, 161, 163–4,
    182, 190, 200, 202–3, 209–13,
    216, 218
atheism 10, 13, 22, 23–4, 26–7, 130–1,
    132, 135–6
Atwood, Margaret 15, 25
Auerbach, Erich 16
Augustine of Hippo, St 68, 76, 100, 104, 135
Avison, Margaret 53

Bach, Johann Sebastian 61, 144
Bachelard, Gaston 189, 209, 210, 214, 218
    imagination, ideas of 210, 218
Baden, Hans Jürgen 43
Balakrishnan, Purasu 172
Balthasar, Hans Urs von 1, 2, 10, 19, 21,
    37–42, 47, 60
    criticism of 39
    *Die Apokalypse der deutschen Seele* 37
    Guardini, comparison with 40–2
    his influence in Latin America 42
    modernity, relationship to 38
    theological-literary hermeneutics of
        37–42
Balthus, Balthasar Klossowski de Rola 202
Barnes, Julian 14, 15
Barth, Karl 126
Barthes, Roland 16, 178, 189, 196–8
    Ignatius Loyola, and 196–8
Basil the Great (or Basil of Caesarea) 53
Bates, Milton 129
beauty 4, 67–71, 144, 248
    *claritas* 84
    *integritas* 82–3
    *proportio* 81–2
    in Thomas Aquinas; *see* Thomas
        Aquinas
being 4, 22, 35, 47, 60, 71, 91, 92–3,
    94–106, 130, 144, 159, 161–70,
    190–3, 203, 215–16, 219
belief 1, 6, 9, 13, 26, 35, 37, 41, 131–2,
    139–42, 179, 240
Benedict of Nursia 92, 158
Benjamin, Walter 17
Berlin, Irving 141
Berlin, Isaiah 141
Berlioz, Hector 63

Bernanos, Georges 38
Bernard of Clairvaux, St 92
*Bhagavad Gita* 172
Bible 13, 14, 15, 21, 25, 26, 40, 56, 61, 63,
      64, 79, 109, 151, 153
    Genesis 79, 119, 145
    Exodus 14, 79, 81
    Deuteronomy 79, 151
    1 Samuel 77
    Job 61, 63
    Psalms 78, 79, 118, 152, 153, 154, 157,
      158
    Hosea 78, 79
    Jonah 14
    Matthew 79, 109, 121
    Mark 15, 79
    Luke 77
    John 78, 152, 226
    Romans 79, 109, 113–114, 120, 125,
      158
    1 Corinthians 77, 79
    2 Corinthians 121, 125
    Galatians 125
    Ephesians 22, 78
    Philippians 118
    2 Timothy 152
    2 Peter 152
    Revelation 63, 201
Bilson, Thomas 109
Blake, William 1, 15, 20, 25, 209, 222
    imagination, ideas of 109
Bloom, Harold 13, 20, 21, 111, 116, 118
Bonaventure, St 92, 146
Bonnefoy, Yves 5, 86, 189, 190, 194, 195,
      202–204
    as a poet-painter 202–204
Borde, Pascale 77, 79, 82, 83, 84, 85
Bossy, John 240, 241
Botton, Alain de 23, 26
Boyle, Nicholas 20, 21, 26, 68
    *Sacred and Secular Scriptures* 20–1
Brahms, Johannes 61
Bremond, Henri 5, 177–8
    *Prayer and Poetry* 177
Brentano, Clemens 32

Breslin, James 225
Brooke, Rupert 21
Brother Lawrence 221, 229
Brown, John Russell 122, 124, 125

Calvin, John 242
Calvino, Italo 179
Câmara, Hélder 228
Canisius, Peter 243
Carey, John 245
Cassirer, Ernst 133,134
Cecil, Robert 241
Certeau, Michel de 212–14, 215, 216,
      217–19
    'mystics' 212–13, 217
    *Mystic Fable* 212–13, 217, 218, 219
    'Mystic Speech' 216
Chenu, Jean Marie-Dominique 20–1
Chesterton, G.K. 21
Chrétien, Jean-Louis 70
Christ, *see* Jesus
Christology 14, 73–4, 79, 93, 102, 110,
      113–14, 118–19, 171
Cicero 82
Cinthio, Giovanni Battista Giraldi 111
Cixous, Hélène 5, 189, 190, 191–2, 193,
      194–6, 197, 198–9, 200–3
    Heidegger, comparison with 192–4
    Ignatius, similarities with 198–201
    as a poet-thinker 198–202
    reading, ideas of 191–2
    writing, views of 200
Claudel, Paul 38
Coghill, Neville 118, 120, 125
Coke, Sir Henry 112
Coleridge, Samuel Taylor 1, 17, 155
Collinson, Patrick 240
communion 77, 83, 92, 95, 225, 230
Conley, Verena Andermatt 192
Constable, Henry 6, 239–41, 243–50, 252–3
    conversion of 239, 241
    as a devotional poet 246–8
    images of the Virgin Mary 6, 240–52
      *see also* Mary, Mother of God
    secular verse of 243–5

contemplation 5, 11, 32, 34, 58, 59, 69, 75, 77, 81, 84, 96, 106, 138, 158–60, 161, 166, 178–84, 189–91, 194–6, 201–2, 221–6, 234
Contini, Gianfranco 91, 103
conversion 6, 56–7, 58, 64, 167, 169, 183–4, 195, 222, 232–4, 239–46, 252
Copernicus 3
Coulson, John 12
Courtès, Pierre-Ceslas 71
Crashaw, Richard 251
Crashaw, William 251
  *The Jesuites Gospel* 251
creativity 5, 56, 57, 59, 64, 71–2, 131–46, 177, 182, 193, 194, 200, 202–3, 210, 211–19, 226–34
criticism 2, 9–27, 36–42, 44–7, 117–18, 167, 189, 190, 214, 223–7, 230, 248
Crotty, Terence 76
Curtius, Ernst Robert 67, 68
Czapiewski, Winfried 68

Daniel, Samuel 243
Dante Alighieri 3, 4, 17, 33, 65, 91–106, 136
  *Commedia* 91–6, 102, 103
    as an imaginary journey 91–3
    *Inferno* 94, 95, 95–99
    *Paradiso* 91, 92–4, 95, 99–100, 100–101, 102–3, 104–6
    his use of images 93–5, 102–3, 104
Darwin, Charles 3
Dasseleer, Pascal 68
Dawkins, Richard 23
De Bruyne, Edgar 68
*Dei Verbum* 152, 153
Delacroix, Eugène 202
Delorme, Jean 72
Derrida, Jacques 16, 71, 198–9, 201
  Cixous, spiritual companion of 198
Descartes, René 18
desire 35, 95, 98, 99, 138, 168, 214–18, 248, 252
Desmond, William 3, 59, 60

Detweiler, Robert 12, 13, 19, 20, 22, 43, 189, 194, 197
  *Breaking the Fall: Religious Readings of Contemporary Fiction* 189
  *Gelassenheit* 194
  Jasper, collaboration with 13, 19, 20
  Kermode, compared with 22
  literature and religion in conversation 13
  postmodernism, in relation to 12, 13, 19
  reading religiously, ideas of 189, 197
  Scott and Steiner, compared with 13
devotion 6, 73, 80, 151, 224, 229, 239–53
Dickinson, Emily 53
discernment 3, 55, 56, 60, 65, 180, 184–5, 196–8, 199
Dominic, St 195
Donne, John 6, 151, 245
Dostoyevsky, Fyodor 25, 34, 35, 38, 40
Drakakis, John 123
Drayton, Michael 243
Droste-Hülshoff, Annette von 32
Duffy, Eamon 240
Duncan, Robert 223
Dyer, Sir Robert 246

Eagleton, Terry 9, 11, 12, 12–13, 20, 23–4, 26–7, 124, 191
  *The Illusions of Postmodernism* 23
  'Religion for Atheists' 23, 27
  literature and religion, views of 27
  tragedy, ideas of 24
Eckhart, Meister 161, 194
Eco, Umberto 68, 69, 84
Eichendorff, Joseph Freiherr von 32
Eliot, T.S. 9, 11–12, 13, 21, 22, 65, 161–74
  *Four Quartets* 151, 163, 165, 167, 171, 173
    'Burnt Norton' 158
    'The Dry Salvages' 166, 172–3
    'East Coker' 163, 165–6, 167, 168, 170–1
    'Little Gidding' 173–4
  'Ash-Wednesday' 151, 170
  'Religion and Literature' 11–12

'The Hollow Men' 170
  as 'worldmaker' 161–74
  *Bhagavad Gita,* reference to 172
  Heidegger's 'world-making' applied to
    his poetry 161–2, 163, 169
  religious imagination in 167–75
  Ricoeur's ideas of imagination applied
    to 162–3, 166–7, 167–9, 172–4
  Van Gogh in relation to 165–6
Elizabeth I, 240, 244, 245, 246, 247, 248
Emerson, Ralph Waldo 154
  'The Poet' 154
Empson, William 12, 13
Erasmus, Desiderius 112
eucharist 77, 79–85, 232–3
Eurydice 215
*eutrapelia* 10, 21–2, 24, 26
existence 17, 31, 94–5, 138, 146
  as human 42, 57, 92, 96, 97, 99, 66–70,
    209, 230
experience xi, 1, 3, 5, 15, 18, 56, 58, 72,
    80, 84, 85, 141, 142, 161–2, 164,
    177, 178–85, 193, 195, 196, 202,
    209–19, 221–2, 224, 227–30, 232,
    234

faith 13, 20, 23, 25, 40, 42, 54–8, 61, 63,
    65, 68–70, 72, 77–9, 82, 83–4, 139,
    184, 221, 222, 225, 226, 227, 230,
    232–3
Farrer, Austin 12
Feuerbach, Ludwig 131
fiction 25, 26, 32, 80, 129–46, 213
Fiddes, Paul 20, 21, 126
Flannery, Austin 44, 152
Francis of Assisi, St 195, 245
Franssen, Paul J.C.M. 245
Freud, Sigmund 3, 136, 140–1
Frye, Northrop 1, 10, 14–15, 17, 21, 24
  *An Anatomy of Criticism* 15

Gadamer, Hans Georg 16–17
Gallagher, Lowell 123
Gallagher, Michael Paul 184
*Gaudium et Spes* 44

Gauthier, R.A. 85
Gelpi, Albert 230
Giacometti, Alberto 202
gift 3, 4, 59–60, 65 ,123, 146, 164, 194,
    197, 202, 215, 228
Gilbert, Sandra 194
Gilson, Etienne 68, 73
Girard, René 25, 58
God 4, 17–18, 20, 21, 24, 33, 45, 55,
    56, 58, 59–60, 64, 68, 69, 70–4,
    76–81, 83–5, 92–6, 100, 102,
    104, 106, 110, 112–13, 117–19,
    121, 123, 125–6, 129–46, 151–4,
    155–6, 157–8, 161, 173, 178,
    184, 196–7, 198, 201, 222, 226–7,
    230–1, 242, 251
Goethe, Johann Wolfgang von, 33, 38,
    39–40, 40, 155
Gordon, Lyndall 167
grace 4, 5, 59, 61–4, 84, 101, 102, 110,
    119–26, 157, 177, 185, 194, 221,
    224, 230, 234
Grayling, A.C. 26
Grundy, Joan 240, 243, 244
Guardini, Romano 31, 32, 33–7, 38, 40–2,
    47
  compared to Balthasar 38, 40–2, 47
  criticism of 37
  Rilke, his focus on 36
  theological-literary hermeneutics of,
    33–7, 40–2
    close reading, importance for 37
    Dostoyevsky, his interest for 35
    Hölderlin as 'seer' 35
    inspired by Max Scheler 34
    modernity, his relation to 35
    poets as seers 35
Guigo II 158
Guite, Malcolm 64–5
Gy, Pierre-Marie 83

Hackett, Helen 245, 246, 247
Hahn, Friedrich 43
Haigh, Christopher 240
Hartman, Geoffrey 155

Hass, Andrew 11, 12
Haupt, Sabine 39
Heal, Bridget 242, 243
healing 57–8, 62, 171, 193
Heaney, Seamus 1, 64–5
heart 55, 75, 77–8, 97, 102, 113, 123, 158,
    184, 214–15, 217–18, 225–6, 232
Heidegger, Martin 18, 22, 161–2, 163,
    169, 190, 191, 192–4, 201, 202
    'The Origin of the Work of Art' 163–5,
        166
    'What are poets for?' 192–3
    artwork , importance of 162, 163–4
    concept of freedom compared to
        Ricoeur's 169–70
    *geworfenheit* 169
    poetry, ideas of 191
    the poet as a maker, idea of 191
Heller, Erich 213, 218
Herbert, George 6, 65
hermeneutics 2, 11, 13, 14, 15, 16, 18, 31,
    32, 36–7, 39, 42–3, 45–6, 56, 120,
    137, 165, 184, 194, 200–1
history 15, 38–9, 45–6, 55, 57, 67–8,
    74n9, 77, 83, 94–5, 152, 156, 184,
    191, 227, 240–2
Hitchens, Christopher 23, 26
Hofmann, Peter 39
Hölderlin, Friedrich 22, 34, 35, 36, 190,
    191, 192, 193
Holst, Gustav 61
Homer 154
hope 21, 45, 57, 64, 65, 72, 75, 78, 82–3,
    93, 161, 167–74, 193, 202–3, 233,
    249
Hopkins, Gerard Manley 12, 34, 38, 40,
    151, 156–8
    'God's Grandeur' 157–8
    'The Starlight Night' 157
    inscape 157
Hopper, Edward 202, 203
humanism 13, 21, 23, 26, 155
humanity 22, 24, 44, 45, 82, 83, 92, 95,
    106, 113, 124, 126, 141, 155, 168,
    234, 250, 251

Hume, David 53, 213
Hutchison, Ben 211

idea 4, 20, 58, 69, 74, 92–103, 129,
    134–40, 191, 230
Ignatius of Loyola 5, 65, 178–9, 179–80,
    181, 183–4, 184–5, 189, 190, 194,
    194–9, 200, 201, 203, 228
    *Spiritual Exercises* 5, 178–81, 183–5,
        190, 196–7, 199, 201, 228
        Barthes's interpretation of 178–9,
            196–8
        dynamic of 178
        imaginative reading as spiritual
            transformation 178–80, 181–5
        inner motions in 180, 184
    the pilgrim poet 195–8
image 4, 77, 91–107, 110, 112, 125, 130,
    133, 138, 146, 211, 222, 225
imagination 53–8, 125–6, 134, 209, 227
    artistic creation and God's imaging
        145–6
    Christian theology and 125
    double reality of 59–60
    emergence of 53
    imaginative epoché 173
    in the *Spiritual Exercises* 182
    Miłosz on 3
    mysticism and 209–20
        in Levertov 220–36
        in Rilke 209–20
    poetic imagination 1, 163
    productive imagination 162–3
        four categories of 163
    reading, in relation to 180
    religious 1, 3, 4, 5, 54, 59–65, 126,
        168–9, 171, 227
        criteria for defining 59–64
        'faithful attention' connected to
            224
        Henry Constable's religious belief
            in relation to 239–52
        Ignatius's 65
        non-explicit 65
        religious reading and 189–190

transformation as a consequence of 143
immanence 59–60, 63, 137, 144, 209, 214,
    217, 222, 225, 229, 232, 234
incarnation 3, 57, 58, 60, 64, 73–4, 77, 85,
    102, 151, 155, 156, 172, 197, 201,
    222, 225, 226, 233, 234
Inge, Dean William Ralph 222, 225, 234
inspiration 4–5, 152, 153, 155, 222–4,
    226, 227
interpretation 16, 17n5, 18, 31, 33–47,
    58–9, 129, 133, 140, 152, 182, 189
Ion 155
Iser, Wolfgang 180, 183
Ivens, Michael 196

Jackson, Donald 61
James (the apostle) 92
James I (King) 109, 112, 241
James, William 5, 212, 214, 222, 234
    his definition of mysticism 212
Jardine, Alice 192
Jarrett-Kerr, Martin 12
Jasper, David 11, 12, 13–14, 19, 20, 24,
    43, 194
    *Literature and Theology* (1987) 10–11
    Detweiler, collaboration with 13, 19,
      20
    hope in religious return 13
    postmodernism, in relation to 19–20,
      24
    the Chalcedonian formula, views of
      14, 20
Jay, Elisabeth 9, 14, 15
Jesus 19, 24, 37, 44–5, 58, 73–4, 76, 77,
    78, 79, 82, 83, 84, 85, 93, 103, 109,
    110, 114, 118, 119, 121, 152, 171,
    172–3, 179, 180, 189, 232, 250,
    251, 252
John (the apostle) 92
John of Damascus 100
Johnson, Trevor 243
journey 91–4, 173, 183–4, 190–1, 210,
    218, 222, 225, 228–30
Julian of Norwich 174, 221, 229, 231, 234
Jung, Carl 3

justice 109–26

Kafka, Franz 18
Kant, Immanuel 18, 53, 70, 140, 143–4,
    155
Kearney, Richard 1, 172, 191
Kermode, Frank 1, 10, 14, 15–17, 22, 24
    theological-literary hermeneutics of
      44–6
      character of approach 44
      hermeneutical principles 45
      method of structural analogy 46
      seven characteristics 45
Kipling, Rudyard 21
Klemm, David E. 13
knowledge 1, 14, 46, 55, 58, 69–70, 72–4,
    77, 84, 131, 135, 145, 168, 170,
    173, 179–80, 203, 209, 222, 231
Kovach, Francis J. 68
Kramer, Kenneth 171, 172
Kranz, Gisbert 33
Kreitzer, Beth 242
Krishna 172–3
Kristeva, Julia 246
Kuschel, Josef-Karl 1, 2, 10, 19, 35, 40,
    44–6

language 17–18, 25, 45, 67–86, 131,
    156–7, 158, 163–4, 166–74, 179,
    191–2, 196–8, 200, 211–16, 221,
    222–9, 240, 243–53
Lash, Nicholas 19
Lawrence, D.H. 12, 64
Lawrence, William 117
Leavis, F.R. 11, 12, 27
*lectio divina* 70, 73, 158–9
Lever, J.W. 109, 111, 117
Levertov, Denise 5, 221–34
    'Origins of a Poem' 224–5
    'Some Notes on Organic Form' 224–6,
      229–30
    *The Stream and the Sapphire* 222,
      225–6, 227–8, 232
    Ignatius's *Exercises*, views of 228
    imagination and mysticism in 221–36

her poetry as sacramental 231–3
incarnational mysticism and 221,
233–4
inspired by Julian of Norwich 229–32
writing as religious act 224
Lispector, Clarice 200, 201
literature and theology 9–30, 31–49
in the English-speaking world 10–27
in the German-speaking world 31–49
liturgy 67, 77, 84, 151, 153, 232, 233
Lochbrunner, Manfred 37, 38, 39, 40
Locke, John 53
Lonergan, Bernard 57, 61
love 55–6, 57, 60, 65, 76, 83, 92–3,
95–101, 106, 110, 113, 120–6,
145–6, 155, 203, 230, 243–52
Luther, Martin 14, 78, 153, 170, 242
Lynch, William F. 3, 12, 57–8

Mahler, Gustav 61
Maimonides, Moses 134
Malick, Terrence 63–4
*The Thin Red Line* 62
*The Tree of Life* 61, 64
*To the Wonder* 63
Mariology 6, 239–43, 246–53
Marion, Jean-Luc 59
Maritain, Jacques 68, 73
Marotti, Arthur 243
Martz, Louis 246
Mary, Virgin Mother of God 239, 248, 249
images of the Virgin 239
as humble maid 242
as Queen of Heaven 239, 241–3,
246–8, 250–2
as *Virgo Lactans* 249
*see also* Constable, Henry
Matthew (the apostle) 152, 153
McCabe, Herbert 23, 137
McCracken, Hunter (*The Tree of Life*) 62
MacCulloch, Diarmaid 242
McEwan, Ian 25
McKerrow, R.B. 112
McKinnon, George 19
Maitland, Sara 14

Martens, Harry 227
meaning 12n1, 15, 17, 18, 20, 32, 37, 39,
41, 46, 55–6, 71–4, 77, 123, 133–5,
139–40, 143, 144, 158–9, 162,
163–5, 168, 170, 173, 183–4, 191,
197, 212–13
*Measure for Measure* 109, 110–19
*The Merchant of Venice* 119–25
Merton, Thomas 221
metaphor 19, 20, 56, 125, 126, 131, 136,
140, 153, 163, 166–8, 171, 190,
212, 214, 216–17, 222, 225, 231,
243, 244
metaphysics 5, 11, 17n5, 39, 68, 69, 71–2,
79, 81, 133–4, 168, 213
Miłosz, Czesław 3
Michel, Alain 67, 77, 79, 82, 83, 84, 85
Michelangelo 133
Miles, Margaret 133, 250
Mills, Ralph 223
Milton, John 15, 20, 25
mind/intellect, intelligence 5, 55, 69, 70,
71, 80–1, 91, 103n11, 132–46, 159,
183, 184, 209, 212–13, 217–19,
224–6
Mitchell, Stephen 211
modernism 5, 12, 13, 17, 18, 71, 200, 210,
219
modernity 13, 33, 34–5, 38–9, 41, 43,
45–6, 54, 55, 212
Mommaers, Paul 210–11
Mongeau, Gilles 68
Montrose, Louis 247
Mörike, Eduard 34, 37
Moses 79, 135
movement xi, 3, 5, 33, 38, 65, 77, 83, 92,
93, 125–6, 132, 145, 159, 170, 172,
180, 190–2, 194, 196, 199, 200,
203, 211
Mozart, Wolfgang Amadeus 61
Müller, L. 68
mystery 3, 18, 20, 59, 60, 64, 65, 74–6, 79,
83, 125–6, 162, 165, 166, 171, 174,
177, 178, 179, 184, 203, 213, 223,
226, 230–4

mysticism 5, 177, 209–10, 222
    Dean Inge on 222
    in Levertov 221–34
    in Rilke 209–19
    mystic and poet, connection of 177,
        210, 211
    'mystics', as a style of writing 212–19
    poetry as mystical gesture 211–12
myth 2, 14–15, 25, 97, 103, 130, 169,
        198, 201

Nashe, Thomas 112
Nazianzen, Gregory 100
Newman, John Henry 1, 3, 54–5, 59, 65
Newton, Isaac 3
Nietzsche, Friedrich 132, 170
Nussbaum, Martha 3, 54–5, 56
    on imagination 55–6
Nuttall, A.D. 118

objectivity 1, 15, 46, 69, 144–5, 161–2,
        182
Oliver, Mary 159
    'White Flowers' 159
Olson, Charles 226
    'Projective Verse' 226
*The Oxford Handbook of Literature and
    Theology* 9, 10, 14

Pack, Robert 223
Panofsky, Erwin 68
Pareyson, Luigi 182
    interpretation compared to
        performance 182
Paul (the apostle) 79, 109, 110, 113–14,
        115, 120, 121, 125, 126, 152,
        158
Peel, Sir Robert 54–5
Péguy, Charles 38
Penn, Sean (*The Tree of Life*) 62
Perkins, William 118
Perniola, Mario 184
Peter (the apostle) 92, 106, 152, 228
phenomenology 94, 161, 164, 166, 167,
        210, 211

philosophy xi, 1, 3, 32, 35, 36, 39, 42, 54,
        59, 62, 76, 79–80, 92, 94, 133–4,
        155, 162, 167, 169, 200
Pickstock, Catherine 73
Pitt, Brad (*The Tree of Life*) 62
Plato 132, 142, 155
Plotinus 68
poetics 45, 59, 67–8, 71, 82, 191, 202,
        210–14, 217, 221–6, 228–30,
        233
poetry 129, 133, 134, 142–3, 144, 154,
        190, 191, 192, 193, 213, 216, 218
    Heidegger's 'What are poets for?'
        192–3
    as sacramental art 154–6
    as secular scripture 155
    devotional poetry of Henry Constable
        239–55
    directed to silence 158, 159
    inspiration connected to 155
    King James Bible and poetic language
        153
    mystical poetry, examples of 219,
        209–34
    poet as priest 224
    poet as *Weltvollendender* 213
    poetics, in relation to 191
    Psalms and 152–3
    scripture in relation to 151–4, 156
    theology compared to 125–6
    reading of 158–204
    as active contemplation 5, 189–204
    as free reconstruction 179
    as performance 182
    as prayer 177
    as process of conversion 184
    as spiritual experience 177–85
    as spiritual transformation 5, 173
    exercise of 178–9
    Ignatian rules, in relation to 184–5
    *lectio divina,* compared to 158–9
    the reader as traveller 183
    the reader as 'world-maker' 174
    the role of the 'religious imaginary' in
        194

*poiesis* 191, 213, 215, 218
Pope, Alexander 154
   on Shakespeare 154
Pope Paul VI 152
postmodernism/postmodernity 2, 12, 13,
   14, 17, 19, 20, 23, 24, 26, 47, 54,
   71, 198, 200
Poussin, Nicolas 202
prayer 56, 61, 62, 64, 65, 70, 76, 82, 84, 85,
   121, 126, 157, 158, 159, 177–8,
   196, 199, 201–2, 222, 224, 234
pre-modern 32, 34, 39–40, 60
projection 56, 130–1, 134, 162, 163, 167,
   168
prophet 23, 33, 35–6, 40, 53, 55, 56, 57,
   78, 81, 154, 218
Proust, Marcel 25, 55, 177
Pseudo-Cyril of Jerusalem 100
Pseudo-Dionysus the Areopagite 82
Pullman, Philip 25–6

Quinn, M. Bernetta 130, 134

Raabe, Wilhelm 34
Rahner, Hugo 21–2, 199
Rahner, Karl 1, 60, 126, 185
rationality 13, 18, 54–60, 85, 95–6, 110,
   125, 134, 137, 209
reader 3–5, 26, 31, 34, 65, 154–8, 174,
   179–85, 194, 197n8, 202, 211–19
reading 2, 5, 21, 26, 56, 70, 121, 152,
   158–60, 177–85, 189–203, 216
realism 62–3, 72, 79, 80, 144, 170, 225
reality 4, 14, 33, 45–6, 55, 72, 122, 125,
   129–46, 161–74, 209–12
reason 1, 54–5, 70, 85, 95, 99, 125, 134,
   140, 156
religion xi, 2, 9, 11–13, 20, 23–7, 32, 42,
   54–5, 59, 123, 129–33, 136–41,
   168, 171, 189, 197, 224, 233, 239
resurrection 24 , 72, 83, 91, 93, 102, 168,
   170–1, 232–3
revelation 5, 13, 15, 25, 35, 37, 46, 56, 72,
   74, 85, 125–6, 156, 162, 201, 223
Richards, I.A. 27

Richardson, Joan 136, 141
Ricoeur, Paul 14, 55, 162–3, 166–7,
   167–9, 172–4
   concept of freedom, compared to
    Heidegger's 169–70
   'epoché', meaning of 162, 166, 173
   'Ethics' 167, 168
   *Figuring the Sacred* 56
   'Lectures on Imagination' 162
   poetic language and surplus of being
    in 168
   poetic and religious imagination
    according to 171–2
   religious symbolism according to 168
   role of imagination, his views on 56–7,
    162–3
Riddel, Joseph 138
Rilke, Rainer Maria 5, 34, 36, 38, 40, 56,
   64, 133, 145, 192, 209–12, 213,
   214–19, 234
   *The Notebooks of Malte Laurids Brigge*
    211, 213, 215, 217, 218
   *Sonnets to Orpheus* 210, 213, 214, 215,
    216, 217, 218
   as a mystic 214
   his poems as mystical gestures 218–19
Rimbaud, Arthur 85
Roethke, Theodore 159
Roser, Isabel 199
Rosier-Catach, Irene 68
Rowling, J.K. 25–6
Rushdie, Salman 24
Ruskin, John 177
Ryan, Marie-Laure 179
Ryan, Salvador 250

sacrament 20, 60, 73, 77, 80n14, 82, 84,
   103, 111, 151, 154–5, 230–3
St John's Bible Project 61, 63, 64
Santayana, George 129
Scheler, Max 34
Schlegel, Wilhelm 32
Schneider, Reinhold 38, 41
Schoenberg, Arnold 18
scholasticism 34, 67, 68, 71, 93, 138

Schoot, Henk J.M. 68, 73–4
Schrenk, Gottlob 110
Schröer, Henning 43
Schweiker, William 13
Scott, Nathan A., Jr 12–13, 17, 18, 43
scripture 5, 11, 13, 14–21, 22, 23, 25, 26,
    40, 56, 61–4, 70, 72–3, 76–9, 81,
    92, 121, 135, 151–60, 221, 226,
    227, 239
Seneca 118
Sexton, Anne 227
Shakespeare, William 3, 4, 10, 20, 22–3,
    25, 33, 58, 109–10, 111–13, 116,
    118, 119–20, 122, 123, 125, 126,
    154–5, 243
    *All's Well that Ends Well* 117
    *King Lear* 23
    *Macbeth* 23
    *Measure for Measure* 4, 109–10,
        110–19, 117, 118, 119, 126
    *The Merchant of Venice* 4, 119–25, 126
    *Troilus and Cressida* 117
    law and divine mercy in 109–26
    religious imagination in 117–19, 125,
        126
Sharp, R.A. 17
Shaw, George Bernard 22, 53
Sheldrake, Philip 212
Shell, Alison 117, 245, 246
Shuger, Debora 117, 118
Silvayn, Alexander 122, 124
Simons, Hi 129, 130
Smith, Lorrie 224
Socrates 155
Sölle, Dorothee 43
soul 35, 37, 41, 53, 84, 91–7, 99–100, 111,
    113, 115, 121, 131, 153, 177, 180,
    184, 193, 196, 200
Southwell, Robert 246
spirit 59, 92, 93, 94, 98, 103–4, 117–24,
    145, 152, 153, 154, 155, 159, 179,
    180n3, 185, 194, 199, 210, 223
*The Spiritual Exercises*; *see* Ignatius of
    Loyola
Sri, P.S. 172

Steiner, George 1, 10, 12, 13, 14, 17–19, 20,
    22–4, 25, 26, 27, 59–60, 86, 210
    'A Reading Against Shakespeare' 10,
        22–3
    *Real Presences* 17, 18, 26, 59
    contrasted with Eagleton 23–4
    criticism of 19
    deconstructionism, in relation to 19
    as an 'Iliad' critic 17
    Nathan Scott on 17
    religious responsibility of art according
        to 18
Stevens, Wallace 1, 3, 4, 65, 129–46, 156
    'A Child Asleep in Its Own Life' 144–5
    'Imagination as Value' 133
    'Modern Poetry' 141–3
    'Two or Three Ideas' 131–2
    criticism of his aesthetic 145
    fiction as value 140
    fictive conception of God 135
    God, imagination and reality in
        129–46
    poetry and religion according to 129,
        130–1, 132
    religious imagination and poetic
        imagination 136
    role of poetry according to 142–3
    'supreme fiction' 134, 136–9, 140–1,
        143
        abstract quality of 137–8
        as replacement for God 140
        compared to the Word 146
        compared with Thomas Aquinas's
            theology 144–6
Strong, Roy 247
Stubbes, Phillip 112

Tanner, Kathryn 68
Taverner, John 61
Taylor, Charles 3, 55–6
    Ricoeur in relation to 55–7
Taylor, George 162–3, 166–7
Teresa of Avila 213
text 15, 26, 45, 72, 119–23, 124, 178–84,
    189, 195–8, 200

theology 137–8
  embedded in poetry, *see* Thomas
    Aquinas
  literature and 9–49
  use of images 94, 95, 125–6
    of the Virgin Mary, *see* Mary
  works of art, in relation to 60–4
Thomas (the apostle) 78
Thomas Aquinas 3, 4, 67–86, 92, 94,
    104–5, 137, 185
  *Adoro te Devote*
    beauty in 81–4
    language in 76–81
  *Lauda Sion* 67, 70
  beauty, ideas of 68–70
  language, view of 70–4
    Christological foundation of 73–4
    as an instrument of vision 70
  poet and theologian 67–86
  poetry 67
    eucharistic poetry and revelation
      85–6
Thompson, Iain 164
Thoreau, Henry David 230
Tillich, Paul 1, 2, 10, 12, 13, 42–3, 45
  influence abroad 43
  Kuschel's criticism of 45
  his method of correlation 42–3, 46
  theological-literary hermeneutics of
    42–3, 45
Tolkien, J.R.R. 21
Tolstoy, Leo 22
Torrell, Jean-Pierre 68, 70, 78, 85
tragedy 17, 22, 24, 57, 58, 61, 58, 61,
    96
Trainar, Marie (Geneviève) 76
transcendence 18, 19, 20, 21, 23, 27, 35,
    55, 56, 59–60, 61, 63, 64–5, 69–70,
    83, 84, 85, 125–6, 143–4, 161, 164,
    182, 209, 214, 221, 225, 227, 248
transformation 3, 4, 5, 54–9, 61, 63, 64, 81,
    125, 142–3, 156, 162–3, 165–73,
    177–85, 190–204, 213, 217–18,
    230, 232, 242
Treanor, Lucia 84

truth 1, 4, 21, 35, 40, 45, 46, 58, 70, 72, 73,
    75, 77, 95–7, 133–4, 139–40, 141,
    143, 144–5, 156, 163–5, 181, 201,
    229, 232
Turner, Victor 241
Tyndale, William 153

Vaihinger, Hans 140
Van Gogh, Vincent 163, 164, 165–6
Valdés, Mario 56
Vallet, Pierre 68
Vanhoozer, Kevin 167, 168, 169
Vattimo, Gianni 218
Velázquez, Diego 232
Venturi, Robert 12
Vico, Giambattista 53–4
vision 59, 68, 70, 72, 83, 84, 140, 169, 179,
    201, 231, 233, 248

Walsham, Alexandra 240
Walton, Heather 190, 201
Ward, Graham 24
Warnock, Mary 1
Whetstone, George 111
Whitman, Walt 153–4
  *Leaves of Grass* 154
    'As Adam Early in the Morning'
      153–4
Wielockx, Robert 68, 74, 80–1, 83
Wiesner-Hanks, Merry 242
Wilder, Amos Niven 43
will 14, 93, 95, 96, 100, 101, 113, 139, 161,
    168, 173, 184, 239
Williams, Rowan 4, 25–6
Williams, William Carlos 223, 226, 230, 232
Winterson, Jeanette 14
Wittgenstein, Ludwig 10, 22–3
  lack of appreciation of Shakespeare 10,
    22–3
Wordsworth, William 155–6
  *The Prelude* 155–6
Wright, Terry 12–13, 17, 43
Würffel, Stefan Bodo 39
Wyschogrod, Edith 198, 200
  hagiography, view of 198–9

Xenophanes 130

Yalom, Marilyn 250, 251
Yates, Frances 246–7
Yeats, W.B. 18, 24, 65

Young, Julian 164
Yourcenar, Marguerite 179

Ziolkowski, Theodore 37
Žižek, Slavoj 21